FACING MOUNT KENYA

THE TRIBAL LIFE OF THE GIKUYU

BY

JOMO KENYATTA

WITH AN INTRODUCTION BY

B. MALINOWSKI

VINTAGE BOOKS

A DIVISION OF RANDOM HOUSE

NEW YORK

T O

Moigoi and Wamboi and all the
dispossessed youth of Africa: for
perpetuation of communion with
ancestral spirits through the fight
for African Freedom, and in the
firm faith that the dead, the living,
and the unborn will unite to rebuild
the destroyed shrines.

INTRODUCTION

"ANTHROPOLOGY begins at home" has become the watchword of modern social science. Mass-observation and "Northtown" in England; "Middletown" in U.S.A.; the comprehensive studies of villages and of peasant life carried out in Eastern Europe—notably in Rumania and Poland; the new drive in French folklore undertaken by Rivière and Varagniac—all these are directing the technique, method, and aims of anthropology on to our own civilisation. Even Volkskunde, the study of the German people by German scholars, though partly mystical and largely misused, is none the less an expression of the sound view that we must start by knowing ourselves first, and only then proceed to the more exotic savageries.

In all this we do not even debate the point as to whether an educated and trained member of a community is entitled to observe it with profit and competence. We do not place taboos on Psycho-analysis, because the psycho-analyst himself may be of the same race and culture as his patient, and at times even in the same neurotic condition. We do not send our Behaviourist to Central Australia because, being white, he might be unable to study white children. The English economist is allowed to work on the commerce and banking of the City of London, and the French jurists have given us excellent analyses of the Code Napoléon.

Yet when an African writes a book about his own tribe, it seems almost necessary to justify his claims. I shall not make any such attempt or gesture because, in my opinion, the book speaks for itself. Mr. Kenyatta also does not argue the point whether "Anthropology begins at home" is as true of Africa as of Europe. It obviously is. Mr. Kenyatta has acted upon the principle and produced an excellent monograph on African life and custom.

As every good ethnographer ought to do, the Author shows his credentials in his Preface. He has gone through the African course of training. He became, later on, practically acquainted with administrative and economic issues of East African policy. As to his training in Anthropology, I can add one or two points which he himself is not in a position to make. For several years past Mr. Kenyatta has been a member of my discussion class at the London School of Economics. He was thus associated in research and discussion, in original contribution and extempore critical activity with a number of brilliant, experienced and highly competent young scholars, many of whom had done their own term of field-work, and all of whom had had years of previous academic training. In this group he was able to play an active, indeed creative part, giving us illuminating sidelights, inspired by the inside knowledge of an African, but formulated with the full competence of a trained Western scholar. The present book bears full witness of his ability to construct, and his clarity of thought and expression.

There is one quality in the book to which I would like to draw special attention. Mr. Kenyatta is outspoken and honest to an extent rarely found in students of social science: he recognises the dangers of his own bias. "In the present work I have tried my best to record facts as I know them, mainly through a lifetime of personal experience, and have kept under very considerable restraint the sense of political grievances which no progressive African can fail to experience" (Preface). In fairness to Mr. Kenyatta, and as a matter of wisdom in any co-operation between Europeans of goodwill and Africans who have suffered the injury of higher education, we have to recognise the fact that an African who looks at things from the tribal point of view and at the same time from that of Western civilisation, experiences the tragedy of the modern world in an especially acute manner.

For, to quote William James, "Progress is a terrible thing." It is terrible to those of us who half a century ago were born into a world of peace and order; who cherished legitimate hopes of stability and gradual development; and who now have to live through the dishonesty and immorality of the very historical happenings. I refer to the events of the last few years which seem to demonstrate once more that Might is Right; that bluff, impudence, and aggression succeed where a decent readiness to co-operate has failed. The first seeds of this new historical demoralisation, let us remember, were indeed planted, not by Fascism or Communism, but by the frauds, the imbecilities, and the impotence of democratic statesmanship, which led us into the World War; then into the ensuing injustices and betrayals of the Peace Treaties. German National Socialism and the other totalitarianisms have been largely manufactured and fomented through the ill-applied brutality, then the weakness, of the Allied policies.

"The African is not blind," Mr. Kenyatta reminds us. The educated, intellectual minority of Africans, usually dismissed as "agitators," are rapidly becoming a force. They are catalysing an African public opinion even among the raw tribesmen. A great deal will depend upon whether this minority of "agitators" will be made to keep a balanced and moderate view of economic, social and political issues, or whether by ignoring them and treating them with contempt we drive them into the open arms of world-wide Bolshevism. For on this will depend the general drift of African opinion from one end of the Dark Continent to the other.

It is amazing how, for instance, the Abyssinian venture has organised public opinion in places and among natives whom one would never have suspected of having any complicated views on the League of Nations, on the Dual Mandate, on the Dignity of Labour, and on the Brotherhood of Man. But about Abyssinia most Bantu and Negroes have their views. They have been organised into a hatred of European encroachment and into a contempt for the debility of those powers and movements which ranged themselves on the side of Africa, and then, through weakness and incompetence, abandoned the cause of Africa and let it go by default. Again, the mismanagement of the "Chinese incident" is uniting the world of coloured peoples against Western influence and above all against Great Britain and the United States, for even to one who is black, brown, or yellow, *noblesse oblige.*

Mr. Kenyatta has wisely refrained from using any such language as appears in my last sentences. He presents the facts objectively, and to a large extent without any passion or feeling. That some of this is contained in his presentation of facts is a help and not a hindrance. For if the present book does nothing more than help us to understand how Africans see through our pretences, and how they assess the realities of the Dual Mandate, it will be rendering a great service. From this point of view the chapters on land tenure, on economic life, on the marriage system, and, last but not least, on religion and magic, deserve a careful scrutiny. Any African bias contained in them is all to the good.

There is perhaps a little too much in some passages of European bias. I might have been tempted to advise the writer to be more careful in using such antitheses as "collective" v. "individual," in opposing the native outlook as "essentially social" to the European as "essentially personal." At many points unnecessary comparisons are introduced and European expressions such as Church, State, "legal system," "economics," etc., are used with somewhat superfluous implications. When we read of "a woman specialist . . . who has studied a form of surgery from childhood," and who performs an operation "with the dexterity of a Harley Street surgeon," the picture is amusing but not helpful. I am not aware that a Harley Street specialist had ever been placed side by side with the old Gikuyu practitioner to be compared with her. Principles of asepsis are certainly not prominent in the ritual surgery of any African tribe.

In another context Mr. Kenyatta himself warns us against the dangers of misusing European terminology. "The average European observer, not trained in comparative sociology . . . thinks of a tribe as if it must be analogous to the European sovereign state." Indeed, to use such expressions as "State," "Sovereignty," "Church," is only profitable if these terms be re-defined completely so as to make them applicable to the African culture. In the following statement, however, Mr. Kenyatta obviously runs counter to his own judicious advice and the rules of terminological caution. "To make use of European terminology, it might be said that religion in Gikuyu is 'State established,' but it would be even more true to say that Church and State are one." Since, however, as we have been rightly told, the word State cannot be well applied, nor yet the word Church, while an Established Religion carries with it a multitude of unnecessary implications, it might have been better not to introduce a somewhat misleading and quite superfluous simile, and to describe the condition in terms of concrete detail. This is so abundantly given, however, that such criticisms are really due to a cavilling pedantry which I am using on this book to express my very high opinion of its quality.

The chapter on magic is especially important and valuable because of the abundance of texts, of the details given as to the ritual and the ingredients employed, and the inside information on the psychology of act and situation alike. Some anthropologists may question here the reinterpretation of the real processes which underlie magic. "It can be safely said that this (i.e. magic) is one way of transmitting thoughts telepathically from one mind to another," we are told by Mr. Kenyatta. "It seems that, through concentration, the magician or the possessor of love magic is able to penetrate into the mental mechanism of the person with whom he desires to establish communication. In this form the magician's suggestions are easily transmitted by means of vibration to the brain, and then to the mind."

I submit that Mr. Kenyatta would still have to supply some evidence as to how these "vibrations" are produced, how they act on the brain, and thence on the mind. But the author disarms all criticism when he tells us: "There is something in it which can be classified as occultism, and, as such, it cannot be dismissed as merely superstition." For, indeed, how can *we* criticise Mr. Kenyatta for believing in the reality of those magical vibrations and the possibility of penetrating the mental mechanisms of others, in occultism and telepathy or spiritism? How can we criticise him, and exonerate the great English physicist who believes in table-rapping and spooks; or accept as civilised the two or three of our present Cabinet Ministers who believe in Christian Science, or the Oxford Group Movement, or spiritism? Do the religious convictions of those who accepted Hitler as God, who had faith in the omnipotence of Mussolini or in the omniscience of Stalin, belong to savagery or to civilisation, to superstition or to faith?

We are thus led to the reflection that Europe is as deeply immersed in occultism; that superstition, blind faith and complete disorientation are as dangerous a canker in the heart of our Western civilisation as in Africa. Indeed, since we know better, and have all the means to combat superstition among us, Mr. Kenyatta's somewhat ingenuous remarks should lead us to search our own hearts and not to indulge in another supercilious attack on the African's liability to superstition. There is more superstition among us; it is more dangerous as well as more despicable than anywhere among the most primitive tribe.

The present book will thus be useful, inspiring, as well as entertaining and instructive, in a variety of ways and for a multitude of readers. It is one of the first really competent and instructive contributions to African ethnography by a scholar of pure African parentage. Through his upbringing Mr. Kenyatta combines to an unusual extent the knowledge of Western ways and Western modes of thought with a training and outlook essentially African. As a first-hand account of a representative African culture, as an invaluable document in the principles underlying culture-contact and change; last, not least, as a personal statement of the new outlook of a progressive African, this book will rank as a pioneering achievement of outstanding merit.

B. Malinowski

Department of Anthropology,

University of London

PREFACE

THE COUNTRY of the Gikuyu,[1] whose system of tribal organisation will be described in this book, is in the central part of Kenya. It is divided into five administrative districts: Kiambu, Fort Hall (Murang'a), Nyeri, Embu, and Meru. The population is approximately one million. Owing to the alienation of agricultural and pastoral land, about 110,000 [2] Gikuyu live mostly as squatters on farms on European land in various districts of Kenya. The rest of the population inhabits the Gikuyu Reserve and the towns. The Gikuyu people are agriculturists; they herd large flocks of sheep and goats, and, to a less extent, cattle, since their social organisation requires a constant supply of stock for such varied purposes as "marriage insurance," pay-

[1] The usual European way of spelling this word is Kikuyu, which is incorrect; it should be Gikuyu, or in strict phonetic spelling Gekoyo. This form refers only to the country itself. A Gikuyu person is Mu-Gikuyu, plural, A-Gikuyu. But so as not to confuse our readers we have used the one form Gikuyu for all purposes.

[2] "We see no reason to doubt the general accuracy of the statement that the number of Kikuyu now resident outside the reserve is in the general neighbourhood of 110,000, and supporting calculations are given in the memorandum, which had been filed with the original record of the evidence." (*Report of the Kenya Land Commission*. September, 1933, § 499.)

ments, sacrifices, meat feasts, magical rites, purification
ceremonies, and as means of supplying clothing to the
community.

The cultural and historical traditions of the Gikuyu
people have been verbally handed down from generation to generation. As a Gikuyu myself, I have carried
them in my head for many years, since people who
have no written records to rely on learn to make a
retentive memory do the work of libraries. Without
note-book or diary to jot down memoranda, the African learns to make an impression on his own mind
which he can recall whenever it is wanted. Throughout
his life he has much to commit to memory, and the
vivid way in which stories are told to him and their
incidents acted out before his eyes helps the child to
form an indelible mental picture from his early teaching. In every stage of life there are various competitions arranged for the members of the several age-
groups, to test their ability to recall and relate in song
and dance the stories and events which have been told
to them, and at such functions parents and the general
public form an audience to judge and correct the
competitors.

Like any other Gikuyu child, therefore, I acquired
in my youth my country's equivalent of a liberal education, but while I lived among my kinsfolk there was
no obvious necessity for writing it down. But during
my anthropological studies and visits to various countries in Europe, I had the opportunity of meeting men
and women who were keenly interested in hearing about
African ways of life. I then realised the necessity to set
down in black and white the knowledge which had
hitherto remained in my head, for the benefit both of
Europeans and of those Africans who have been detached from their tribal life. Before setting to work
I realised the difficulty which faced me owing to my
lack of training in comparative social anthropology,

and accordingly set about finding ways and means to acquire the necessary technical knowledge for recording the information scientifically. It was my friend and teacher, Professor Malinowski, who made this possible for me through the International Institute of African Languages and Culture, and I wish to place on record my appreciation of his unfailing help and encouragement, both in study and in the arrangement of my material.

I wish to express my gratitude to those many friends, both European and African, who have been good enough to read and discuss parts of my manuscript and to give their frank opinions of it. Their criticisms and suggestions have been helpful. I am indebted to Dr. Raymond Firth for his careful reading of the manuscript and his technical advice on anthropological points. And to my brother Moigai for taking photographs of initiation ceremonies and for checking information on ritual points; and to my father and other elders, who gave him their help.

I owe thanks also to my enemies, for the stimulating discouragement which has kept up my spirits to persist in the task. Long life and health to them to go on with the good work!

Thaaaai—to the members of the Gikuyu Central Association, my comrades-in-arms of the past, present, and future. In this work as in all our other activities, their co-operation, courage, and sacrifice in the service of the Gikuyu people have been the inspiration and the sustaining power.

In the present work I have tried my best to record facts as I know them, mainly through a lifetime of personal experience, and have kept under very considerable restraint the sense of political grievances which no progressive African can fail to experience. My chief object is not to enter into controversial discussion with those who have attempted, or are attempting, to describe the same things from outside observation, but to let the truth speak for itself. I know that there are many scientists and general readers who will be disinterestedly glad of the opportunity of hearing the Africans' point of view, and to all such I am glad to be of service. At the same time, I am well aware that I could not do justice to the subject without offending those "professional friends of the African" who are prepared to maintain their friendship for eternity as a sacred duty, provided only that the African will continue to play the part of an ignorant savage so that they can monopolise the office of interpreting his mind and speaking for him. To such people, an African who writes a study of this kind is encroaching on their preserves. He is a rabbit turned poacher.

But the African is not blind. He can recognize these pretenders to philanthropy, and in various parts of the continent he is waking up to the realisation that a running river cannot be dammed for ever without breaking its bounds. His power of expression has been hampered, but it is breaking through, and will very soon sweep away the patronage and repression which surround him.

The reader will undoubtedly wish to know my credentials for writing the book. Merely to have been born and bred in the Gikuyu country may seem to him a vague qualification, so I will give a more explicit account of the sources of my knowledge.

I have said that as a boy I received the usual education of Gikuyu boys, and the legends in the chapters on Kinship and Government, and elsewhere in the book, are some of those which I absorbed from my elders during early training in custom and tradition, and later used to relate to my juniors as an evening amusement. The terms of kinship are those which I have heard and used for years among my own kinsmen. As my grandfather and father were polygamous,

I was born into a wide kinship group with several degrees of relationship.

Following the tribal custom, I had to pass through the several stages of initiation along with my age-group, *kehiomwere,* and can therefore speak from personal experience of the rites and ceremonies. Although men do not witness the physical operation on the girls, they are not ignorant of its details, as the young initiates of both sexes talk freely to each other about it afterwards. Moreover, one of the operators was my aunt, Waco, and in visiting her homestead as a child, I naturally picked up the details of the process by hearing conversations between her and other women.

I participated in the activities of my age-group, and was chosen as its leader. Afterwards, through my knowledge of the outside world, I came to take a leading part in the progressive movements among the Gikuyu generally, and still hold that position. As the General Secretary of the Gikuyu Central Association, I started and edited the first Gikuyu journal, *Muigwithania,* in 1928–1930. This gave me the opportunity to tour all over the Gikuyu country and to meet many people, old and young, with whom I have discussed various aspects of cultural problems, political, social, religious, educational, and others. In due course I have passed three stages of eldership (*Kiama kia mbori ithato*), and this has enabled me to participate in Councils of Elders and to learn their procedures in various parts of the Gikuyu country. As a member of the warrior class, I not only have a practical knowledge of the Gikuyu methods of warfare, but have lived in the Masai country at a place near Ngare Narok, where I came in close contact with Masai military methods and learnt much about them, and have also visited many other tribes.

As for magic, I have witnessed the performance of magic rites many times in my own home and elsewhere.

My grandfather was a seer and a magician, and in
travelling about with him and carrying his bag of
equipment I served a kind of apprenticeship in the
principles of the art. Besides this, I have lived in a
place called Gaturi in Central Gikuyu, a district well
known for its magical practices, and there came into
contact with many magicians, or witch-doctors, and
learnt a great deal about their ways. I have also had
opportunities of meeting and discussing the subject
with other magicians, both from coastal and up-country
tribes.

Information about the new religious cult came my
way in 1930–31, on my return from a first visit to
Europe. A deputation from its members visited me at
that time, and I learnt much from them about their
activities and ideas.

I can therefore speak as a representative of my people, with personal experience of many different aspects
of their life. Finally, on the vitally important question
of land tenure, I can claim to speak with more than
ordinary knowledge, as I have explained in a note at
the beginning of Chapter 2. The Gikuyu have chosen
me as their spokesman before more than one Royal
Commission on land matters. One was the Hilton
Young Commission of 1928–29, and a second was the
Joint Committee on the Closer Union of East Africa,
in 1931–32. Before this Committee I was delegated
to present a memorandum on behalf of the Gikuyu
Central Association. In 1932 I gave evidence in London before the Morris Carter Kenya Land Commission,
which presented its Report in 1934. I have studied
and taken part in various discussions of this Report,
and disputes arising out of it, among others the one
about the removal of the Gikuyu people from their
ancestral home in Tigoni; a matter which has been
widely discussed in the Press and the House of Commons.

I make special mention of these points, because to anyone who wants to understand Gikuyu problems, nothing is more important than a correct grasp of the question of land tenure. For it is the key to the people's life; it secures for them that peaceful tillage of the soil which supplies their material needs and enables them to perform their magic and traditional ceremonies in undisturbed serenity, facing Mount Kenya.

JOMO KENYATTA

London

CONTENTS

FACING
MOUNT KENYA

MAP OF THE GIKUYU COUNTRY

1

TRIBAL ORIGIN AND KINSHIP SYSTEM

THE GIKUYU tribal organisation is based on three most important factors, without which there can be no harmony in the tribal activities. For the behaviour and the status of every individual in the Gikuyu society is determined by the three governing principles which we will categorically enumerate here. The first is the family group (*mbari* or *nyomba*), which brings together all those who are related by blood; namely a man, his wife or wives and children and also their grand- and great-grandchildren. The second is clan (*moherega*), which joins in one group several *mbari* units who have the same clan name and are believed to have been descended from one family group in the remote past. It is obvious that, owing to the polygamous system of marriage, a family or *mbari* unit increases rapidly, and in one generation it is possible for a *mbari* to have a hundred members or more. Thus in a few generations the number increases to several thousands, which renders it impossible for a *mbari* to live together in a group where they could refer to one another as father, mother, sister, brother, uncle, aunt, grandfather, grandmother, etc.

When these identities of blood relations disappear, the only bond left between a group which once was united by close blood relation is the *moherega* identity. This knits together distant relatives and facilitates the feeling of rendering mutual support in all important matters in the interest and the welfare of the *moherega*. In perpetuation of this feeling, representatives of a *moherega* generally meet on occasions of big events, such as marriage ceremonies and initiation or circumcision ceremonies. In such gatherings, the elders bring with them a young member each from their respective *mbaris*. The younger members of the *moherega* are introduced to one another, and they are told how their lineage links their particular *mbari* to the *moherega*. This information is given to the youths so that when they grow up and take the responsibility in the leadership of their own *mbaris,* they will be in a position to conduct wisely the affairs of their family group, and at the same time to follow the correct line of their ancestors in promoting the unity of the whole of the *moherega*.

The third principle factor in unifying the Gikuyu society is the system of age-grading (*riika*). As we have seen, the *mbari* and the *moherega* system help to form several groups of kinsfolk within the tribe, acting independently; but the system of the age-grading unites and solidifies the whole tribe in all its activities.

Almost every year, thousands of Gikuyu boys and girls go through the initiation or circumcision ceremony, and automatically become members of one age-grade (*riika rimwe*), irrespective of *mbari, moherega,* or district to which individuals belong. They act as one body in all tribal matters and have a very strong bond of brotherhood and sisterhood among themselves. Thus, in every generation the Gikuyu tribal organisation is stabilised by the activities of the various age-grades, of old and young people who act harmoniously, in the political, social, religious and economic life of the Gikuyu.

With these few opening remarks, we will proceed at once to describe the "behaviour patterns" which are the key to understanding the relationship existing between various individuals within a kinship group. To do this effectively, it is necessary to take as our starting-point the tribal legend which will throw light on the origin of the Gikuyu system of kinship.

According to the tribal legend, we are told that in the beginning of things, when mankind started to populate the earth, the man Gikuyu, the founder of the tribe, was called by the Mogai (the Divider of the Universe), and was given as his share the land with ravines, the rivers, the forests, the game and all the gifts that the Lord of Nature (Mogai) bestowed on mankind. At the same time Mogai made a big mountain which he called Kere-Nyaga (Mount Kenya), as his resting-place when on inspection tour, and as a sign of his wonders. He then took the man Gikuyu to the top of the mountain of mystery, and showed him the beauty of the country that Mogai had given him. While still on the top of the mountain, the Mogai pointed out to the Gikuyu a spot full of fig trees (*mikoyo*), right in the centre of the country. After the Mogai had shown the Gikuyu the panorama of the wonderful land he had been given, he commanded him to descend and establish his homestead on the selected place which he named Mokorwe wa Gathanga. Before they parted, Mogai told Gikuyu that, whenever he was in need, he should make a sacrifice and raise his hands towards Kere-Nyaga (the mountain of mystery), and the Lord of Nature will come to his assistance.

Gikuyu did as was commanded by the Mogai, and when he reached the spot, he found that the Mogai had provided him with a beautiful wife whom Gikuyu

named Moombi (creator or moulder). Both lived happily, and had nine daughters and no sons.

Gikuyu was very disturbed at not having a male heir.
In his despair he called upon the Mogai to advise him
on the situation. He responded quickly and told Gikuyu
not to be perturbed, but to have patience and everything would be done according to his wish. He then commanded him, saying: "Go and take one lamb and one
kid from your flock. Kill them under the big fig tree
(*mokoyo*) near your homestead. Pour the blood and
the fat of the two animals on the trunk of the tree.
Then you and your family make a big fire under the
tree and burn the meat as a sacrifice to me, your benefactor. When you have done this, take home your wife
and daughters. After that go back to the sacred tree,
and there you will find nine handsome young men who
are willing to marry your daughters under any condition
that will please you and your family."

Gikuyu did as he was directed by the Mogai or Ngai,
and so it happened that when Gikuyu returned to the
sacred tree, there he found the promised nine young men
who greeted him warmly. For a few moments he could
not utter a word, for he was overwhelmed with joy.
When he had recovered from his emotional excitement,
he took the nine youths to his homestead and introduced them to his family.

The strangers were entertained and hospitably treated
according to the social custom. A ram was killed and a
millet gruel prepared for their food. While this was
being made ready, the youths were taken to a stream
nearby to wash their tired limbs. After this, they had
their meal, and conversed merrily with the family and
then went to bed.

Early the next morning Gikuyu rose and woke the
young men to have their morning meal with him. When
they finished eating, the question of marriage was discussed. Gikuyu told the young men that if they wished

to marry his daughters he could give his consent only if they agreed to live in his homestead under a matriarchal system.

The young men agreed to this condition, for they could not resist the beauty of the Gikuyu daughters, nor the kindness which the family had showed them. This pleased the parents, for they knew that their lack of sons was now going to be recompensed. The daughters, too, were pleased to have male companions, and after a short time all of them were married, and soon established their own family sets. These were joined together under the name of Mbari ya Moombi, i.e. Moombi's family group, in honour of their mother Moombi.

The nine small families continued to live together, with their parents (Gikuyu and Moombi) acting as the heads of the Mbari ya Moombi. As time went on, each family increased rapidly, and Gikuyu and Moombi had many grand- and great-grandchildren. When Gikuyu and Moombi died, their daughters inherited their movable and immovable property which they shared equally among them.

During the time of mourning for the death of their parents they continued to live as one family group as before. But as the number of members of each individual family group multiplied, it was found impossible to live together and to follow the system of classificatory nomenclature without forming more family sets and clans.

It was then decided that each of the nine daughters should call together all her descendants and form one clan under her own name. Thus the nine principal Gikuyu *meherega* clans were founded. The names of the main clans are: (1) Acheera; (2) Agachiko; (3) Airimo; (4) Amboi; (5) Angare; (6) Anjiro; (7) Angoi; (8) Ethaga; (9) Aitherando. Besides these there are others which are more or less variations of the original ones.

After the system of kinship was extended from Mbari ya Moombi to several *mbaris* and *meherega,* it was then thought necessary to bring all these groups under one strong bond of kinship, in which they could act in solidarity and regard one another as members of one big family.

This large group was then formed and given the ancestral collective name of Rorere rwa Mbari ya Moombi, namely, children or people of Moombi or Moombi's tribe. In this, women continued to be the heads of their family groups and clans for some generations. But somehow the system changed from matriarchal to patriarchal.

It is said that while holding superior position in the community, the women became domineering and ruthless fighters. They also practised polyandry. And, through sexual jealousy, many men were put to death for committing adultery or other minor offences. Besides the capital punishment, the men were subjected to all kinds of humiliation and injustice.

Men were indignant at the way in which the women treated them, and in their indignation they planned to revolt against the ruthless women's administration of justice. But as the women were physically stronger than the men of that time, and also better fighters, it was decided that the best time for a successful revolt would be during the time when the majority of women, especially their leaders, were in pregnancy.

The decision was hailed by the men who were very anxious to overthrow the rule of the opposite sex. At once the men held a secret meeting in which they arranged a suitable date to execute their plan. On the day appointed to carry out the initial stage of the revolt, the men started to act enthusiastically. They embarked on a campaign to induce the women leaders and a majority of their brave followers to have sexual intercourse with them. The women were unfortunately deceived by the flattery of the men, and blindly agreed to their inducements without knowing the wicked plan the men had made to overthrow the women's rule.

The men, after completing the first act, quietly waited for the result. After six moons had elapsed the men then saw clearly that their plan had materialised. At once they organised into groups and finally carried out the revolt without much resistance. For the brave women were almost paralysed by the condition in which they were. The men triumphed, took over the leadership in the community and became the heads of their families instead of the women. Immediately steps were taken to abolish the system of polyandry and to establish the system of polygamy.

The men also decided to change the original name of the tribe as well as the names of clans which were given under the matriarchal system, to new ones under the patriarchal system. They succeeded in changing the name of the tribe from Rorere rwa Mbari ya Moombi to Rorere rwa Gikuyu (i.e. Gikuyu nation or the Children of Gikuyu). But when it came to the changing of the clan names, the women were very infuriated and strongly decided against the change which they looked upon as a sign of ingratitude on the part of the men. The women frankly told the men that if they dared to eliminate the names which stood as a recognition that women were the original founders of the clan system, the women would refuse to bear any more children. And to start with, they would kill all the male children who were born as a result of the treacherous plan of the revolt.

The men were very much afraid of the women's strong decision, and in order to avoid the conflict, they allowed the original names of the clans to remain unchanged. And the nine main clans in the Gikuyu tribe are still known under the names of the nine Gikuyu daughters who were the founders of the Gikuyu clan system. The proper names of these daughters from which the clan names as given on page 7 were derived are: (1) Wacheera; (2) Wanjiko; (3) Wairimo; (4) Wamboi; (5) Wangare; (6) Wanjiro; (7) Wangoi; (8) Mwethaga or Warigia; (9) Waithera. And these are the common women's names in the Gikuyu society nowadays.

Up to this point we have been following the description of how the Gikuyu kinship system was founded. With that as our background, we will proceed to analyse the behaviour patterns which govern the relations between the members of one kinship group.

In the Gikuyu family group, as in other forms of tribal organisation, there are certain rules of behaviour which must be strictly observed in order to keep the group in harmonious relationship. These "behaviour patterns" (*metugo ya nganyiiti,* as they are called by the Gikuyu), are very important, and though fundamentally similar in the family groups to be found almost in every part of the world, they no doubt differ considerably under the influence of such factors as patrilineal and matrilineal descent, the division of labour and responsibility between men and women in every society.

The Gikuyu society is organised and functions under the patrilineal system. The father, who is the head of the family, is called *baba* (my or our father), *ithe* (father, his or her), *thogwo* (father, your). The father is the supreme ruler of the homestead. He is the owner of practically everything, or in other words, he is the custodian of the family property. He is respected and obeyed by all the members of his family group. His position in the community depends largely on the type of homestead he keeps, and how he manages it, because the capability of good management of one's homestead is taken as a testimonial that one is able to manage public affairs.

It is etiquette for a son or daughter to talk to the father in a gentle and polite tone, and the parent, except when reprimanding or correcting his children, is required by custom to reciprocate the compliment in the same way as his children extend it to him.

The members of his children's age-grade address him in the same manner as his children do. It is considered impolite to address the father by his own name or names; his children speak of him as "my or our father," other children address him as "father of So-and-so." Unless he is a rascal, they dare not mention his name in private or in public, except when mentioning it in a collective sense, that is, in referring to the family group, such as *Mbari ya Moigai* (Moigai's family), or *Ng'undo ya Moigai* (Moigai's land), etc.

The mother is called *maito* (my or our mother), *nyina* (his, her or their mother), *nyokwa* (your mother). The term "mother" is considered as an honourable form of address, and one which is desired by every woman in Gikuyu society. When a woman reaches the stage of motherhood she is highly respected, not only by her children, but by all members of the community. Her name becomes sacred and she is addressed by her neighbours and their children as "mother of So-and-so." To maintain her prestige, she must be hospitable to visitors and render assistance to her neighbours when they are in difficulty or in need.

The worst thing that a man can do to infuriate another is to dare to mention his mother's name in an indecent way. This would result in a fight to defend the sacred name of the mother. The great attachment and respect shown to the mother by her children is due to the fact that she is their nurse, and has daily closer contact with them than the father. She feeds and looks after the clothing and ornaments of the children. When they are in trouble, they first go to their mother, to appeal or confess to her. If the matter needs the atten-

tion of the father, it is the mother who takes it before
him and tactfully explains the children's needs to her
husband. In many cases the mother manages to get
conciliation between the father and the children and
avoid a conflict.

In a Gikuyu family, especially when there is more
than one wife, the mother is the immediate head of
her family set, namely, her hut, her children, her personal ornaments and household utensils, as well as her
cultivated fields with the crops thereon and granaries.
In these respects she is her own mistress as far as
other wives are concerned.

The relations between wives are those of partnership
based on the collective possession of the husband, and
not on the ownership of the property within the precincts of a wife's hut or granary. The wives address one
another as *moiru wakwa* (my partner or co-wife). Each
wife is materially almost independent of the other. The
head wife has no superior authority over the rest. But
she is only respected for her seniority in age, provided
that she lives up to it. Her main official duty in the
homestead is to take a leading part in the religious and
other ceremonies performed in the interest of the
family group. With regard to work, she does her own
work in the same way as the rest, according to the
recognised rules in the homestead.

The co-operation in cultivating the land, planting
the seeds or harvesting, depends entirely on mutual
agreement between the wives and their husband. Each
wife addresses her husband as *mothuri wakwa* (elder
mine or my husband). The husband addresses his wife
as *mutumia wakwa* (lady mine). Collectively he addresses them as *atumia akwa* (ladies mine). They address him collectively as *mothuri wito* (elder ours).
This form of address is extended symbolically to each
member of the husband's age-grade. And he, too, ad-

dresses the wives of the members of his age-grade in the same manner as "lady or ladies mine."

The brother of the husband is given a nickname as a sign of endearment. He, too, reciprocates in the same way, and sometimes a present is necessary as a sign of naming. The sister of the wife is addressed by the husband as *maramu,* which is something like "my sister-in-law." All the wife's other relatives, including her parents, are addressed individually as *mothoni wakwa,* and collectively, *athoni akwa,* i.e. my relative-in-law and relatives-in-law respectively.

The wife addresses the husband's parents as *maito* or *baba,* i.e. my mother or father, as the case may be. They address her by her father's name as daughter of So-and-so. This is a sign of endearment and respect to the parents.

We have examined the relation between wife or wives and husband, and also between relatives on both sides. It is necessary then to turn our attention to the social behavior existing between the children in a family group, and again the relation between them and other members of both paternal and maternal family groups.

The bond of kinship between the children of the same mother is strengthened by the mother. Male children address one another as *moro wa maito,* i.e. son of our mother. Female children address one another as *mware wa maito* (daughter of my or our mother). A brother refers to his sister as *mware wa maito,* and the sister to his brother as *moro wa maito.*

As regard to seniority in age, the elder child is addressed by the younger one as *mokoro wakwa* (my senior), the parents refer to such a child as *irigithathi* (first child). The first-born is regarded as a centre of affections and a precious possession of the parents, especially that of the first wife. The younger child is addressed by the elder one as *moruna wakwa* (my

follower or one who followed me). The last child is
known as *kehinganda* (one who closed the womb),
such a child is held dear, particularly by the mother.
The relation between the children of one father and
different mothers is strengthened by the father. They
address one another as *moro wa baba* (son of our
father), *mware wa baba* (daughter of our father).

The bond of kinship between the children of the
same mother and father is stronger than that of the
children of one father and different mothers. The feeling between the former is that of inseparables, and it
is said that, having slept in the same womb (*maraire
nda emwe*), and having suckled the same breast (*mon-
gire nyondo emwe*), they are one another's flesh and
blood, and as such they ought to live for one another.

On the other hand the children of the same father
and different mothers behave to one another in a different way. The feelings between them is that of separate
family sets linked up and kept together by the father.
And as long as the father is alive, the connection-link
is very strong. But when the father dies, they are free
to break up the common homestead and establish
separate homesteads together with their respective
mothers. After this the family group which once was
kept and functioned together under the father's direction and co-operation, becomes two or three distinct
family units acting almost independently.

This is how sub-clans are started. In the first place
the sons of the same father and different mothers continue to perform collectively their religious and other
sacrificial ceremonies. They do this generally during
their lifetime. But after they are dead the relation between their sons begins to drift apart slowly until the
divergence reaches a point where collective action or
participation in religious or other private functions of a
family is no longer considered necessary. At this juncture the only bond left between such a group of people

is that of a common distant ancestor with whom all commune according to the needs of their particular family group.

In many cases, especially in a small family group of one or two wives, close relation between the members is maintained for many generations, and the authority of the father is always passed to the next generation through the elder son in each generation. In perpetuation of the kinship system girls count very little on their parents' side; their function becomes more important later on in their husband's homesteads.

If a man dies without a male child his family group comes to an end. This is one thing that the Gikuyu people fear dreadfully, and it can be said to be one of the factors behind the polygamous system of marriage. There is no doubt that perpetuation of family or kinship group is the main principal of every Gikuyu marriage. For the extinction of a kinship groups means cutting off the ancestral spirits from visiting the earth, because there is no one left to communicate with them. And so when a man has more than one wife and many children, his soul rests in peace with the feeling that, after death, it will not be wandering in the wilderness or lose contact with the earth, for there will always be someone to hold communion with.

RELATION BETWEEN CHILDREN AND THEIR FATHER'S RELATIVES

In the Gikuyu society behaviour towards the father's relatives is entirely different from that accorded to the mother's relatives. All his brothers are addressed by his children by the name of "father ours," according to their age in comparison to that of the real father. If it be an elder brother he is addressed as *baba mokoro* (elder father, my or our), the younger brother is called *baba monyinyi* (small or younger father, my or ours).

They in turn address the children in the same way as their own. Sometimes these relations depend on the position of the fathers, if they are rich and entertain the children nicely they hear more of "our elder father, our younger father," but if they are not in a position to give the children treats, they hear less of the beloved form of address. Hence a Gikuyu saying that *"Motheni ndetagwo baba mokoro kana monyinyi,"* that is, a poor man does not command the respect of being called "elder or younger father."

The form of address used between the children of brothers is that of *moro* or *mware wa baba mokoro* or *monyinyi* (son or daughter of my or our elder or younger father, as the case may be). A sister of the father is called *tata* (aunt). The relation between her and her brother's children depends on whom she marries and the distance between her husband's homestead and that of the brother. If there is mutual agreement between the two families and frequent visits are exchanged from both sides, the children become well acquainted with their aunt and respect her as one of the close relatives and one who entertains them. But unlike her brothers, who are looked on as fathers and have supreme authority over the children, she has very little influence in affairs concerning the children or the homestead of her brothers, except in social functions.

Her children and those of her brothers address one another as *moihwa* (cousin), there is a strong bond of kinship between them, and whenever they pay a visit to one another, the host provides a special meal for the guest. Even when they are just passing by, it is considered as a bad omen not to visit the homestead of your cousin or to leave it without eating something, no matter how little it may be. This is illustrated by a Gikuyu saying that *"moihwa ndaimagwo ronyeni,"* which means, a cousin cannot be denied a meal.

GRANDPARENTS ON BOTH SIDES

Grandparents are called *guuka* (grandfather) and *coco* (grandmother). The affection between them and the children is very great. Symbolically the children belong to the same age-group as their grandparents. The name given to the first male child is that of his paternal grandfather, and at the time of birth it is announced that it is "he" who has come. Similarly the second male child will represent his maternal grandfather. In religious ceremonies the children are treated in the same manner as their grandparents. The same thing applies to a female child. Owing to the supreme authority which grandparents have in the family group the children, while with them, are given the feeling that they are with their equals. Sometimes the children spend more time with their grandparents, especially the grandmother, than with their own parents. A boy is called by his grandmother "my husband," and a girl is called "my co wife." The grandfather calls the boy *wakine,* "my equal," and the girl *mohiki wakwa,* "my bride." This form of address is, of course, used figuratively and as a sign of endearment.

When the grandparents are not living near the homesteads of their daughters or sons, the children pay frequent visits to their grandparents and stay with them for some time. Sometimes it becomes difficult to get the children to return to their parents' homesteads, for they feel more free in playing and joking with their grandparents than they would with their own parents.

MOTHER'S RELATIVES

As we have seen that the behaviour pattern towards the father is extended to his brothers and sisters, in the same way that towards the mother is extended to her relatives. The important members of her family group, who enter into functions of the kinship system, are the father, mother, brother, and sister. Her mother and father, as stated above, treat their daughter's children with great respect and love.

The mother's sister is called *tata,* the same as the father's sister, but the relation between her and the children of her sister is entirely different. She is looked upon by the children in the same way as their real mother. The affection and indulgence that she gives to the children and the sympathetic attitude towards them is even greater than that the children can expect from their own mother. Children like to visit or to be visited by their aunt, and whenever such a visit is made it is always an occasion of rejoicing and feasting. The children of both sisters address one another as *moro* or *mware wa tata* (son or daughter of my or our aunt), the behaviour pattern between them is almost like that of brothers and sisters.

The mother's brother, who is called *mama* (my or our uncle), is the only one in the family group who enjoys that title. For there is no uncle on the father's side, because those who might be called uncle, according to European system of kinship, are called "fathers" in the Gikuyu society. The uncle's relation with his sister's children is that of fatherly love and affection. He has a certain influence over the children. For instance, before children can be allowed to pierce their ears as a sign of approaching the circumcision ceremony, his permission must be obtained. A gift of five sheep or goats is made by the father to the uncle at a time when the permission is required.

Visits are made to the uncle's homestead, but not so frequent as those made to the mother's sister. The reason being that in his homestead, unlike that of his sister who is ruler of her house, the entertainment of the children is in his wife's hands. And unless he has a very good and hospitable wife, the children would feel rather nervous at visiting him, except at the time of a ceremonial feast when children are accompanied by their mothers.

RELATIVES BY MARRIAGE

We have discussed the behaviour patterns and terms used among the husband's and wife's immediate relatives. But as a marriage brings together all members of two distant clans, it is necessary to describe the relation existing between the two groups.

After a marriage contract is signed between two families all clan members of both sides become united. They regard one another as *mothoni* (relative by marriage). The behaviour towards one's relative-in-law is bound up with the word *mothoni,* which means one who is bashful or polite. Therefore it follows that every *mothoni* must treat another with politeness. In the case of a woman the politeness tends to be bashful, especially in the presence of her relatives-in-law. She must not eat in their presence or utter unpleasant words. She must cover her body properly when sitting or passing near them. She must speak in a sweet and polite tone when talking to them, etc.

The same thing applies to a man. He must show politeness to his mother-in-law or any other member of her age-group. He must give up his seat to her, get out of the way while she is passing. He must cover his body properly in her presence and not use any vulgar language while speaking to her or in her hearing. The father-in-law may not enter the house of his daughter-in-law before she becomes a mother, and as a sign of politeness he must give a sheep or goat on entering her house.

With regard to economics, both sides give each other a great deal of mutual help. In agriculture, relatives by

marriage generally help one another. Cultivation rights
are, moreover, given to a relative by marriage who
has not sufficient land of his own to maintain himself
and his family. There are numerous gifts exchanged
among them, especially in times of ceremonies connected with initiation, marriage, or religion. For example, if a man is having his son or daughter circumcised, and has not sufficient grain to entertain
visitors and friends who attend the initiation ceremonies,
he will send to his relatives-in-law to supply the necessary food and drink, knowing that they would ask for
the same help if they were similarly placed. This
exchange of gifts is governed by the principle of "give
and take."

2

THE GIKUYU SYSTEM
OF LAND TENURE

THE RULES governing land tenure, like many other social customs, were taught to me by my father, who is a landowner. As I was his first son he was careful to give me all necessary information about land tenure, to equip me to discharge my duties as *moramati* in future years. In this way I acquired the knowledge which is a normal part of every Gikuyu's education, especially if he is a first-born. But in addition to this I have been a witness to many land transactions and disputes, both public and private, in various parts of Gikuyu; for instance, I acted as private interpreter to Chief Kioi in his big land case which, after several hearings before the *Kiama,* was brought to the Supreme Court in Nairobi in 1921. I was elected as a spokesman of the Gikuyu Central Association when we presented our case before the Hilton Young Commission in 1928; afterwards, when the report came up for discussion in Parliament, I was delegated to present the Gikuyu point of view with regard to land and other matters to the Secretary of State for the Colonies in 1929, and have continued to do so when the occasion has arisen.

Because of these experiences, my knowledge of Gikuyu land tenure is not merely due to the fact that I am a Gikuyu, but is the result of great interest and specialised study, both of recorded precedents and of those tribal evidences which are handed down from generation to generation.

In studying the Gikuyu tribal organisation it is necessary to take into consideration land tenure as the most important factor in the social, political, religious, and economic life of the tribe. As agriculturalists, the Gikuyu people depend entirely on the land. It supplies them with the material needs of life, through which spiritual and mental contentment is achieved. Communion with the ancestral spirits is perpetuated through contact with the soil in which the ancestors of the tribe lie buried. The Gikuyu consider the earth as the "mother" of the tribe, for the reason that the mother bears her burden for about eight or nine moons while the child is in her womb, and then for a short period of suckling. But it is the soil that feeds the child through lifetime; and again after death it is the soil that nurses the spirits of the dead for eternity. Thus the earth is the most sacred thing above all that dwell in or on it. Among the Gikuyu the soil is especially honoured, and an everlasting oath is to swear by the earth (*koirugo*).

Owing to the importance attached to the land the system of land tenure was carefully and ceremonially laid down, so as to ensure to an individual or a family group a peaceful settlement on the land they possessed. According to the Gikuyu customary law of land tenure every family unit had a land right of one form or another. While the whole tribe defended collectively the boundary of their territory, every inch of land within it had its owner.

The following terminology is used to denote the landholders' position:

1. *Mwene ng'ondo* or *githaka,* the individual owner of land who has acquired it either by purchase or through inheritance or by acquiring first hunting rights.

2. *Moramati,* a trustee, who acts as the guardian to the younger members of his family group.

3. *Mohoi,* one who acquires cultivation rights on the *ng'ondo* or lands of another man or family unit, on a friendly basis without any payment for the use of the land.

4. *Mociarwa,* a man who is adopted into the family of a clan other than his own by means of a special religious ceremony.

5. *Githaka kia ngwataniro,* land held by two individual families as joint property (this practice was rare).

6. *Mothoni,* a relation-in-law of the first degree, who acquires cultivation or building rights, or both.

7. *Mothami,* a man who acquires cultivation and building rights on the *githaka* of another man or clan.

8. *Borori wa Gikuyu,* territory of the Gikuyu, this term denotes the political unit of all lands within the tribal boundary. The term emphasises that the land belongs exclusively to the Gikuyu. Undoubtedly this is what the Europeans have misinterpreted to mean "Tribal ownership or communal land."

Having given these outlines, we will at once proceed to describe how the land was originally acquired and the traditional sanctions under which the Gikuyu system of land tenure was maintained prior to the coming of the Europeans into the country. To do this effectively it is best to start from a tribal legend connected with the old man Gikuyu, the founder of the tribe, from whose name that of the country and of the people is derived.

According to the tribal legend, which as a boy I heard from my grandfather's talk with other elders, and which many of our people are familiar with, we

are told that from the beginning of things, Ngai or
Mogai (God or Divider or Benefactor), when he was
dividing the world into territories and giving them to
the various races and nations that populate the globe,
gave the man Gikuyu a territory full of the good things
of nature. The Mogai commanded Gikuyu to establish
a home for himself and his descendants. Gikuyu and
his wife, Moombi, built their first homestead at a place
called Mokorwe wa Gathanga, and had many children.
As time went on, the people increased rapidly owing
to the multiplicity of wives and good nourishment from
the soil. Soon the land, which was held as the family
land, became densely populated. For this reason some
of the people decided to move southward and try to
acquire more lands from the forest dwellers.

In the forests there lived a race of people called
Gumba (pigmy), who were engaged in hunting. They
were very short and strong. Their homes were built
underground, they were shy and did not like to mix
freely with the strangers. To avoid meeting other people
they dug tunnels (*miungu*) connecting different sections
of their underground villages. As soon as they saw a
stranger they ran into the tunnels, which were cunningly concealed; then they would run quickly underground and reappear at the other end. The Gikuyu
were very much astonished, for they thought that these
people had magic for opening the earth and disappearing therein at will.

As far as the story of these people goes, there is no
clear indication of any land transactions between them
and the Gikuyu people, but it is said that they disappeared underground and no one knows what became
of them. Their disappearance is attributed to the failure
of their magic, which they used to perform while
entering into their underground homes. And it is supposed that when the earth swallowed them, they were

not able to perform their magic to permit them to return to the surface.

Our theory on this question is that it is not likely that this race of early hunters was swallowed by the earth, as we are led to believe by the tribal legend, but that there are two ways in which the disappearance of the Gumba could definitely be explained. Firstly, that they moved farther west towards the Congo forests where similar types of people are to be found. But when we consider the distance between the Congo forest and the Gikuyu country, and the hardship which the Gumba would have encountered on their journey to Congo, we are inclined to think that the movement did not take place.

If that is so, then the only possible way to account for the disappearance of the Gumba is that they inter-married with the early Gikuyu pioneers who ventured into the forests, and perhaps lost their contact with the other main sections of the Gikuyu, and, therefore, settled in the forests in the same way as Gumba.

There is strong reason to support the latter theory, for soon after the Gumba had disappeared as a race, there came into being another race of hunters known as Ndorobo or Aathi, who seemed to have grown like mushrooms in the forests. Unlike their predecessors, they were not short in stature, but something between the Gumba and the Gikuyu. Also they did not live underground, but built their homes on the surface, almost on similar lines to those of the Gikuyu home-steads. Their language, too, was similar to the Gikuyu. To a certain extent the two tribes could understand one another with little difficulty.

With these evidences it would not be assuming too much to say that the interbreeding between the Gumba and the Gikuyu was responsible for the disappearance of the Gumba as a distinct race, and the producing of the Ndorobo or Aathi, who became the new owners and the masters of the forests, as we shall see later.

The Ndorobo established friendly relations with the Gikuyu, and, as the people continued to move southwards, land transactions started between the two tribes who lived side by side. The Ndorobo were not interested in cultivating the land, their main occupation was hunting and collecting wild honey in the forests. Apart from land transactions they traded with the Gikuyu. By barter they sold their honey and skins of animals to the Gikuyu, who in turn gave the Ndorobo grains, yams, sugar-canes, bananas, and other fruits of the soil.

As the time went on the Gikuyu, who had not enough land to cultivate in the congested areas, started to buy lands from the Ndorobo. All the lands which were bought in this way were held under private ownership or as a family joint property. In fact, there was not in any part of the Gikuyu, as far as memory goes, any land that belonged to everybody, or what is called "no man's land." The term "communal or tribal ownership of land" has been misused in describing the land, as though the whole of it was owned collectively by every member of the community.

The Gikuyu defended their country collectively, and when talking to a stranger they would refer to the country, land, and everything else as "ours," *borori wiito* or *borori wa Gikuyu,* to show the unity among the people. But the fact remained that every inch of the Gikuyu territory had its owner, with the boundary properly fixed and everyone respecting his neighbour's. In the Report on the Gikuyu Land Tenure, paragraph 22, it is recorded that: "——there are several places in the Nyeri and Fort Hall districts where one may stand and see more than a thousand acres at a stretch with scarcely an acre uncultivated, and the disputes which occur, though complicated and troublesome, are surprisingly few." In former days no man could dare go and cultivate another man's land without first obtaining the necessary permission from the rightful owner or owners. The sense of private property vested in the family was highly developed among the Gikuyu, but the form of private ownership in the Gikuyu community did not necessarily mean the exclusive use of the land by the owner, or the extorting of rents from those who wanted to have cultivation or building rights. In other words, it was a man's pride to own a property and his enjoyment to allow collective use of such property. This sense of hospitality which facilitated the communal use of almost everything, has been mistaken by the Europeans who misinterpreted it by saying that the land was under the communal or tribal ownership, and as such the land must be *mali ya serikali*, which means Government property. Having coined this new terminology of land tenure, the British Government began to drive away the original owners of land.

In the following pages we will describe the system of land tenure, showing how the land was first acquired, and how it passed from individual ownership to family or clan ownership. In doing so we will base our analysis on the eight different types of land holding or land rights.

In dealing with the private ownership of land we will begin our description from the time when the Gikuyu people started to move southward and established contact with the Ndorobo, from whom the land, especially in South Gikuyu, was bought. Before this time, although some form of private ownership of land existed, the system was not so obvious, as there was no property exchanged in acquiring the possession of the land. In the first place the land was given to the Gikuyu by the Mogai, the Lord of Nature. Secondly, by the fact that the Gikuyu was the first to establish his homestead on the land. Thirdly, that when the people started to multiply and to form their own individual family groups,

each family group pegged out a portion of the forest
and reserved the first rights of cultivation and hunting
therein. In those days the claim of having cleared the
original forest was the basic principle of absolute
ownership of land. In other words, a man acquired the
right to own the land through the labour he spent in
developing it. For this reason it was necessary for the
whole family to join forces in order to clear sufficient
land for their present and future needs. Fourthly, when
the land which the Mogai had given to the Gikuyu was
thickly populated and no more forests left to be pegged
out, people moved towards the forests in the south.
Here, the forests having been owned by the Ndorobo,
there was no possibility of a man just going into the
forest and establishing his claim by merely clearing
the original forest. This being the case, the Gikuyu who
were anxious to own the land, on seeing that the
Ndorobo were willing to sell, at once started to purchase
it. Thus a new form came into being, of owning the
land by purchase, instead of owning by acquiring the
first rights of hunting or clearing the original forests.

In order to clarify the two systems last mentioned,
under which the lands were acquired, let us take the
words from the Report on the Gikuyu Land Tenure
issued in 1929. In paragraph 24 the following statement is made: "It is most interesting to consider why
it is that the tribal theory is in most respects intact
in Nyeri and Fort Hall, while in Kiambu it has been
modified greatly in favour of the individual owner-
cultivator and the sectional head."

The reason for this difference is that in Nyeri and
Fort Hall there hardly existed any land transaction between the Gikuyu and Ndorobo, and even if any
purchase of land from the Ndorobo had taken place
in these districts it would have happened so far in the
remote past that the incident has faded from the
memory of the present generation. Most probably there

were no Ndorobo in either Fort Hall or Nyeri, for the Mokorwe wa Gathanga, the place where the Gikuyu are believed to have originated, is somewhere in these districts. If that is so, there could not have been any land transactions between the Gikuyu in the two districts and the Ndorobo, unless there is evidence to prove that both the Gikuyu and the Ndorobo originated at the same place. But as far as we are aware, there is no such evidence in the tribal historical legends.

The next point in connection with the slight difference between the system of land tenure in the Kiambu district and that which exists in the Nyeri and Fort Hall districts, is that in the former case the land was actually bought from the Ndorobo. In the Kiambu district the land transaction between the Gikuyu and the Ndorobo is a recent occurrence, and there are people still living who took part in purchasing the land from the Ndorobo.

At the same time there are single families who bought the land, and as they have not yet increased to form a clan unit the land is still in the hands of the first purchaser, and as such he has the rights of private ownership. For example, if a man whom we will call A bought land before he was married, that land was his own private property during his bachelorhood. When he married B, the land became the joint property of husband and wife. In this case we will assume that A had no relatives or he was independent of such relatives. He cleared a part of his land for his wife to cultivate; that part cultivated by his wife became her own or she had full cultivation rights, while the soil still remained the property of the husband. Let us say that a man had sixty acres of land. The first wife might have cultivated two acres; she would refer to this part as "my garden" (*mogonda wakwa*), and the rest as "our land" (*githaka giito*). Next A married a second wife C, and cleared another part of his land for her in

the same way as for B. The land which remained uncultivated belonged to all three. The wives could call
it "our land," while their husband called it "my land"
(*githaka giakwa*). Now each wife had her garden or
gardens according to her capacity in cultivation. No
one, except perhaps her husband, would encroach upon
her cultivated pieces of land. If any of the wives wanted
a new garden, her husband would clear another piece
from the uncultivated land.

After some time the family began to increase. Let
us imagine that each wife had three sons and perhaps
some daughters. But as female children do not take
part in the ownership of land, we will leave them out,
because, having no system of spinsterhood in the
Gikuyu society, women do not inherit land on their
father's side; they play their part in the family or clan
in which they marry.

To return to our analysis, Mr. A with his two wives
B and C had six sons. The sons following their father's
example married two wives each. In this way the land
which used to be the private property of Mr. A, and of
which he had absolute ownership, was now shared by
several persons who had full cultivation rights, namely,
the father, his two wives, the six sons with their twelve
wives, making a total of twenty persons who called the
land "ours," and the father who retained the title of
"my land" (*ng'ondo yakwa*).

For our analysis let us suppose that the twelve wives
followed the example of their mothers-in-law and had
an average of three sons each. This would bring the
number of the land claimants to fifty-six persons, all
having full cultivation rights, and each regarding the
piece under cultivation as "my garden." The other uncultivated land or fallow land would be regarded by all
collectively as "our land," while Mr. A still called the
whole of the land "my land." If we take daughters into
consideration, as they also had to use land before

marriage, we will find that while Mr. A was still living he might have had about seventy or more people of his own as nucleus of his *mbari* or clan unit.

As time went on this group of people became a big community and the land which all regarded as "our land" could no more support them. When a family group reached this point, the more prosperous members of it went and bought lands somewhere else and started the same proceeding as we have already described; but those who were not in a position to buy land became *ahoi* or *athami,* i.e. they acquired cultivation or building rights on the lands belonging to another family group or clan unit.

The above description gives a clear picture contradicting what is called communal ownership of land, a term which presupposes that the land belonged to every Dick and Harry in the community. This could not be the case for, as we have shown, the land did not belong to the community as such, but to some individual founders of various families who had the full rights of ownership and the control of the land.

Unlike the European, the African kinship tie is so strong that all a man's children and grandchildren, including great-grandchildren, are considered as forming the family group, and as such they must stick together.

To clarify the above statement let us take the case of a man who bought or acquired the first hunting rights of land while a bachelor, and was afterwards forced by circumstances to become monogamous instead of polygamous. In this case we will suggest that fate so decided that the man had only one son and many daughters, which means that there were only two persons who could call the land "ours" and the father who called it "mine," and who had full or outright ownership of that particular land. On his death he transferred his rights to his son according to the customary law of inheritance. So it is clear that unless there were many sons in a family group, the land remained the private property of the man who bought it or of his son who inherited it.

BUYING AND SELLING LAND

After land was bought from the Ndorobo, any man who held such land, through purchase or inheritance, had full rights to sell it outright or give it to any one as he liked without consulting any one, except the elders who acted as the ceremonial witnesses in all land transactions. By inheritance we mean a single son inheriting the land from his father who had no other relatives.

When a man has many sons he is no more alone, his interests are interwoven with those of his children, and since they are flesh of his flesh, bone of his bones, he shares his land and all his property with them. He could not sell his land without consulting them unless he was a very bad man, who did not care for the future of his family. Cases of this nature are very rare in the Gikuyu community but even when it occurred the elders of the village or district would intervene and plead with the father for the welfare of his children.

LAND INHERITANCE

After the death of the father the land passed on to his sons, the eldest son took his father's place. At this juncture the system of land tenure changed a little, there was no one who could regard the land as "mine," all would call it "our land." The eldest son who had assumed the title of *moramati* (titular or trustee) had no more rights than his brothers, except the title; he could not sell the land without the agreement of his brothers who had the same full cultivation rights on the pieces of land which they cultivated as well as those which were cultivated by their respective mothers.

At this stage the land had now become family or *mbari* land, under the name of the original owner (*Mogori Githaka* or *Mwene Githaka*). For instance, if the original owner was Kamau, his *mbari* would be known as *mbari ya Kamau* (the Kamau's family group), and the land as *ng'ondo* or *githaka kia mbari ya Kamau,* i.e. the land of Kamau's family group. Through this process the land passed from one man to his sons and then it was actually vested in the clan's name.

The above statement shows clearly that the Gikuyu system of land tenure was never tribal tenure, nor was there any customary law which gave any particular chief or a group of chiefs any power over lands other than the lands of their own family groups. A chief could only give cultivation or building rights to a *mohoi* or *mothami* on his own land or that of his *mbari,* but in this case he could do so only if he was a *moramati.* Otherwise he had no power to give or sell land outside the boundary of his own personal property.

The policy of making a chief a trustee or investing him with the power of allotting "tribal or communal lands," is entirely new and foreign to the Gikuyu democratic principles. The power to decide land disputes was invested in the councils of elders (*kiama*), who conducted all land transactions. Any chief who participated in these councils did so in his capacity of an elder (*mothuri wa kiama*), and not as a chief.

Up to this point we have been following the Gikuyu system of land tenure, from the founder of the tribe to the Gumba and Ndorobo, the master of the forests; and then to the first purchaser and his family. We have now reached the juncture where the administration of the land has passed to the *moramati.* Having done so, it is necessary to add a short description of the *moramati* and his duty to his brothers on whose behalf he acts as a trustee.

A *moramati* owes his position to his seniority in age, and to being the first son of the first wife. And in a case where the first wife had no sons, the first son of the second wife became the heir. The duty of the *moramati* was to see that the land was properly used, and to carry out the wishes of his dead father. *Moramati* had no more cultivation or building rights than his brothers. Agriculturally he was only the ceremonial figurehead and master of his own pieces of cultivated fields in the same way as his father's wives, brothers and sisters. If any of them wanted to clear a piece of virgin land, he or she was at liberty to do so, provided that there was no taboo or custom prohibiting cultivation of that particular piece of land.

If an outsider wanted to acquire cultivation or building rights, as a *mohoi* or *mothami,* such rights could only be given by the *moramati* with the consent of other members of the family group. In the first place the *moramati,* before giving such rights, would see to it that there was enough land for the needs of his group. Secondly, he would not grant cultivation rights on the fallow land that had previously been cultivated by any of his juniors, unless they had abandoned the cultivation of such land altogether.

Before a man was given cultivation or building rights his character and past history were carefully scrutinised to make sure that he was not a trouble-maker. A *mohoi* or *mothami* was given permission to settle on the land only on the understanding that he would respect the rights of the members of the landowning family and keep peace with them. As a sign of his adherence to this agreement he had to give a calabash or gourd of beer to the *moramati* or his representative, whenever he had an occasion of brewing beer. This obligation was strictly applied to a man who had been given cultivation and building rights (*mothami*), but if he had only cultivation rights (*mohoi*), his obligation to give beer was only when he had brewed sugar-cane beer from the land given to him.

A *mothami* was further obliged to help in case of any work of emergency such as building houses or cattle-pens. If a *mothami* behaved decently his family and that of the landowner sometimes joined in teamwork for mutual benefits. On the other hand, a breach of the contract on the part of a *mothami* meant withdrawal of his rights and removal from the land. The authority to carry this out was invested in the hands of the *moramati*. If a *mothami* or *mohoi* refused to quit the land, he was taken before the *kiama* (council of elders), who naturally gave judgment in favour of the *moramati*. But in any case a *mohoi* or *mothami* was given sufficient notice to find another land and also to harvest his crops. Apart from the beer which was given as a token of friendship and respect, there was no payment of rent of any kind for the use of the land. The cultivation or building rights were given purely as a matter of friendship and not on a business basis.

There was another situation necessitating a change in the position of the *moramati;* for instance, if he mismanaged the land and a quarrel arose between him and his juniors, the village council (*kiama gia itora*) was summoned to divide up the land equally among the male representatives of the family group. But this was only done when all effort to seek conciliation had failed. When the land was divided up, the *moramati* was left to himself and his own immediate family, i.e. his wife or wives and their children. The rest, if they wanted to continue the management of their land under one head, appointed one of themselves as the new *moramati* and carried on with their affairs as before.

When the land was thus divided up, the old *moramati* could sell his own portion to anybody else, and perhaps move away and buy land in another district. According to the customary law of land tenure, if one of the brothers wanted to sell out his share, the relatives had the first option so as to avoid a stranger coming in their midst. The one whose right was bought out, and his descendants, lost all claims to the original ancestral land, and were treated as mere strangers.

Before the sanction for the sale of such land was given, the matter was carefully scrutinised by the *kiama* in order to preserve kinship unity in connection with the ancestral land. For the selling out of his rights in the family land was the last thing that a man could do to sever the relation with his kinsfolk. In perpetuation of the kinship unity it was considered right and proper for a man to reserve his rights in the ancestral land, so that if misfortune should befall him in his ventures, he could always return to his ancestral home and be received with joy by his kinsfolk.

PASTURE LAND AND PUBLIC PLACES

It is important to mention that in every district there were pasture lands where livestock grazed in common. There were also salt-licks (*moonyo*) and mineral springs (*irori*), the access to which was free to all those in the district. In addition to these there were public places (*ihaaro*) reserved for meetings and dances. And also public roads and paths (*njera cia agendi*), as well as sacred groves where national sacrifices were offered to Ngai.

Public opinion entered strongly in the management of the above-mentioned lands, for although in reality these lands were owned by different individual families, in actual uses they were treated as common lands. Whenever a salt-lick or a mineral spring was found on any land, whether cultivated or uncultivated, the owner could not prevent other people in the district from sending their livestock to such places. But in the case of a poor man who had no other land, he was given another piece of land by the elders of the district. But for pasture lands there were permanent grass or bush lands reserved for that purpose. Generally these lands were situated some distance from the homesteads, some of them were considered not good for cultivation except along the rivers where sugar-cane, bananas, and *ndoma* (arum lily) were cultivated.

Near homesteads there were also pasture lands, owing to the system of cultivating the lands in rotation, and besides this there was also woodland, reserved for building materials and firewood. The use of such land for grazing was restricted to the family group possessing it. They could give or withhold the permission to outsiders.

If we consider for a moment the pasture lands, salt-licks, public meeting and dance places, the woodlands, including big forests along the frontier of the Gikuyu and the neighbouring tribes, we will at once see that there were big tracts of lands used for other purposes than cultivation and which were equally important to the community.

It is of these lands that the early European travellers reported that they had seen huge lands "undeveloped" and "unoccupied." To them it may have seemed so, but to the Gikuyu every inch of their territory was useful in some way or another. To a Gikuyu these lands were no more unoccupied than moorlands in England, for if a Gikuyu were asked to make a report on such moorlands, he would naturally report that these lands are undeveloped and unoccupied. The mere absence of large herds of sheep and goats on the lands, and the lack of bananas, yams and sugar-cane cultivation would be sufficient evidence to convince him that those lands were not put to "proper uses." Just in the same way the Europeans did not justify the usefulness of bush land in Africa where they expected to find cultivated grass-land for pasture.

CEREMONY OF MARKING
THE BOUNDARY

In analysing the Gikuyu system of land tenure the most important aspect and deciding factor as to the ownership of land is the ceremony of marking the boundary. This was performed only when absolute land sale took place. In the case of a *mohoi* or *mothami, mociarwa* or *mothoni,* no such ceremony could be performed between them and the landlord, for they had only been given cultivation or building rights.

It was only when the purchaser had paid or agreed to pay the number of sheep and goats required as the price of the land, that the two parties concluded an agreement in the form of a ceremony. This was done in the presence of the principal elders of the district who acted as witnesses. Before buying and selling of land took place, there was a preliminary ceremonial discussion between the seller and the buyer. According to the etiquette of the people, no man could go directly to another and tell him that he wanted to buy his land. The same applied to the seller, he could not advertise the sale of his land publicly; the reason being that the land was regarded as the mother of the people, and as such the selling or buying of it must be treated matrimonially.

Therefore, the correct approach was that when a man wanted to buy another man's land, he would brew a small beer and take it to the landowner in the same way as if he were proposing marriage to his daughter. After sipping the beer ceremonially, the two men would then join in a conversation, talking in parable something like this: "Well, son of So-and-so, I brought you this small beer to tell you that within your homestead I have seen a beautiful lass. I hope you will excuse me when I say that I am madly in love with her. My great desire which urged me to come here to-day is to ask you if you will accept me as your son-in-law. I am sure that you, being a man of great experience, will not fail to see the admiration I have in my heart for your beautiful lass. And I know that you will not fail to give your consent to my humble request."

Through such a conversation the landowner would know at once what his guest really wanted. Then, in the same parable language, they would agree or disagree. If they agreed about the price of the land they would fix a date and invite the elders of the district to be present as ceremonial witnesses.

On the day appointed, the elders gathered on the land in question, where the two parties wishing to enter into symbolical matrimony awaited them. The seller of the land was asked to testify by an oath that the land he was selling was his own property, that he or his ancestors were the original and rightful owners. And that he was satisfied with the number of sheep and goats he had asked as the price of his land, and that later he would not ask the purchaser to give him more than what had been already agreed to. Then the elders turned to the purchaser and asked him to take oath and declare that he had willingly agreed to buy the land and to give the number of sheep and goats asked for it; that the animals he was giving were his own or family property, and that there was no dispute as to the ownership of such property in his family group or outside it.

When the above declaration was concluded, the purchaser provided a ram, which was slaughtered on the spot where the declaration was made. The contents of the stomach were taken out, then the elders formed a procession with the seller and the purchaser at the head of it. They moved slowly chanting a ceremonial melody connected with the fertility of the soil. The landowner pointed out the boundary of his land which he was selling, at the same time the ceremonial elder sprinkled the contents of the stomach along the line, while the rest planted trees and lilies (*matooka*) as a permanent boundary mark.

The elders, in their ritual tones, uttered curses against anyone who should cunningly or maliciously remove the boundary mark of his neighbour. When the marking of the boundary was completed, all sat down at the centre of the land, two small pieces were cut from the skin of the ram, the purchaser put one on his right wrist and so did the seller. This act of uniting the two men in the land transaction, who now regarded one another as relatives-in-law, concluded the ceremony of marking the boundary.

After the elders had finished their official duty they joined in a meat feast and sometimes in beer drinking. The elder who sprinkled the contents of the stomach along the boundary line was given a ewe as the reward for his laborious duty. The official name of the ritual gift is known as *"mwate wa kuhura njegeni,"* i.e. a ewe for dusting off aching caused by a stinging creeper called *njegeni*.

According to the Gikuyu system of land tenure no man could claim absolute ownership of any land unless he or his ancestors had gone through the ceremony of marking the boundary, which was the Gikuyu form of title-deed. The boundary trees and lilies so ceremonially planted were highly respected by the people. They were well looked after and preserved. The history connected with such lands was passed from one generation to another. No man dared to remove his neighbour's boundary mark, for fear of his neighbour's curses and out of respect for him.

If one of the boundary trees or lilies dried out, fell

down, or was rooted up by the wild animals, the two neighbours would visit the spot and perhaps replace it, but if they could not agree as to the actual place where the mark stood, they called one or two elders who, with a little ceremony, replanted the tree or lilies. But in a case of a big dispute, especially where a fire had destroyed boundary marks, a full council of elders was called to replant the tree and lilies.

LAND TENURE AND THE COMING OF THE EUROPEANS

In the foregoing analysis we have traced how the land was formerly acquired and how the rules governing the system of land tenure were laid down. Further, we have shown the relations between the landowner and his immediate family, and the relations between that group and those who acquired cultivation or building rights. Later on we will show how this generosity of giving temporary cultivation or building rights to strangers was extended to the Europeans when they arrived in the Gikuyu land. Before entering into this discussion it is necessary first to give a short account of the prophecy of a great Gikuyu medicine man, Mogo wa Kebiro, who predicted the coming of the Europeans and the result thereof.

MOGO WA KEBIRO AND HIS PREDICTION

Once upon a time there lived in Gikuyuland a great medicine man known as Mogo or Moro wa Kebiro. His national duty was to foretell future events and to advise the nation how to prepare for what was in store. We are told that one early morning the prophet woke up trembling and unable to speak; his body covered with bruises. His wives on seeing him were very frightened and in a state of hysteria, not knowing what

had happened to their husband, who went to bed in
perfect health the previous evening. Horror-stricken,
the family summoned the ceremonial elders to his side
with a view to offer a sacrifice to Ngai (God) and to
inquire what the great man had foreseen that had so
frightened him.

When the ceremonial elders arrived, a male goat
(*thenge*) was immediately slaughtered and Mogo wa
Kebiro was seated on the raw skin. The senior elder
among the gathering took the blood of the animal,
mixed it with oil, and then this mixture was poured on
the head of the great seer as an anointment. At the
same time the ceremonial elders, saturated with religious
beliefs, recited ritual songs as supplication to Ngai.
Soon Mogo wa Kebiro regained his power of speech.
With his usual prophetic voice he began to narrate what
he had experienced during the previous night. He told
the elders that during his sleep Ngai (God) had taken
him away to an unknown land. There the Ngai had
revealed to him what would happen to the Gikuyu
people in the near future. On hearing this he was hor-
rified, and in his endeavour to persuade Ngai to avert
the evil events coming to the Gikuyu, he was badly
bruised and exhausted and could not do anything but
obey the Ngai's command to come back and tell the
people what would happen.

After a little pause, Mogo wa Kebiro continued his
prophetic narrative. In a low and sad voice he said that
strangers would come to Gikuyuland from out of the
big water, the colour of their body would resemble that
of a small light-coloured frog (*kiengere*) which lives in
water, their dress would resemble the wings of butterflies; that these strangers would carry magical sticks
which would produce fire. That these sticks would be
very much worse in killing than the poisoned arrows.
The strangers, he said, would later bring an iron snake
with as many legs as *monyongoro* (centipede), that this

iron snake would spit fires and would stretch from the big water in the east to another big water in the west of the Gikuyu country. Further, he said that a big famine would come and this would be the sign to show that the strangers with their iron snake were near at hand. He went on to say that when this came to pass the Gikuyu, as well as their neighbours, would suffer greatly. That the nations would mingle with a merciless attitude towards each other, and the result would seem as though they were eating one another. He also said that sons and daughters would abuse their parents in a way unknown hitherto by the Gikuyu.

Mogo wa Kebiro urged the people not to take arms against the coming strangers, that the result of such actions would be annihilation of the tribe, because the strangers would be able to kill the people from a far distance with their magical sticks which spit deadly fires. The warriors were very angry when they heard this statement and said that they would take up arms and kill the iron snake and the strangers. But the great seer calmed them and told the warriors that the best thing would be to establish friendly relations with the coming strangers, because the spears and arrows would not be able to penetrate the iron snake, and therefore the warriors' attempt to fight the strangers and their snake would be futile.

The great medicine man advised the people that when these strangers arrived it would be the best policy to treat them with courtesy mingled with suspicion, and above all to be careful not to bring them too close to their homesteads, for these strangers are full of evil deeds and would not hesitate to covet the Gikuyu home-land and in the end would want to take everything from the Gikuyu.

When the people heard what Mogo wa Kebiro had predicted they were very disturbed and did not know what to do except wait and face the coming danger.

Many moons afterwards, about 1890 or thereabout, the
predicted danger began to appear, for sure enough,
the strangers dressed in clothes resembling the wings
of butterflies started to arrive in small groups; this was
expected, for prior to their arrival a terrible disease,
called *ndigana* or *nyongo,* had broken out and destroyed
a great number of Gikuyu cattle as well as those of the
neighbouring tribes, the Masai and Wakamba. The
incident was followed by a great famine, which also
devastated thousands of the tribesmen.

The first few Europeans who passed near the Gikuyu
country were more or less harmless, for they passed
through along the borderline of the country between
the Gikuyu and Masai or between Wakamba and the
Gikuyu. They were thus directed according to the
prediction of the great medicine man. The Europeans
with their caravans kept coming and going the same
way from the coast to Lake Victoria and Uganda. In
their upwards and downwards journeys they traded with
the Gikuyu with little or no conflict. At last, misled by
European cant, the Gikuyu thought that the Europeans
with their caravans did not mean any harm and be-
friended them. Forgetting the words of Mogo wa Kebiro
to treat the Europeans with courtesy mingled with
suspicion and not to bring them near their homesteads,
the Gikuyu began to welcome the Europeans in close
proximity to their homesteads.

At this stage it is interesting to give a short narrative
of how the Gikuyu came to lose their best lands. When
the Europeans first came into the Gikuyuland the
Gikuyu looked upon them as wanderers (*orori* or
athongo) who had deserted from their homes and were
lonely and in need of friends. The Gikuyu, in their
natural generosity and hospitality, welcomed the wanderers and felt pity for them. As such the Europeans
were allowed to pitch their tents and to have a temporary right of occupation on the land in the same

category as those Gikuyu *mohoi* or *mothami* who were given only cultivation or building rights. The Europeans were treated in this way in the belief that one day they would get tired of wandering and finally return to their own country.

These early Empire builders, knowing what they were after, played on the ignorance and sincere hospitable nature of the people. They agreed to the terms of a *mohoi* or *mothami,* and soon started to build small forts or camps, saying that "the object of a station is to form a centre for the purchase of food for caravans proceeding to Uganda," etc. For "Kikuyu was reported a country where food was extraordinarily abundant and cheap." [1]

The Gikuyu gave the Europeans building rights in places like Dagoretti, Fort Smith and others, with no idea of the motives which were behind the caravans, for they thought that it was only a matter of trading and nothing else. Unfortunately, they did not realise that these places were used for the preliminary preparations for taking away their land from them. They established friendly relations with the Europeans and supplied them with food for their caravans, taking it for granted that naturally the white wanderers must undoubtedly have their own country, and therefore could not settle for good in a foreign land, that they would feel home-sick and, after selling their goods, would go back to live in their homesteads with parents and relatives.

The belief that the Europeans were not going to live permanently in Africa, was strengthened by the fact that none of them seemed to stay very long in one place. Therefore, reasoning from this, the Gikuyu naturally came to the conclusion that one day all the Europeans in Africa would pack up bag and baggage and return to their own country in the same way as they came. It

[1] *The Rise of our E. African Empire,* by Lord Lugard, p. 323, vol. 1.

was a common saying among the Gikuyu until a few years ago that *"Gotire ondo wa ndereri, nagowo Coomba no okainoka,"* which means that there is no mortal thing or act that lives for eternity; the Europeans will, no doubt, eventually go back to their own country. This saying was taken up as a lamenting slogan, and was sung in various songs, especially when the wanderers started to show their real motive for wandering.

The early travellers reported that "Kikuyu promised to be the most progressive station between the coast and the lake. The natives were very friendly, and even enlisted as porters to go to the coast, but these good relations received a disastrous check. Owing largely to the want of discipline in the passing caravans, whose men robbed the crops and otherwise made themselves troublesome, the people became estranged, and presently murdered several porters." [1] This was the beginning of the suffering and the use of the sticks which produced killing fire, as Mogo wa Kebiro had predicted in his prophecy of the coming of the white men. For soon after the above incident, we are told that the Gikuyu were "taught a lesson," they were compelled to make "the payment of fifty goats daily, and the free work of three hundred men to build the fort they had destroyed." [2]

After this event the Gikuyu, with bitterness in their hearts, realised that the strangers they had given hospitality to had planned to plunder and subjugate them by brute force. The chief, Waiyaki,[3] who had entered into a treaty of friendship with the strangers, was afterwards deported and died on his way to the coast. People were indignant for these acts of ingratitude on the part

[1] *The Rise of our E. African Empire*, by Lugard, p. 535, vol. 2.
[2] *Ibid.*, p. 536, vol. 2.
[3] "I made treaties with Eiyaki (Waiyaki) and several other chiefs, who came from considerable distances to perform the ceremony of blood-brotherhood." (*Rise of our E. African Empire*, by Lugard, p. 329, vol. 1.)

of the Europeans, and declined to trade with them, thinking that the Europeans and their caravans would get hungry and move away from the Gikuyu country; but soon the Gikuyu were made to know that "might is right," for it is reported that "from this country of teeming abundance, where in a few days I obtained many thousand pounds of food, the officer finds it impossible to purchase a single bag of grain," and parties were sent out regularly to take it by force!—and "large armed parties were necessary to procure firewood and water." [1]

The prediction of Mogo wa Kebiro was slowly being fulfilled, for soon afterwards the Kenya-Uganda railway (the iron snake) was completed. And the Europeans, having their feet firm on the soil, began to claim the absolute right to rule the country and to have the ownership of the lands under the title of "Crown Lands," where the Gikuyu, who are the original owners, now live as "tenants at will of the Crown." The Gikuyu lost most of their lands through their magnanimity, for the Gikuyu country was never wholly conquered by force of arms, but the people were put under the ruthless domination of European imperialism through the insidious trickery of hypocritical treaties.

The relation between the Gikuyu and the Europeans can well be illustrated by a Gikuyu story which says: That once upon a time an elephant made a friendship with a man. One day a heavy thunderstorm broke out, the elephant went to his friend, who had a little hut at the edge of the forest, and said to him: "My dear good man, will you please let me put my trunk inside your hut to keep it out of this torrential rain?" The man, seeing what situation his friend was in, replied: "My dear good elephant, my hut is very small, but there is room for your trunk and myself. Please put your trunk in gently." The elephant thanked his friend, saying:

[1] *Blue-Book Africa*, No. 8, 1893, p. 2.

"You have done me a good deed and one day I shall
return your kindness." But what followed? As soon as
the elephant put his trunk inside the hut, slowly he
pushed his head inside, and finally flung the man out
in the rain, and then lay down comfortably inside his
friend's hut, saying: "My dear good friend, your skin
is harder than mine, and as there is not enough room
for both of us, you can afford to remain in the rain
while I am protecting my delicate skin from the hail-
storm."

The man, seeing what his friend had done to him,
started to grumble, the animals in the nearby forest
heard the noise and came to see what was the matter.
All stood around listening to the heated argument between the man and his friend the elephant. In this tur-
moil the lion came along roaring, and said in a loud
voice: "Don't you all know that I am the King of the
Jungle! How dare anyone disturb the peace of my kingdom?" On hearing this the elephant, who was one of the
high ministers in the jungle kingdom, replied in a soothing voice, and said: "My Lord, there is no disturbance
of the peace in your kingdom. I have only been having
a little discussion with my friend here as to the possession of this little hut which your lordship sees me oc-
cupying." The lion, who wanted to have "peace and
tranquillity" in his kingdom, replied in a noble voice,
saying: "I command my ministers to appoint a Commission of Enquiry to go thoroughly into this matter and
report accordingly." He then turned to the man and
said: "You have done well by establishing friendship
with my people, especially with the elephant who is
one of my honourable ministers of state. Do not
grumble any more, your hut is not lost to you. Wait
until the sitting of my Imperial Commission, and there
you will be given plenty of opportunity to state your
case. I am sure that you will be pleased with the find-
ings of the Commission." The man was very pleased by

these sweet words from the King of the Jungle, and innocently waited for his opportunity, in the belief that, naturally, the hut would be returned to him.

The elephant, obeying the command of his master, got busy with other ministers to appoint the Commission of Enquiry. The following elders of the jungle were appointed to sit in the Commission: (1) Mr. Rhinoceros; (2) Mr. Buffalo; (3) Mr. Alligator; (4) The Rt. Hon. Mr. Fox to act as chairman; and (5) Mr. Leopard to act as Secretary to the Commission. On seeing the personnel, the man protested and asked if it was not necessary to include in this Commission a member from his side. But he was told that it was impossible, since no one from his side was well enough educated to understand the intricacy of jungle law. Further, that there was nothing to fear, for the members of the Commission were all men of repute for their impartiality in justice, and as they were gentlemen chosen by God to look after the interests of races less adequately endowed with teeth and claws, he might rest assured that they would investigate the matter with the greatest care and report impartially.

The Commission sat to take the evidence. The Rt. Hon. Mr. Elephant was first called. He came along with a superior air, brushing his tusks with a sapling which Mrs. Elephant had provided, and in an authoritative voice said: "Gentlemen of the Jungle, there is no need for me to waste your valuable time in relating a story which I am sure you all know. I have always regarded it as my duty to protect the interests of my friends, and this appears to have caused the misunderstanding between myself and my friend here. He invited me to save his hut from being blown away by a hurricane. As the hurricane had gained access owing to the unoccupied space in the hut, I considered it necessary, in my friend's own interests, to turn the undeveloped space to a more economic use by sitting in it myself; a duty which any of you would undoubtedly have performed with equal readiness in similar circumstances."

After hearing the Rt. Hon. Mr. Elephant's conclusive evidence, the Commission called Mr. Hyena and other elders of the jungle, who all supported what Mr. Elephant had said. They then called the man, who began to give his own account of the dispute. But the Commission cut him short, saying: "My good man, please confine yourself to relevant issues. We have already heard the circumstances from various unbiased sources; all we wish you to tell us is whether the undeveloped space in your hut was occupied by anyone else before Mr. Elephant assumed his position?" The man began to say: "No, but——" But at this point the Commission declared that they had heard sufficient evidence from both sides and retired to consider their decision. After enjoying a delicious meal at the expense of the Rt. Hon. Mr. Elephant, they reached their verdict, called the man, and declared as follows: "In our opinion this dispute has arisen through a regrettable misunderstanding due to the backwardness of your ideas. We consider that Mr. Elephant has fulfilled his sacred duty of protecting your interests. As it is clearly for your good that the space should be put to its most economic use, and as you yourself have not yet reached the stage of expansion which would enable you to fill it, we consider it necessary to arrange a compromise to suit both parties. Mr. Elephant shall continue his occupation of your hut, but we give you permission to look for a site where you can build another hut more suited to your needs, and we will see that you are well protected."

The man, having no alternative, and fearing that his refusal might expose him to the teeth and claws of members of the Commission, did as they suggested. But no sooner had he built another hut than Mr. Rhinoceros charged in with his horn lowered and ordered the man to quit. A Royal Commission was again appointed to look into the matter, and the same finding was given. This procedure was repeated until Mr. Buffalo, Mr. Leopard, Mr. Hyena and the rest were all accommodated with new huts. Then the man decided that he must adopt an effective method of protection, since Commissions of Enquiry did not seem to be of any use to him. He sat down and said: *"Ng'enda thi ndeagaga motegi,"* which literally means "there is nothing that treads on the earth that cannot be trapped," or in other words, you can fool people for a time, but not for ever.

Early one morning, when the huts already occupied by the jungle lords were all beginning to decay and fall to pieces, he went out and built a bigger and better hut a little distance away. No sooner had Mr. Rhinoceros seen it than he came rushing in, only to find that Mr. Elephant was already inside, sound asleep. Mr. Leopard next came in at the window, Mr. Lion, Mr. Fox, and Mr. Buffalo entered the doors, while Mr. Hyena howled for a place in the shade and Mr. Alligator basked on the roof. Presently they all began disputing about their rights of penetration, and from disputing they came to fighting, and while they were all embroiled together the man set the hut on fire and burnt it to the ground, jungle lords and all. Then he went home, saying: "Peace is costly, but it's worth the expense," and lived happily ever after.

3

ECONOMIC LIFE

DIVISION OF LABOUR

IN THE PREVIOUS CHAPTER we have been discussing the land tenure, which is the most important factor, as we shall see presently, in our analysis of the economic life of the Gikuyu, for the supply of material needs depends entirely on the land.

The chief occupations among the Gikuyu are agriculture and the rearing of livestock, such as cattle, sheep and goats. Each family, i.e. a man, his wife or wives and their children, constitute an economic unit. This is controlled and strengthened by the system of division of labour according to sex. From the homestead to the fields and to the tending of the domestic animals, every sphere of activity is clearly and systematically defined. Each member of the family unit knows perfectly well what task he or she is required to perform, in their economic productivity and distribution of the family resources, so as to ensure the material prosperity of the group.

The best point for starting our analysis of the division of labour is from the homestead and then moving gradually to the fields. In house-building the heavy work of cutting timbers and putting up the framework falls on men. Carrying and cutting of the grass for thatching and plastering the wall with clay or cow-dung is the work of women. Men build fences around the homestead or gardens and also cattle-pens. They are the night watchmen to protect the crops against the wild animals.

The entire housework naturally falls within the sphere of women's activities. They cook, bring water from the rivers, wash utensils and fetch firewood from the forests or bush. They also perform the task of carrying the loads on their backs. According to the tribal customs which govern the division of labour, no man would dare to indulge in any of these activities except in a case of emergency, or otherwise he would scandalise the women and it would be difficult for such a man to get any girl to marry him. He would be given a nickname, *kihongoyo* or *moburabureki,* something like "Nosy Parker." Women are afraid of a man of this character, for they say that if he could perform women's work, what is the use of getting married, for how can a wife and husband be doing the same thing at the same time?

In cultivating the fields men clear the bush and cut big trees, and also break the virgin soil with digging-sticks or hoes. Women come behind them and prepare the ground for sowing seeds. Planting is shared by both sexes. Men plant bananas, yams, sweet potato vines, sugar-canes, tobacco, and also provide poles for propping up bananas and yams. Women plant maize, various kinds of beans, millet and sweet potato vines.

Weeding is done collectively. Cutting drains or water-furrows and pruning of banana plants, as well as making roads and bridges, is the work of men. Harvesting is done chiefly by the women. Tending of cattle, sheep and goats, and also slaughtering and distributing the meat and preparing the skins, is entirely the men's duty. Dress-making, pottery and weaving of baskets is exclusively women's profession. Wood-carving, smith's work, bee-keeping and hunting are men's occupations.

Women take responsibility for grinding corn and millet,
for making gruel, and pounding grains in wooden mortars. They also pound sugar-canes for making beer.

The brewing of beer is done jointly by both men and
women. Men cut the canes from the field and peel them,
and the women carry the canes home. While the women
are pounding, the men are busy mixing the substance
of the sugar-canes with the water and squeezing or
wringing the juice out of it, and also straining the
juice into fermenting gourds. Trading is done by both
sexes. Carrying and selling grains at the markets is
chiefly done by women, while taking sheep and goats or
cattle to the markets and selling them is the job of men.

AGRICULTURE

The land being the foundation rock on which the
Gikuyu tribal economy stands, and the only effective
mode of production that the people have, the result is
that there is a great desire in the heart of every Gikuyu
man to own a piece of land on which he can build his
home, and from which he and his family can get the
means of livelihood. A man or a woman who cannot
say to his friends, come and eat, drink and enjoy the
fruit of my labour, is not considered as a worthy member of the tribe.

A family group with land to cultivate is considered
as a self-supporting economic unit. The group work
harmoniously with a view to satisfying their immediate
needs, and with the desire to accumulate wealth in the
form of cattle, sheep and goats. These are acquired
through effective tillage of the land, except in a very few
cases nowadays where some people are able to get
money in some other ways than selling their products.

CHILDREN IN ECONOMIC ACTIVITIES

Children begin their activities in production when they are young as a part of their training in agriculture and herding. When children are very young they are left at home minding small babies, or are taken by their parents to the field where they are allowed to play in a corner of the cultivated field. Soon the children get interested in the work and are ambitious to participate in gardening. As soon as they are able to handle a digging-stick they are given small allotments to practice on.

The children are very proud of their small gardens and take great interest in learning how to become good agriculturalists. Parents help them to plant seeds and teach them how to distinguish the crops from the wild plants or weeds. For sometimes children keep on rooting out growing crops together with weeds, until gradually their eyes get to recognise what are weeds and what are crops. The children are very enthusiastic in their work, and frequently like to take their playmates and proudly show them round the small gardens, saying: "Look how our crops are growing nicely, surely we are going to have a good harvest, and then we can have a big feast as a result of our labour."

As a child grows, its sphere of activities in gardening increases. Instead of small fields, a large one is provided according to the capability of the child. Of course, the work is done collectively. The crops thus cultivated are in the care of the mother, who is the managing director of food supply in the homestead.

The children co-operate with their parents in production and distribution of the family's resources and wealth until the time of marriage. When a girl marries, if her husband's homestead is near, she continues to cultivate her childhood gardens and takes the crops home for the use of herself and her husband. On the

other hand, if she goes far away to live, she leaves the
gardens to her mother. In the case of a boy, he takes
full control of his gardens when he marries. For although he still co-operates with his parents in the general economy of the family group, he and his wife are
now responsible for supplying and satisfying their own
immediate material needs.

SEASONAL CALENDAR

In the Gikuyu country there are four seasons and two
harvests in one year. These are divided as follows: (1)
The season of big rain (*mbura ya njahe*) from March to
July; (2) the season of big harvest (*magetha ma njahe*),
between July and early October; (3) short rain season
(*mbura ya mwere*), from October to January; (4) the
season of harvesting millet (*magetha ma mwere*), from
January to March. There are various names attached to
these seasons, according to the activities pursued during
each season, such as clearing virgin land (*matuguta*),
protecting millet from the birds (*marira ma mwere*),
etc., but the names mentioned above are the main divisions of the seasonal calendar.

PREPARING FIELDS FOR PLANTING

Where land is available the system of cultivating it in
rotation is the most favoured, for it gives a farmer or
peasant an opportunity of getting a new field every
four or five seasons, and at the same time letting the
old one rest fallow. In this way a peasant is able to get
good crops without using manure, because most of the
Gikuyu land is very fertile. In cases where land is not
available, especially nowadays owing to the alienation
of the Gikuyu lands, people depend entirely on turning
their land over and over again to renew it.

During the hot season a family group gets together

and prepares their fields ready for planting. Every member of the group has his or her own fields for various seasonal crops, such as maize, a variety of beans, sweet potatoes and European potatoes and other vegetables. All these are planted at once when the rain starts. They are the mainstay of the Gikuyu diet.

Permanent crops such as yams, sugar-canes, bananas, can only flourish in particular soils in various localities. The planting of these is a matter for individuals and for the custom of different districts. These are not crops that everyone in the community can afford to grow on account of the suitable soil and water they require. In some districts, especially Fort Hall and Nyeri, these articles of food are plentiful, but in other districts they are looked on as somewhat of a luxury.

It would be tedious to describe here planting ceremonies or magic connected with the economic activities in the fields, as the magic which enters into the economic life of the people is dealt with in Chapter 10 on religion and ancestor worship.

To avoid repetition of magical aspects we will proceed to analyse the work and crops in the fields. Apart from the crops mentioned above, there are three kinds of crops which are planted in rotation, namely, millet (*mwere*), tree peas (*njogo*), and *njahe*, a very nourishing kind of beans used mostly to feed women after child-birth. *Njogo* and *njahe* are planted during the big rain season, and *mwere* during the short rain season. The reason being that if *njahe* and *njogo* are planted during the short rain season, the result will be failure, because they are very slow-growing crops and need plenty of water. The same with *mwere;* if it is planted during the big rain, it will grow taller and taller, and bear very little or no grain at all. From a scientific and economic point of view, obtained from years of trial and error, the planting of crops and weeding of the gardens are done according to the seasonal calendar.

CLEARING WEEDS

When crops are about four or five inches high the weeding of the ground is started. During this time people join in a collective weeding. Four or five persons or more form a group for team-work, they cultivate one man's field one day then next day another man's field, and so on until they clear weeds from all their fields. Another way of cultivating the fields is by inviting a group of friends, ten or more, and providing them with a feast of beer or gruel and other edibles. This is not looked upon as a reward for the work done, but as hospitality to one's guests.

After a man has informed his friends about the work he wants them to help in, a day is fixed, generally three days ahead. On the day appointed, the friends meet in the garden or field early in the morning and start to work enthusiastically, singing cultivation songs. Sometimes they will challenge cultivators in the next field and compete with them in work and songs. About midday, when the sun becomes hot, they have finished clearing a big field. At this juncture they retire and start feasting joyously for having completed the work of helping their friend.

If a stranger happens to pass by at this time of enjoyment after labour he will have no idea that these people who are now singing, dancing and laughing merrily, have completed their day's work. For after they have cleaned off the dust which they got from the fields, they look, in all respects, as though they have been enjoying themselves the whole day. This is why most of the Europeans have erred by making general remarks that "the African is a lazy being and likes to bask in the sun, while his wife or wives work for him," not realising that the African in his own environment does not count hours or work by the movement of the clock, but works with good spirit and enthusiasm to complete the task before him. In this way an African is able to work better and quicker in his own field, where he is his own master, than when employed by the Europeans where he has to be bossed about.

To turn to our analysis of the work in the fields, the correct method of ensuring a good crop is, that while the crops are growing the fields are weeded over and over again until there are no more weeds growing there. Then comes a time of relaxation waiting for the harvest. This is a period of numerous dances and songs and performing various ceremonies, especially if a good harvest is expected. About this time one of the quick-growing kinds of bean (*mboco*) is ripe, and is taken as a supplement to food prepared from the grains stored during the previous harvest.

MARKETING

At this time people have finished the heavy work of weeding and there is little to do in the fields except that the crops are in need of protection against the birds. This work is generally done in rotation, one member of the family group taking charge of the field one day and another the next day. This gives all the members of the group an opportunity of participating in dances and visiting the markets to sell or buy.

Marketing begins when crops are ripe and have not yet dried to be harvested. Various things are taken to markets, principally bananas, yams, a variety of beans, tree peas, maize, millet, potatoes and sugar-canes. In these markets one finds all kinds of ornaments, articles of clothing, from skins of animals to the Lancashire cotton, different types of agricultural implements, running from digging-sticks to hoes made in Birmingham or in Japan. There are also sheep and goats, milk and butter-fat, etc.

There are two ways of exchanging goods, one by

barter and the other by money. The former is predominant, for the majority of the people still adhere to the old form of exchanging one article for another. For instance, if one man has beans and he wants yams, he goes to the man who has yams and is in need of beans and tells him: "I have my beans and I want your yams." Then they argue as to how many yams to a basket of beans. If they agree they exchange there and then; if not, each goes his own way, looking for someone else who will agree with him, for the exchange depends entirely on individual buyer and seller.

There are also fixed prices for certain goods dictated by the seasonal law of supply and demand. For instance, if a man wants a cultivating-knife he goes to a smith who has fixed a general price for each of his articles according to their sizes. For example, a small knife is exchanged for a small basket of millet or two small baskets of beans. Again, if a woman wants an ornament she goes to a man or a woman who has them and there exchanges two heaps of sweet potatoes or one heap of yams for a bracelet or an ear-ring.

In the markets things are bought and sold in small and big quantities by people who have too much of one thing and too little of the other. Take the case of a man who is about to stage a big ceremonial feast, and perhaps has not cultivated sufficient grain to enable him to display his generosity to his friends. He takes one of his sheep or goats to the market and exchanges it for three or four big baskets of millet or for any other commodity that he lacks. If a man has too many cows and fewer sheep and goats, he takes one of his cows, especially one that has no religious implications within the family group, and exchanges it for ten or more sheep and goats. Sometimes there are people who have been working for wages and have saved a few shillings after paying their poll or hut taxes. When one such returns to his home and wants to own a few of these valued animals, which are the recognised standard of wealth among the Gikuyu, he goes to the market and makes a good bargain with the people who have brought their sheep and goats to raise sufficient money for the Government taxes. In these markets one can buy almost any conceivable thing that is available in the tribe. It is considered a sign of industry to be selling grain in the markets, for it proves that one has not only cultivated sufficient for the family, but also a surplus for accumulation of wealth.

HARVESTING

In many cases the harvesting-time is the busiest period for the majority of women, for the simple reason that they are the managing directors of the food supply in their respective family groups. Therefore it is considered right and proper for the women to handle the grain and store it according to the immediate and future needs of the family. The work of harvesting is almost divided equally between men and women. For while the women do the actual harvesting and carrying the harvest home, the men cut or root out maize or millet stalks, burn them and spread the ashes in the field as a part of the manuring and to kill certain insects. Men also make new granaries or repair the old ones.

When the harvesting is completed, a woman's first thought is to store sufficient grain to last her family until the next harvest. After she has done so, and there is surplus grain left, she consults with her husband. Then, if there is something that the family needs, the surplus grain is sold immediately in the markets to satisfy the needs. If there are no immediate needs, the surplus grain is kept back and sold later when there is a scarcity of that particular grain in the markets.

The stored grain is dished out carefully by the wife, with the view neither to be wasteful nor starve the family. She prepares family menus with a variety of daily changes to balance the diets. For example, if she had prepared sweet potatoes and gruel for to-day's meal, to-morrow she will cook a mixture of beans, maize, greens and perhaps bananas. Although food is changed almost daily, the wife takes great care not to exhaust the supply of one article of food. So when there is plenty of beans and maize, and less bananas and sweet potatoes, she cooks more of what is abundant and less of what is scarce.

A wife who manages efficiently the economic affairs as well as other duties in her family group, is highly respected not only by her group but by the entire community.

ECONOMIC VALUE OF SHEEP AND GOATS AND CATTLE

We have seen that in the Gikuyu society almost every man has a garden or gardens from which his immediate needs are supplied. We have also dealt with the economic aspects of the crops raised in these fields, and how they are bartered in the markets or sold for money. Little has been mentioned about the marketing of domestic animals, but up to this point we have not yet discussed the economic value of these animals. It is therefore necessary to give a short description of how the Gikuyu look upon their cattle, sheep and goats.

To a Gikuyu the cattle in the first place are merely a display of wealth, for a man to be called rich he must own a number of cattle. Because, while every family has a number of sheep and goats, say, from one to hundreds, only a small minority own cattle, and therefore to own a cow or two is the first sign of being a wealthy man.

Apart from being the display of wealth, cattle play a part in the economic life of the people. To start with, cow's milk is used for babies by those who can afford it. The milk is very little used in the Gikuyu diet except by those who own a number of cows. Hides are used for various purposes, for bedding, making sandals and straps for tying and carrying firewood and other loads. As a source of meat or butter supply, cattle play a very small part. Cows are never killed for food, except at a time of famine, but bulls and oxen are now and again slaughtered for occasional meat feasts (*kerugo*), and this is regarded as luxurious and only practised by well-to-do persons.

Cows give the owner a prestige in the community, but are never killed for any particular sacrificial or religious ceremonies, except in very rare cases or when a bull or ox is substituted for a male goat or a ram. As economic assets cattle play a part in the marriage ceremony, where a cow or more is given as marriage insurance (*roracio*), but there, too, cattle are given as a substitute for sheep or goats, each cow being valued at ten sheep or goats and a bull or an ox at five sheep or goats.

In former days cattle had very little economic value to the owners, apart from the fact that such owners were looked on as dignified, respected rich men. The milk was not sold, but used by the herdsmen and by visitors, especially warriors, who were the protectors of the villages against Masai or other raiders. The rich men, who naturally had more property to be protected, were responsible for feeding the warriors in the way of milk and providing oxen for meat feasts (*irugo*) to keep the warriors in good healthy condition.

Sometimes the owner of cattle hardly had the pleasure of drinking his cows' milk, especially if they were far away from his homestead. In spite of this the owner of a large number of cattle was sentimentally satisfied by praise names conferred upon him by the community in their songs and dances. Nowadays some people, especially those who are near European towns, do sell their milk and derive a good income from it. This income could be improved by introducing a better breed instead of keeping a number of cows which give very little milk. From the economic point of view the present breed of cattle reared by the Gikuyu is very poor, and it would be a great advancement if the Government could help the people to secure a few good bulls for breeding, and gradually replace the inferior types of cattle with better ones. This method would automatically improve the problem of congestion in grazing areas which faces the country at present, for people would learn the value of keeping a few cows which would be useful economically, instead of keeping a large number of cattle for sentimental satisfaction.

SHEEP AND GOATS AS STANDARD CURRENCY

In the Gikuyu country, before the introduction of the European monetary system, sheep and goats were regarded as the standard currency of the Gikuyu people. The price of almost everything was determined in terms of sheep and goats (*mbori*). This system still operates among the majority of the Gikuyu people who have not yet grasped the idea of a monetary system and its value.

These domestic animals play an important role in the economic, religious, and social life of the Gikuyu. A man with a number of sheep and goats feels no less than a man with a large bank balance. The people look upon these animals as a good investment which gives them a yearly income, for if a man has two or three good sheep or female goats within a year they increase to six or more, and people consider this a good profit. They would argue saying that money is not a good investment, for one shilling does not bear another shilling, whereas a sheep or goat does. This, of course, is due to the ignorance of money speculation, and so they say it is better to buy a sheep or a goat instead of keeping shillings which, if buried in the ground (the only form of saving money the majority of the people know), would rot and lose their value.

Sheep and goats, unlike cattle, are used for various religious sacrifices and purifications. They are the chief means of supplying the people with meat, while the skins are used as articles of clothing. Finally, without them a man cannot get a wife, for it is sheep and goats that are given as *roracio* (marriage insurance). If a man has cash money and he wants to get married he must, in the first place, buy cattle or sheep and goats, because the parents of the wife-to-be will not accept cash money as *roracio*. To them coins have very little meaning and have no religious or sentimental associations within the people's custom.

The real value of money is only realised when a man takes it and buys a cow or sheep and goats, or pays the Government taxes, otherwise money as such has little function inside the Gikuyu country. With all the disadvantages connected with the rearing of sheep and goats, they are still regarded generally as the only means of expression of wealth. By disadvantages we mean that in some cases young men have been ruined by spending years earning money to buy these highly valued animals and sometimes sickness invades a homestead and kills every one of them in a few days. This means a loss of ten or thirty pounds, which if it had been put in a savings bank, would have remained there and helped the young man to improve his standard of living. This is a question which is very difficult to settle, for some people would argue that the animals give better profit yearly, whereas shillings do not multiply quickly and do not give the same sentimental satisfaction. But let us hope that gradually people will be able to decide which one of the two systems is suitable for their advancement.

TRADING WITH THE NEIGHBOURING TRIBES

We have given a description of how the Gikuyu exchange goods amongst themselves in the markets, and the types of articles sold and bought. Having done so, we will now enter into discussion of how the Gikuyu trade with their neighbours, i.e. the Masai and Wakamba. The articles of special value in trading with the Masai are spears, swords, tobacco, gourds and red ochre. The Masai, who are not agriculturalists, and who regard the cultivation of soil as a crime against their gods, depend almost entirely on the Gikuyu for the supply of the three last-mentioned articles. Although the Masai have their own blacksmiths, the spears made by the Gikuyu were and still are regarded as the best.

There are inter-tribal markets where these goods are exchanged, but, apart from these markets, sometimes a group of men organise into a trading guild and take their goods into the heart of the Masai country. In former days this kind of trade was conducted in the homestead of a friend who acted as the guide and protector of his friends and their goods.

The Gikuyu, after collecting their trading goods, would send for their friend or friends in Masailand, asking them to meet the traders at the frontier and conduct them into the country. Thus goods were taken to villages, and, after exchanging them for sheep, the Gikuyu would return escorted by their friends to the frontier to avoid any molestation by the hostile warriors who would only be too glad to have someone on whom to blood their spears. The same thing happened when the Masai wanted to enter into Gikuyuland for the purpose of trade.

Nowadays the trade between the two tribes is mostly restricted to trading centres. Only those who can afford to pay heavy licence fees to the British Government can open a trading store in these centres.

As regards trade with the Wakamba, there are no special articles as in the case of the Masai. In fact the Wakamba being agriculturists grow almost the same crops as the Gikuyu. The two tribes are racially and linguistically identical. It can be said that in the beginning of things the Gikuyu and Wakamba were brothers, but how and why they came to part is a matter requiring some investigation.

In former days there was very little hostility between the two tribes, and their trade depended on seasonal harvests. If there was a shortage of food in Gikuyuland and abundance in the Wakamba country, the Gikuyu went and bought grain from the Wakamba, the exchange being sheep and goats or cows and sometimes ivory. The same thing happened in the case of the Wakamba. Apart from these contacts, there were frequent and friendly visits from both sides for trading or other purposes.

We may mention here that soft chains, snuff-boxes or carriers, bows and arrows, witchcraft and herbal medicines were among things exchanged in trading, or given as presents to friends, in reciprocity, which is the basic principle of friendship. The friendly relations between the Gikuyu and the Wakamba is still the same, except that free visiting is now prohibited, and only those who have a special pass from the British Government can visit either Gikuyu or Wakamba country or other tribes.

4

INDUSTRIES

IRONWORK

FOR CENTURIES the Gikuyu people have developed the technique of procuring iron ore from the sand, and so the use of iron tools has been well established in the Gikuyu country from time immemorial. In Gikuyu legends and stories we are told how, in the beginning of things, the animals were divided into two sections for domestication purposes. The divider, Mogai, gave one section of the animals to men and the other to women. At this time people did not possess any iron tools; they used wooden knives and spears. The women took to slaughtering their animals for food and other purposes; they did this with wooden knives, and it took a long time to kill and skin one animal. The legends go on to tell us that owing to the pain inflicted on the animals through this slow process of killing and skinning with blunt wooden knives, the animals could not stand it much longer. One night, when the women were sleeping, the animals gathered together and decided to run away from these cruel human beings. All the animals possessed by the women ran away and scattered in the forests and plains; at the same time they selected their own chiefs and leaders and defended themselves from being captured by the human beings. The lion and leopard were chosen as the defenders of jungles; the elephant, buffalo and rhinoceros as the defenders of the forests; the hippopotamus as the defender of rivers and lakes, and so on. From this time the animals which were possessed by the women became wild animals, and the men's animals, which at that time were not used for killing, remained domesticated.

Women tried hard to get their animals back from the forests and jungles, but they did not succeed; they pleaded with the Mogai to help them get their animals back, but Mogai would not listen to their petition, for he said that the women had treated their animals cruelly and therefore he had given them freedom to roam freely in the forests, plains and jungles. When the men saw the crisis which had befallen the women they held a conference and decided to send a delegation to the Mogai and ask him what they should do with their animals, which were increasing by leaps and bounds. The delegates took with them a fine lamb which was fawn-coloured all over its body. They told Mogai that they wanted to sacrifice the lamb to him, but they did not like to kill and skin it with the blunt wooden knives for fear of losing their herds as had happened to the women. To their request the Mogai replied: "You are wise men, for you have remembered to seek my advice. I can see that you know that I have given you these animals and I have power to take them away from you. For your faith in me I will give you good advice about how to get better tools, not only for sacrifices, but also for your general use. I will make you the masters of your animals with new tools, but I command you to share these with your unfortunate womenfolk."

At this juncture Mogai directed the men to a site in a river-bed and said to them: "Take sand from this site. Dry it in the sun; then make a fire and put the sand therein, and through this process you will get

iron. I will give you wisdom to make better tools and
you will not have to use blunt wooden tools any more."
From this time the Gikuyu, following the advice of
Mogai, entered into the phase of metal or iron culture.

Apart from these legends and stories which have
been handed down from generation to generation, we
have no other records to show exactly when and how
this evolution took place.

The fact that the Gikuyu have been well acquainted
with the technique and the development of ironwork can
be proved by the number of iron implements and ornaments of purely Gikuyu origin which are to be found
in all branches of activities in the Gikuyu community.
The chief iron articles in the Gikuyu society are the
following: spears, swords, digging- and clearing-knives
of different sizes, ear- and finger-rings, arrow heads,
bracelets of various shapes and sizes, axes and fine
chains, hammers and tongs, tweezers, etc.

With these preliminary remarks we will proceed to
describe how the work of procuring iron is done. The
iron is obtained from ore. The method adopted by the
Gikuyu for this purpose of collecting iron ore is that of
washing sand which is secured from certain districts and
in a particular river. The sand is carefully washed in
a river by experienced men; the black substances that
contain ore are put together and are handed over to the
women and children, who help to spread the ore in the
sun to dry. It is worth noting that the whole family of a
smith takes part in the work, and the work is divided
among the group. When a man is busy in the river
washing the sand, his wife or wives and children are
busy spreading the iron ore in the sun to dry. This
method of working may seem primitive in the eyes of
the machine-man of the Western world, but nevertheless the system fulfilled the needs of the community. In
the olden days there was only one great demand for
iron—namely, during the time of initiation, when the

young warriors needed new equipment for war or protection. The chief demand in this direction was for spears and swords. This did not necessarily mean that a new supply of iron was to follow, for there was always a bit of iron in every homestead left over from worn-out tools or those which had broken and could not be mended. These bits of iron were collected and put away to be used in the future for supplying a spear or a sword to the son of the homestead. For this reason the iron production, as mentioned above, was not everyday work. Some smiths had never participated in the work of iron production; they lived on repairs and renewing or joining up together the old bits of iron to produce a new tool or weapon.

After the sand containing iron ore is dried it is carried to the smithy. There it is put in a fire made of a special mixture of charcoals. Some of these are made from a particular tree and others from a special banana plant. The two kinds of charcoals are mixed. The banana charcoal is said to have particular value in smelting iron. Its substances help to put the pure iron together and to separate it from impure matters.

Before the process of smelting is actually started, a short ritual is performed by the smith and his assistants. The ritual consists of sprinkling a little Gikuyu beer over the furnace, accompanied by a few ceremonial words directed to Mogai and the ancestral spirits. In the absence of beer a little water fulfils the ritual duty. After the ceremony of invoking the spirits of ancestors and appealing to Mogai for guidance and protection in the enterprise, the work of smelting iron is proceeded with. Two bellows are employed simultaneously to keep the fire burning. They are worked by assistants, who learn the profession by means of watching the smith doing the work. In other words, they learn by example. The bellows are put in motion, the charcoals are carefully laid, and then the sand is slowly sprinkled over

the burning fire by the trained hands of the smith. The
heat is kept at a regulated temperature by adding the
required amount of charcoals in the furnace. At the
same time the blowing of the bellows is kept in check.
Sometimes the heat is intensified, and at other times it
is slowed down. In this way the temperature is kept
at the required degree, which reduces the ore to metallic
iron, which is technically called "blooms" (*gekama*).

The smith, with his assistants, continues to work from
morning till the evening, especially when they have
plenty of sand containing ore to melt. In the evening the
melted iron is left in the furnace to cool. Early the next
morning the smith, followed by his assistants, takes a
small quantity of beer made of sugar-cane or honey. On
his arrival at the smithy he performs a short ceremony
of greeting the ancestral spirits who have guarded the
work during the night. The ceremony consists of sprinkling the beer over and round the furnace and again
over the working tools. The communion between the
smith and the ancestor spirits in this respect is considered to be of great importance, for the spirits of
ancestors are said to be very closely connected with
ironwork, and especially male spirits. It is believed that
unless these are appeased they can render the ironwork
unsuccessful by causing the tools or weapons which are
made of the iron to break, and thus reduce the popularity of the smith. This belief is founded on the
ground that the male ancestors have had their bitter
experiences as warriors and some of them had met
their deaths in battle-fields in which the iron weapons
were used. And even those who had not met their
deaths in this way have suffered pain in one way or
another, by being wounded either in battle or in the
general activities of a warrior's life.

When the ritual of communing with the ancestral
spirits is completed, the iron "blooms," which have run
together into small lumps, are taken out from the

furnace. These are joined into a big heap by a mass of slag which has flowed during the melting. After the big pile of slag is taken out, the "blooms" are knocked out and collected together. The next step that follows is to heat the "blooms" and hammer a few of them together, according to the quantity required, to make a spear or sword or other iron articles. The irons thus beaten in heaps are known as *mondwa,* and they are sold according to sizes.

If a man wants a spear he will not buy a ready-made spear but the *mondwa,* and then pay the smith for making the spear. Sometimes the same smith fulfils both tasks of selling the *mondwa* and of making the spear. But there are others who do not make iron, and their duty is merely to make articles with material supplied by their customers.

The smith clan holds an important position in the community; members of that clan are respected and feared. In the first place they command respect because of their skill in ironwork, without which the community would have difficulty in obtaining the necessary implements for various activities, for iron implements play an important part in the economic, religious, social, and political life of the Gikuyu. In the second place the smiths are feared for the fact that strong curses rest with the smith clan. If a smith should curse a man or a family there is no form of purification that could cleanse the cursed individual or the group. The curse consists of cutting a piece of red-hot iron on an anvil and at the same time uttering spells, e.g. *Ng'ania wa Ng'ania arutwika ta kiriha geeke. Mahori maake marohehenjeka, ngoro yake erotweka ta kiriha geeke.* This means: "May So-and-so (proper name given) be cut like this iron. Let his lungs be smashed to smithereens. Let his heart be cut off like this iron."

HUT-BUILDING

It is a common ambition of every Gikuyu young man to own a hut or huts, which means implicitly to have a wife or wives. The establishment of a homestead gives a man special status in the community; he is referred to as *muthuri* (an elder), and is considered capable of holding a responsible position in tribal affairs. Thus, it is the desire of every Gikuyu man to work hard and accumulate property which will enable him to build a homestead of his own. There is a proverb in Gikuyu which says: *"Wega uumaga na mocie,"* that is, the quality of a man is judged by his homestead. With these few remarks we will proceed to describe how a hut is built.

Gikuyu huts are of the round type, with wooden walls and grass thatched roofs. The actual building of a hut takes only one day; and as soon as it is completed, a new fire is drilled from sacred fire-sticks, *"githegethi na Geka kia Igongona."* But in case of rebuilding, the fire from the old hut is preserved to be transferred to the new hut. The fire is ritually lit in the new hut, and after a short ceremony of communing with the ancestral spirits the owner moves into the new homestead. Sometimes two or more huts are built simultaneously, as in the case of a man having more than one wife or a large family which could not be housed in one hut. But general custom requires that even a man with one wife should have two huts, one for his wife's private use and one for himself for general use. The woman's hut is called *nyomba*. Here it is taboo for a mere stranger to enter, because *nyomba* is considered as the traditional sacred abode of the family and the proper place to hold communion with their ancestral spirits. All aspects of religious and magical ceremonies and sacrifices which concern the family are centred around the *nyomba*. It is for fear of defilement and ill-luck that strangers are not allowed to cross this sacred threshold. The man's hut is called *thingira;* in this, friends and casual visitors are entertained.

Nowadays the system of having two huts for a man with only one wife is dying out, owing to the heavy burden of hut taxes imposed on the people by the British Government. The result has been congestion, whole families being crowded in one hut, for many such families can hardly maintain their livelihood and at the same time afford to find money for hut taxation.

We have mentioned that a hut is built and occupied in the same day; this statement may puzzle those who are not acquainted with the Gikuyu method of building. To avoid this, let us at once explain how the work that expedites the putting up of a hut is organised. Most important of all is the Gikuyu collective method of working. A few days before the erection of a hut or huts the building materials are collected. In doing this the division of labour according to sex plays an important role. The work of cutting wood necessary for building falls on men; women take the responsibility of providing thatching grass and other materials.

When a family is engaged in the work of building a hut or huts the help of neighbours and friends is necessary in order to expedite the work. A man goes round asking his friends to help him, and at the same time telling them what kind of building materials he would like them to supply him with. In the same manner the wife visits her women friends, requesting them to help in various ways. Those who cannot take part in collecting building materials are asked to help in providing food and drink for the builders' feast, which is called "*iruga ria mwako.*" On the day appointed many of these friends will turn up, bringing with them the required materials for building. The man and his wife or wives receive their helpers joyfully and bid them to sit down and rest. After all have arrived a feast is pro-

vided, consisting of a variety of food and drink. During
the feasting this group of men and women entertain
themselves with traditional songs relating to team-
work. Before they part, a day is appointed when the
actual building of a hut or huts will take place.

It is obvious that without this system of team-work
it would take a man a long time to complete the work,
especially in a community where the system of paid
labour is traditionally unknown. In its place, mutual
help guided by the rules of give and take plays a significant part. In every branch of work reciprocity is the
fundamental principle governing the relationship between a man and his neighbours, and also between
various groups or clans and the tribe. If a man, after
having been asked to give his service, absents himself
without a good reason, especially when his neighbour
has urgent work, such as building a hut or a cattle
kraal, which has to be completed in one day (for it is
feared that should a hut or a kraal be left unfinished
and unoccupied, evil spirits might dwell therein and,
therefore, cause constant misfortune to the future oc-
cupants and their herd), the result will be that the
defaulter will find himself socially boycotted for his
individualistic attitude. When a man has thus been
ostracised, *"kohingwo,"* he will have to pay a fine of
one sheep or a he-goat to his neighbours for his bad
behaviour. When the fine is paid, the animal is slaughtered for a feast, and then, after a short ceremony of
reunion, the man's status as a good and helpful neighbour is re-acknowledged.

After the building materials have been collected, the
head of the family selects a plot where he wishes to
establish his new homestead. In selecting the plot care
is taken to see that the land is not associated with any
ancestral curse or taboo. The plot must also be one that
has been lawfully acquired. The homestead must not be
built on or near a graveyard, or on a place where a

fierce battle has taken place, resulting in loss of lives. Such places are considered as the resting homes for the departed spirits, and to disturb them would mean to invoke their anger.

When these preliminary arrangements have been made, the man prepares sugar-cane or honey beer for the foundation ceremony. Early in the morning, on the day of building a hut or huts, a small quantity of the beer is taken to the selected plot and, in communion with the ancestral spirits, it is sprinkled on the ground where the new home is to be built. Sometimes milk or uncooked gruel, *"gethambio,"* is preferred for this ceremony, according to the custom of the clan to which the individual belongs. After the ancestral spirits have been summoned to join in the work of building, the friends who have gathered to help their neighbour start to clear and to level the ground. Then the foundation is marked according to the size of the hut which a man wants. To make a good circle a kind of string compass is employed. A stick is put in the centre of the circle and a string tied to it, then a man holds one end of the string and, after measuring the required paces, he holds the string tight and then goes round, marking the ground until the circle lines meet. This is called *"gokurura kiea."* When this is done the builders start digging holes in the ground for the outer wall. The holes are about one foot deep and about six inches in diameter. After this the inner circle is marked, which divides the hut into several apartments. Immediately the wall is erected and the roof put on. This completes the men's work in building, leaving the thatching to the womenfolk.

While the women are engaged in thatching, the men retire to a feast which has been awaiting them. During the feasting the men sing songs relating to the art of building; those who are clever and hard workers are highly praised in these songs; at the same time con-

temptuous phrases are uttered for laziness. In some of
the phrases men call on the women in teasing tones,
saying: "Look on those lazy-bones who are working
like chameleons, the sun is going down, do you want us
to make torches for you? Do hurry up and join us in
feasting, and let us utter blessings for the homestead
before the sun is completely gone down." To this the
women answer in chorus, saying: "You men, you lack
the most important art in building, namely, thatching.
A wall and an empty roof cannot protect you from
heavy rain, nor from burning sun. It is our careful
thatching that makes a hut worth living in. We are not
chameleons, but we do thatch our huts like *'nyoni ya
nyagathanga'* (this is the name of a small bird in Gikuyu
which is well known by its sweet songs and the neatness
of its nest)." In many of the Gikuyu cradle stories and
legends *nyoni ya nyagathanga* and its work is highly
praised. This acts as an encouragement to both boys
and girls to become industrious in their future activities
in life. It is characteristic of the Gikuyu people to sing
inspiring songs while performing a task, for it is said:
"to work in a happy mood is to make the task easier,
and to relieve the heart from fatigue." (*"Koruta wera
na ngoro theru ni kohothia wera na konyihia minoga."*)

When the women have finally finished thatching they
join the men in feasting. Before the party comes to a
close the owner of the homestead brings the remainder
of the beer or the milk which has been sprinkled on the
foundation; he hands it to a ceremonial elder, who
after pouring the liquid into a ritual horn, calls upon
those present to stand up. Then the ceremonial elder,
with his hands raised holding the horn, turns towards
Kere-Nyaga (Mount Kenya). In this position he chants
a prayer, calling for a blessing for the homestead and its
future prosperity. The following is the form of the
prayer used for such an occasion:

"Wee Githuri oikaraga Kere-Nyaga; kerathimo geaku nikeo getomaga mecie ethegee. Namo marakara maku, nemo mahukagia mecie. Togogothaitha tweturaneire ohamwe na ngoma cia aciari aito. Togokoria ate orinderere mocie oyo na otome wethegee. Reke atumia ona mahio mathathare. Thaaai, thathayai Ngai, thaaaai."

The following is the translation of the above prayer: "You, the Great Elder, who dwells on the Kere-Nyaga, your blessing allows homesteads to spread. Your anger destroys homesteads. We beseech You, and in this we are in harmony with the spirits of our ancestors: we ask You to guard this homestead and let it spread. Let the women, herd and flock be prolific. (Chorus) Peace, praise or beseech ye, Ngai (God), peace be with us."

After this the homestead is declared open. The next thing is to light the fire which we have mentioned in our earlier description. Two children, male and female, are selected for this ritual; they are looked upon as a symbol of peace and prosperity for the homestead. The ceremonial elder hands the fire to the children and instructs them how to light it; at the same time he gives them the ritual words to be used in this connection. The children enter the hut, with the elder following behind them, to see that the ritual is correctly carried out. Behind this small procession the owner of the homestead and his wife follow carrying firewood to kindle the fire, for it is considered as a bad omen for such a fire to go out. After the fire has been properly lit, things are moved in without any further ceremony.

Let us glance inside a woman's hut. It may be some six paces from the entrance to the fire-place in the centre. The roof is supported at the outside by the wall, in the inside by a series of poles equidistant from the centre. The poles fulfil a twofold purpose; besides supporting the roof, they are the mainstays of partitions which divide the hut into apartments. These apartments depend upon the needs of the occupant—her bedroom is essential, and no less so is the store-room next door to it. Should a daughter live with her mother, her room will be next to the store-room, and should the woman keep one or two animals (sheep or goats) for fattening, they will have their compartment farther round the wall, just inside the door, on the right as you enter. These rooms will occupy the whole of the right inside of the hut, leaving free only the space between the fire-place and the inner circle of poles. Each apartment communicates immediately with this space.

To the left of a person entering the hut is a long partition, extending almost from the door to the woman's bedroom. Between this and the outer wall the

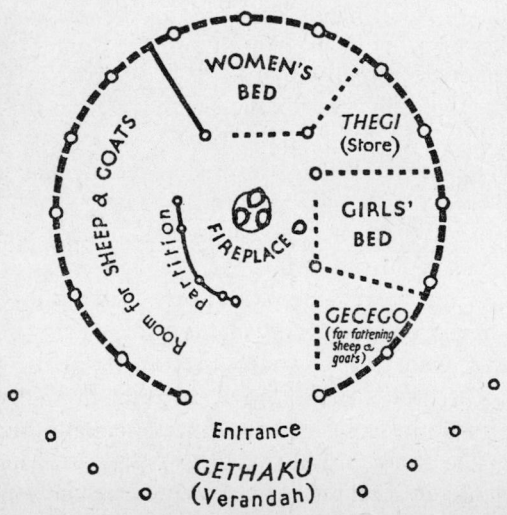

animals sleep at night. The scheme is thus simple; first the fire-place, then the circle in which people may sit, then the outer apartments. The accompanying diagram will make this clear. A woman's hut is considered as the cradle of the family tradition; it has many taboos which, for the harmony and the prosperity of the family, must be strictly observed. Among other things, fire must be lit in the hut every evening, and there must be someone to sleep in it every night. The wife is debarred by custom from having sexual intercourse anywhere else but inside the hut. Sexual intercourse must not take place in the day-time, even with her husband, neither must it be performed whilst food is being cooked, or the food will have to be thrown away, for an act of this nature renders the food unclean and unfit for human consumption. Anyone eating such food will have *thahu* (defilement), and will have to be cleansed by a *mondo mogo* (witch-doctor), for it is feared that unless this is done, disaster will befall such a man.

The man's hut, unlike that of the woman, is very simple; it has only one partition, and sometimes none at all. When there is one, it is used to divide the bedstead from the fire-place. The rest of the hut is left open; this is to provide a large sitting-place for the family and their visitors. For the man's hut is used for general purposes, whereas the woman's hut is strictly used for her private purposes and family matters.

A well-built hut generally lasts for about ten or more years; occasionally the roof has to be re-thatched, especially in the interval between the heavy and the short rains. The wall has also to be repaired every now and again; holes between the wood are filled with cow or sheep dung. This method serves two purposes; in the first place it keeps draughts out, and in the second it preserves the wood and prevents it being eaten by the ants. The wood preserved in this way becomes useful in the future building of new huts, especially when old

ones are pulled down. Some building materials have
been with a family for a considerable number of years,
and they are looked upon as sacred relics.

TYPE OF WEAPONS USED
BY THE GIKUYU

From time immemorial Gikuyu have been well acquainted with ironwork. When and how they discovered this technique is very hard to say; but from the
evidence gathered from the tribal stories and legends it
can be said without hesitation that Gikuyu have been
in possession of iron tools and weapons for many centuries past. In some of the old stories and legends,
which were the only means the Gikuyu had of keeping
records of tribal historical events, we are told how Tene
and Agu, who are the ancestors of the Gikuyu, used
poisoned spears, *kiheti,* or *thiya na ndokoyo,* for hunting elephants and other big game. We are also told of
Ndemi who, unlike their forefathers the hunters, settled
down and began to cultivate the land by means of
cutting down trees with iron tools. The word *ndemi*
is derived from the word *tema,* which means cut, or
gotema, to cut. Hence the word *ndemi* means that which
cuts or one who cuts. The tools and weapons used by
these people were of small types compared to those in
use at present.

With these few remarks we will proceed to describe
categorically the type of weapons which are used by
the Gikuyu to-day. The most important weapons are:
(1) spears; (2) swords; (3) bows and arrows; (4)
shields; (5) a variety of clubs and knobkerries; and
(6) slings. After a boy has passed the initiation ceremony, which gives him the status of a warrior, it is the
duty of his father to supply him with necessary weapons,
for without these he cannot command the respect of
his fellow warriors. The prestige of a family depends

largely on the capability of its sons in their activities amongst the warriors. In the first place the sons are looked upon as the defenders of their family group, and secondly, as the defenders of the collective tribal interests.

In a country like Gikuyu it is necessary to have some kind of weapons, especially spears and swords, not for tribal wars, as some people may think, but for self-defence against the fierce wild animals. It is worth our while here to note that the Kenya Government has put a ban on the Africans carrying dangerous weapons, namely, spears, swords, and bows and arrows. At the same time the Europeans move freely in town and in country carrying all sorts of fire-arms. The Africans, seeing these, marvel at the European conception of "dangerous weapons."

Now let us return to our subject matter, the Gikuyu weapons. We will give a short description of how they are made and the materials they are made from. The spear, the sword, and arrow-heads are made of steel or iron. The work of manufacturing these articles falls on specialised tribal blacksmiths. This profession is generally inherited from father to son. The spear is made in two pieces, the head, *ithombe,* and the foot, *mora;* these are joined together with a piece of very hard wood, *mote wa itimo,* which serves as a handle. The length of a warrior's spear is between five and six feet, while the elder's spear is between four and five feet, with a short wide head and short foot joined together with a long piece of stick. The warrior's spear is called *mwenjerere,* and the one which belongs to elders is called *kiberethi*—the name denotes its wide head. The sword is from two to three feet, with its blade sharp on both sides; it has a wooden handle and a scabbard. In fighting, the sword is the last thing that a man would throw at his enemy; its purpose is for fencing, and a Gikuyu warrior is very proud of his sword, for he can

handle it with great dexterity. The art of fencing is
taught from childhood, and at the time when a man
reaches the stage of a warrior he is well qualified in
the art of fighting.

The arrows are of two types; one with iron heads
and the other with wooden heads. After the arrows are
shaped they are smeared with deadly poison, *ororo,* and
then covered with a leather strap tied around. When
this is done they are carefully put in a quiver and kept
in a cool place. It is against tribal custom for anyone
to use bows and arrows in an ordinary fight; the chief
use for the weapon is hunting, and in former days it
was used in tribal wars. The shield is made of buffalo
hide; the hide is soaked and, in this state, it is put on
a wooden frame, it is then dried and put into shape.
The clubs, or knobkerries, are made in different types
according to the user's taste, the size is also determined
by the strength of the owner, for on many occasions
it has to be thrown at an enemy and, if it is too heavy
or too light, it may be less effective. The entire work of
making these weapons and of carrying them is restricted
to men only.

POTTERY

The Gikuyu have a well-established system of making
earthenware vessels. There are certain clans who spe-
cialise in the pottery industry, and for centuries the
profession has been handed down from one generation
to another. We would like to remind our reader that
the system of division of labour between men and
women, at home and in trades, is very important among
the Gikuyu. In the pottery industry all the work, from
start to finish, is done by women; the digging of the
clay, beating and softening it, the moulding and dry-
ing, the burning of the pots, and finally, marketing—
all these are entirely the tasks of the women. Men are

debarred by custom from approaching the moulding-place, especially when the work is in progress. Men are not allowed to touch any material associated with this work. The presence of a man at the moulding-place is said to have a bad effect on the articles and causes the pots to break when they are put on the fire. Should some of the pots break, as they usually do, during the burning-time, the women always suspect that some ill-behaved man has crept to the spot during the night and has spoiled their work. To avoid this suspicion men keep away from this sacred ground until the work is finished.

As the man holds supreme authority over his smithy, so does the woman in her pottery industry. Both sexes have to obey and respect the custom governing these divisions of labour; anyone disregarding this custom or daring to cross over the prohibited ground is met with a severe punishment, or is ostracised.

The pottery industry is not carried on all the year round, but is restricted to certain seasons. The most favourable time for making earthenware vessels is during the time when crops are nearly ripe, and again after the harvest. It is generally dry at this time, and this makes the clay more suitable for moulding, for the dryer the clay is, the better and more durable the pots become. The industry is carried on with two purposes in view: firstly, to satisfy the family's wants; and secondly, for marketing. The latter is the most important and deciding factor as to whether pots are to be manufactured or not, for unless the potters are satisfied that there is a good market for their articles they will not undertake the task.

Very few potters have good pots for themselves; they sell all the good ones to others, leaving themselves with the bad ones; hence a well-known Gikuyu saying: *"Moombi arugaga na ngeo,"* which means "Potter cooks with broken pots." This shows that the Gikuyu have developed a system of trading far beyond working merely to satisfy immediate or family needs.

Like many other trades, the pottery industry depends entirely on good crops. It is always after a substantial harvest or when one is expected, that the potters are kept busy. During this time of prosperity many marriages are contracted, and this increases the demand for new pots. In keeping with tribal custom, a new bride must always have new pots, as well as other household utensils. These are supplied by her husband.

BASKET-MAKING

The basket industry is again carried on by women, but unlike pottery, there is no restriction on men handling the materials or the baskets while they are being made. The only thing that is taboo for a man is to do the actual work. He may collect the materials and prepare them ready to be used by his female relatives or friends.

The baskets are made of strings from small shrubs called *mogio, mokeo, mwondwe,* and *mogotha.* The barks are chewed or beaten to soften and strengthen them; they are then stretched and put in the sun to dry. The next process is to wind them together into a long string about fifteen feet long. Several of these are made into balls, similar to those which European women use for knitting. When enough strings are prepared the work of knitting the basket, *keondo,* is undertaken. Baskets are of different shapes and sizes according to fashion and taste. The time required to finish a *keondo* depends entirely upon the woman's speed and the leisure time she has in hand. Basket-knitting is looked upon as a spare-time job; it is generally done during conversations or travelling, or going to and from work. The moment a woman reaches her work, namely, weeding in the field or collecting firewood in the forest, the knitting is put aside until the time of going home after work.

Apart from baskets, *keondo* (pl. *ciondo*), there is another kind which we will call trays, *getaroro* (large tray), *getiti* (small tray). These are not knitted, but are sewn. A creeper called *moogo* is cut into several pieces, then these are sewn together.

Getaroro is used for winnowing and spreading grain in the sun to dry; sometimes it is used for carrying grain. The small tray, *getiti,* is used as a dish for serving or keeping food cooked or uncooked. There is no taboo preventing both sexes from undertaking the task of making these articles; but customarily the work falls on men. Very rarely is a woman seen doing it. When a woman is found making *getiti* or *getaroro* it is a sign to indicate that she is a widow and has no male relatives to support her. If a man passing by sees such a woman engaged in making *getiti* or *getaroro* he will not hesitate to seek her acquaintance because she has displayed a symbol of free invitation.

SKIN-TANNING

The skin-tanning industry is one of the most important trades among the Gikuyu; it takes the place of weaving, which is practised in some African communities. The importance of this industry rests on the fact that all the Gikuyu men and women dress nationally in skins. To meet this demand it is necessary for a Gikuyu family to keep a number of sheep and goats and also cattle, not only as a display of wealth, but also as a means of supplying articles of clothing and food.

In every family group there are one or two members specialising in the art of tanning skins and cutting them into shape for making dresses. A man who performs this task is called professionally *"Mohari wa Njoa na*

Motemi Nguo," namely, "Tanner of skins and cutter of dresses." There is a marked difference between a skin suitable for a man's dress and one used for a woman's dress; not only do they differ in quality, but also in the method employed in tanning them. A skin for a woman's dress has to be made thin and soft, for it is said that woman's body is made of a delicate texture, and therefore it must have smooth material to cover it. Therefore, a specialist takes minute care in preparing the materials so as to gain admiration and to reap a good reward from his customers.

It is necessary to give here a short description of the method used in preparing materials for men's and women's clothing. For making a woman's garment the skin is first pegged on the ground to dry; then a specialist takes it and, with his skilled hands, peels off the hair (*kohunyora rooa*), leaving the skin with the required smoothness and thickness. This process needs very careful handling with steady hands; for it is easy to ruin the skin completely if by a slip of the hand one peels off more than is necessary. If a specialist spoils a skin he has to give the owner another one.

Some skins are suitable for the above treatment, but others are treated differently. Instead of peeling off the hair by hand, the hair is scraped off by a knife or by a small axe called *ithanwa rea kohara njoa* which is used for this purpose only. When the task of taking off the hair is completed, the skin is softened by rubbing it in the hands, *gotanduka rooa*. After this the skin is ready to be measured and cut into the required shape. A woman's skirt takes about two skins and an upper garment needs three or four skins. These may be sheep's or goat's, but they arc not of the same value. Goat's skin has more value and it gives longer wear; chief's wives generally wear garments of this material. A woman's clothes consist of three pieces: (1) upper garment, *nguo ya ngoro;* (2) skirt, *mothuru;* (3) apron, *mwengu.*

Let us now turn our attention to men's dress. Man, unlike woman, has only one garment, *gethii.* A young man wears a *gethii* made of kid skins or of a very small calf. These are preferred because of their small and smooth hairs. The *gethii* for young men are made short and cover the body from the shoulders to just below the hips, leaving the legs bare. The only other garment is an apron, *gethere,* which is worn only for ceremonial dances. The elders wear long *gethii,* chiefs and rich men have more elaborate *gethii* made of fur, whilst the lower ranks wear *gethii* made of sheep skins. In former days this rule was strictly adhered to, but nowadays, owing to the introduction of blankets and European clothes, the old custom which defined the correct manner of dress is less observed. There is a great tendency among the young men, from chief to commoner, to adopt the system of wearing European clothes. The only section of the population which is not so much affected is the women. They are more conservative than the men and they look upon the European dress as a piece of ugliness and as a screen to hide deformities. Some will not entertain the idea of having a son-in-law who has adopted the European clothes unless he undresses before a witness.

GIKUYU MUSICAL INSTRUMENTS

Gikuyu people have very few musical instruments, but this, of course, does not mean that they are not musically-minded people. In the musical field the Gikuyu prefer to use their vocal organs more than musical instruments. The majority of their dances and songs are performed without any musical instrument; instead of these, vocalists fulfil the task of supplying the music for a dance or song.

In the whole of the Gikuyu country there are only four different kinds of musical instruments, namely, drum (*kehembe*), large rattle (*kegamba*), small rattle (*njingiri*), and flute (*motoriro*); each of these is used on a separate occasion. In addition to the above list we can mention that there are various kinds of horns which are sounded for ceremonial purposes. These can hardly be described as musical instruments, but we can put them in the same category as bugles.

We will now take the four Gikuyu musical instruments and deal with them categorically, explaining in some detail the role each plays in the life of the community. As far as music is concerned, we can say definitely that the flute is most prominent, and it can be said that a Gikuyu plays his flute with a great sense of humour. It is not played professionally, but for the enjoyment and pleasure it gives to the player.

Generally, this article is made out of bark or shrub, and it is of a temporary nature. A certain shrub, called *mokeo* or *mogio,* is cut according to the size of flute required. The bark is slowly and carefully loosened by twisting the stem gently from one end to the other. Finally the stem is removed, leaving the hollow bark free to be used as a flute. To make the flute effective, holes are cut for producing several notes. There is no cut-and-dried rule as to how a flute may be made or played. The technique depends entirely on the individual's taste. Some people prefer four holes, others six or eight holes. The materials also differ; some people like their flutes made out of bamboo; others prefer the temporary one as mentioned above—which means having a new flute almost every day. Apart from the materials described here, there is no other way of making flutes among the Gikuyu. They do not use metal for this purpose.

The Gikuyu flute is never used for leading a dance or a song. It is played at a time of leisure, or as a comfort when a man is in grief or feeling lonesome. It is mostly used during the dry season when there is less work in the field, especially before the harvest of crops sown during the short rain (*mburu ya mwere*). This season is known as *marira-ini ma mwere*—namely, the season when millet is ripe and is being protected from the birds. This task requires a man to spend a whole day in the fields, starting from about 4 a.m. to about 7 p.m. A high platform (*getara*) is built in the middle of the field, and here a man with a sling keeps a constant watch over his millet. Whenever he sees birds coming towards the millet field he throws stones with his sling to drive the birds away. Millet is highly valued as a special diet; it provides the community with a very nourishing beverage (*ochoro wa mwere*), which plays a very important part in feasts and ceremonies. Birds, too, seem to like this crop very much, and it is not an easy job to keep them away from it. Therefore it is imperative that a man should keep on the look-out until the birds retire to their nests in the evening. In this solitude the flute becomes a comforting companion. A man does not play the flute to amuse himself only, but also to provide soothing melodies for the women-folk in the neighbouring field. Women do not participate in the art of playing flutes, but they are very keen listeners, and a man who is a good player becomes a favourite among his neighbours, especially among the women. Such a man receives tokens (*matego*), in the way of food and drink, from the women, as a sign of their appreciation of his art. During this season there is always great competition among the flute-players.

Apart from this time, during which the flute is played intensively, the only other occasion when it is heard is while a man is walking leisurely, killing time, or while he is away from home in the pasture, herding sheep and goats or cattle. But the latter case is very rare, for some clans will not allow their herdsmen to play the flute while the flock is in the grazing field, for it is feared that sweet melodies might invoke evil spirits and thus bring defilement to the herds. It is also taboo (*mogiro*) to play a flute or to whistle inside a hut, because it is believed that sweet music can easily attract the attention of wandering evil spirits and lure them to come and cause mischief inside the homestead. The playing of the flutes is considered as an outdoor amusement or relaxation, and the art is restricted to the boys and young men. There is no taboo which prevents an old man from playing a flute, but it is one of these social etiquettes which divides various activities according to age; and it is therefore out of place for an old man to indulge in this art.

Next to the flute comes the drum (*kehembe*). Unlike many other African communities, where drums or tom-toms are used intensively, in the functions of the Gikuyu, drums are restricted to a very few ceremonial dances and songs. The use of drums as musical instruments has been adopted only in recent years; the idea was borrowed from the Wakamba, who are the eastern neighbours of the Gikuyu. The method of sending news by tom-toms, which is found in many parts of Africa, does not exist in the Gikuyu country. Its place is taken by horns (*coro*, sing., *macoro*, pl.). The news received from the neighbouring tribes who use tom-toms is relayed throughout the Gikuyu country by means of sounding particular horns, used only for this purpose. This duty was assigned to special trained men who were always in readiness to receive and transmit news. But nowadays this method is very rarely used, owing to the interference of the Europeans with the African institutions and the desire to suppress them by imposing Western "civilisation" on the Africans. The Gikuyu drums are used mainly to supply rhythms to particular swinging dances and songs, called *njong'wa*. The only other occasion when the drums are used is in a procession of young men and young women when they are in a parade, *keonano,* which takes place at the opening of seasonal day dances and songs called *gechukia kia mothenyu* or *kebata.*

Further, there are two kinds of rattles, *kegamba* and *njingiri,* which play an important part in all Gikuyu dances. We will first deal with the large rattles (*kegamba,* sing.; *ciegamba,* pl.). These are made of oval sheets of iron which are cut to the required size, from four to eight inches in length. The ends are filed to a blunt point and then are folded over until the edges are close together, leaving only a very narrow opening; the shape produced resembles a banana fruit. Several iron bullets, *ngaragari,* are put inside the folded iron sheet and, by rolling therein, musical sounds are produced according to the movements of the man who wears it. *Kegamba* is worn fastened below the knee, with a strap which extends above that joint. It is worn only on special occasions, such as war dances, initiation ceremonies, *kebata* and *nguro* dances. The two last-mentioned dances are performed when the warriors are displaying their physical fitness and their dexterity in handling spears and shields; and also their ability to perform high and long jumps while carrying their weapons. This training is necessary, for it prepares the young men to be able to meet any danger with confidence. Through these exercises, Gikuyu men become good runners, and some of them can run many miles without stopping. This is important for a community which has no mechanical aid in travelling, and it becomes useful in times of pursuing an enemy or dangerous animals.

Kegamba is used by men. The only time when women wear it is during initiation ceremonies; its chief use here is to provide rhythm to the dances.

The small rattles, *njingiri,* are made of the same material as the large ones. The shape is the same, but

the only difference is the size. The size of *njingiri* runs
from one to two and a half inches. It is worn in the
ordinary way of life. Its chief use is as an ornament
and to provide walking rhythm, and it is worn on the
lower part of the ankle. Some people prefer to wear
only one of these rattles, but others have sometimes
more than a dozen threaded together on a leather strap.
These rattles are also used in training children in the
proper use of the right hand; the rattles are tied on a
child's wrist, and by tinkling the rattles a child strengthens its right hand. Left-handedness is associated with
bad luck, and parents do their utmost to see that their
children are properly trained in the use of their right
hands.

5

SYSTEM OF EDUCATION
(PRIOR TO THE ADVENT
OF THE EUROPEAN)

THE FOLLOWING PAGES will give a description of some of the many features of the educational system of the Gikuyu people prior to the introduction of European rule. It is to be hoped that the descriptive analysis of the system will illustrate the need for more study of this subject because of its practical value to educationalists, whose assumed function it is to impart Western education to the Africans. There are two strong reasons for the conviction that this study will yield fruitful results. The first is that, like the study of any living thing's growth, it should give the European an understanding of the Gikuyu development from a simpler to a more complex social structure. The study of the Gikuyu system of education should reveal to European educationalists how the character of individuals is formed within the family circle and then within the local group, and then within the whole tribal organisation through a course of initiation ceremonies, and it should give them the process of character formation in the routine of Gikuyu life-history with its numerous age-groupings.

The second reason is that the study of the educational systems of other countries like Germany and Japan has helped other nations to understand the German or Japanese mind. It has shown what are the leading ideas, the scale of values taught to the rising generation, the virtues which are inculcated and the ambitions which are fostered. Therefore, when the Europeans turn to Africa they should ask what is the African's scheme of education, how it works on the growing child, who controls it and what is the mechanism of the process? Making these queries sympathetically, the Europeans will be able to find what are the significant things in the tribal culture, what it is the community regards as all-important and indispensable to its progress and self-maintenance. Careful study of the tribal system of education, the economic, religious, and political aspects of life will no doubt reveal the forces which hold the tribe together and make it happy and strong.

In the following description it will be found that education begins at the time of birth and ends with death. The child has to pass various stages of age-groupings with a system of education defined for every status in life. The parents take the responsibility of educating their children until they reach the stage of tribal education. They aim at instilling into the children what the Gikuyu call *"otaari wa mocie"* or *"kerera kia mocie,"* namely, educating the children in the family and clan tradition. Apart from the system of schools which has been introduced by the Europeans, there is no special school building in the Gikuyu sense of the word: the homestead is the school.

The education of very small children is entirely in the hands of the mother and nurse. It is carried on through the medium of lullabies. In these the whole history and tradition of the family and clan are embodied and, by hearing these lullabies daily, it is easy for the children to assimilate this early teaching without any strain. This is one of the methods by which the history of the people is passed on from generation to generation. At the time when the child begins to learn how to speak, care is taken by the mother to teach the child correct manner of speech and to acquaint him with all important names in the family, past and present. These are given in songs to amuse the child, who is never told that he is being taught. Moreover, the child is left free to listen to these songs when he likes. If the mother notices that he does not like certain songs, she at once introduces others with different phrases and melody embodying the same teaching.

When the child is able to speak, he can answer many questions which are asked gently and naturally to test how much he has learnt. Such questions as these might be asked: What is your name? Who is your father? What is his age-group? What is the name of your grandfather? And your great-grandfather? What is the name of your grandmother? What are their age-groups? Why were they given such-and-such names for their age-groups? This type of question goes back for several generations, and small children are able to answer freely without any effort or strain on their part. These questions are never asked seriously, they are always taken in the form of amusement or conversationally. In this way the history and traditions of the child's family (maternal and paternal) become a stimulating influence in his life and form a fitting background to his environment.

After passing the stage of infancy the education of the child takes a different shape, the child is taught how to sit and walk properly to avoid having bow legs, for a straight figure is admired by Gikuyu. Especially amongst the warriors is it one of the qualities of handsomeness. A man or woman with bow legs is looked upon as an ugly person. As soon as the child can walk the sphere of his education is extended. The lullabies and other songs are continued to soothe children, especially when they are in bad mood; but this age is considered the best time to teach the children how to use their hands in various spheres of tribal activities. At this juncture the parents take an almost equal responsibility, and a system of co-education is introduced in the form of children's games.

The parents do not particularly choose the kind of games their children should play, they are left free to indulge in any games that appeal to them, provided, of course, that the game is not injurious to their health. Anyone observing the children at their play will no doubt be impressed by the freedom which characterises the period of childhood among the Gikuyu. The children do most things in imitation of their elders and illustrate in striking way the theory that play is anticipatory of adult life. Their games are, in fact, nothing more or less than a rehearsal prior to the performance of the activities which are the serious business of all the members of the Gikuyu tribe. The little boys indulge in fighting like big boys. Running and wrestling are very common, and the best performer in these activities is marked out for leadership. They play with small wooden spears, and shields made of banana tree bark, bows and arrows, sling and stones, and acquire no less proficiency in hitting the mark. They play, too, the games of husbands and wives, and build little models of houses and cattle-pens with the material lying nearest to their hands. The little girls plait baskets of grass and grind corn, like their mothers, and make little pots of the local clay and cook imaginary dishes of the same material. The boys play the role of husbands and behave in the same way as they see their fathers do in their respective homesteads.

Of course, not all their games have this aspect of preparation for the serious business of life. Recreation is an essential part of adult activities and those of children. When the child has grown beyond babyhood, the father takes charge of the boy's education, while the mother takes the whole responsibility of the girl's education and a part of the boy's education.

The father has to teach his boy various things. As an agriculturist he has to take him in the garden for practical training. He makes a digging-stick, *moro,* for his boy to play with while the father is doing the actual work of weeding or turning the soil. Through watching his father in these activities, the boy gradually learns how to handle his digging-stick, and thus becomes a practical agriculturist. While this training is going on, special attention is paid to acquainting the child with the names of various plants and roots and their uses, especially those which are used as antidotes for insect or snake bites. If the father is a wood-carver, smith, hunter, bee-keeper, etc., he will teach the boy by examples in the same way. Through moving in the forests and jungles with his father the boy learns about numerous wild fruits and flowers, and comes to know those which are poisonous and those which are edible. Along with these special tasks goes a very important general training. The boy is taught about family, clan and tribal lands, and their boundaries are carefully pointed out to him.

Care is taken to teach the boy how to be a good observer and to reckon things by observation without counting them, as counting, especially of sheep, goats, cattle or people, is considered as one of the Gikuyu taboos, *mogiro,* and one which would bring ill-luck to the people or animals counted. For example, a man with a hundred head of cattle, sheep and goats trains his son to know them by their colour only or by their size and type of horns, while every one of them has a special name.

To test the boy's power of observation and memory,

two or three herds from different homesteads are mixed, and the boy is asked to separate them by picking out all that belong to his herd. Sometimes some of the sheep and goats are hidden, and when the flock comes to rest at midday the boy is given a few minutes in which to inspect *gothorima* and report. His report is very carefully noted by those in charge of the boy's training. If he makes any mistake no harsh remark is made, but quietly he is asked to go through again and point out such-and-such a sheep or goat which has been purposely hidden. By going through the inspection again he would at once notice his mistake. The elder in charge of the herd would ask the boy to trace back in his memory and explain at what time and place he last saw the missing sheep or goat. In this way the weak point in the memory training is noticed and corrected. In the case of a hunter this training is far more intense, because the intricacy of forest paths and the difficulty of tracing animals demand the greatest power of observation. During my boyhood my special task in the family was to look after our cattle, sheep and goats; therefore I had to go through this training, and afterwards taught my brothers.

The mother also takes the same responsibility in teaching her daughter all things concerning the domestic duties of a wife in managing and harmonising the affairs of a homestead. The girl's training in agriculture is the same as that of the boy. The mother is in charge of the co-education of her children. In the evening she teaches both boy and girl the laws and customs, especially those governing the moral code and general rules of etiquette in the community. The teaching is carried on in the form of folklore and tribal legends. At the same time the children are given mental exercises through amusing riddles and puzzles which are told only in the evenings after meals, or while food is being cooked.

There are children's dances held occasionally at

which praise songs are sung. The children merge insensibly into the dances of later years, and it is amazing to see how a small child can capture with his or her feet and bodily movement the complicated, difficult rhythms which have been learned by merely watching their elders and imitating them. These dances are attended by almost every child in the district. Among the spectators parents are prominent, their chief interest being to observe the conduct of the children in public dances and to judge how much they have absorbed the things taught by the parents. Very strong criticism is directed at the parents whose children do not behave according to the approved tribal law of conduct. Such parents are considered to have neglected the important task of preparing their children to become worthy members of the community.

Special care is devoted to physical development, and many of these dances are the means of providing healthy and bodily exercise. In this respect boys have more facility than girls. For apart from these dances, the boys have their games of wrestling, running and jumping, sparring with sticks and shields, lifting weights and stones and clubthrowing. They have district fights, when one gang is matched against another, or champions are put forward in a wrestling match. It can be said that through work and play both sexes get their physical training. The girls have their share in housework, nursing the babies, cutting and gathering firewood and fetching water. The boys are sent out to herd the sheep and goats and the cattle. They help their fathers in stumping the gardens, cutting trees and building.

There is health-teaching for both boys and girls; they learn early that certain things are not safe and regard them as taboos. Children are trained not to go into a house where there is small-pox, not to touch clothes of a leper, nor touch a dead animal, or the bones of a dead man. These and countless other prohibitions are part of the instruction in health and bodily hygiene.

In all tribal education the emphasis lies on a particular act of behaviour in a concrete situation. While the emphasis lies in the sphere of behaviour, it is none the less true that the growing child is acquiring a mass of knowledge all the time. The very freedom which marks the period of childhood gives unrivalled opportunity for picking up all sorts of information about the environment; the child is not handicapped by attending school and listening to formal instruction which is for the most part unrelated to his interests and needs. As he roams the country-side he learns to distinguish a great variety of birds, animals, insects, trees, grasses, fruits and flowers. His interests bring him in contact with these things, since they constitute the furnishings of his play activities. He does not observe or understand them as lessons in natural history, but knows their names and as much about their habits and life-history as he needs for his purpose. When the boy is with his father or the girl is with her mother in the garden, as they constantly are, they learn about the birds they see, the birds that are harmful to the crops, how they can be dealt with, and what birds can be eaten. In the same way they learn the trees that are good for firewood or building, for supporting the yams or propping the bananas, those that resist white ants or make the best bee-hives, stools or grain mortars and pestles. But here again the knowledge is so practical, so much preconditioned by behaviour, that it can be taught and is taught mainly by doing what they are told to do on particular occasions and by not being allowed to do or to touch certain things that are always within their experience.

It is with personal relations, rather than with natural phenomena, that the Gikuyu education is concerned right from the very beginning. Growing boys and girls learn that they have one thing to learn which sums up all the others, and that is the manners and deportment proper to their station in the community. They see that their happiness in the homestead, their popularity with their playmates, their present comforts and their future prospects depend on knowing their place, giving respect and obedience where it is due. Presumption, conceit and disobedience to those above them are grave offences. The whole Gikuyu society is graded by age and the prestige which accompanies a status in age-grouping, and this is done in such a way that even small children are aware of it. It is a commonplace to say that in the Gikuyu society social obligations are arranged and differentiated according to the system of age-groupings, but it is worth while to point out that this obtains in lesser as well as in more important matters. It determines the different salutations used, the manners people may adopt in eating certain foods, the different tasks in homestead or garden; it rules habits of dress or demeanour in the community; and it explains the rights of different people in judging cases, in exercising authority in the clan or family, in ceremonial or religious proceedings.

It is in relation to this social ladder that the child's education must be studied if it is to be understood. His life is marked and his position known by the steps which denote his progress from one stage or status to another. Among the Gikuyu the first and least important is the piercing of the ears, *gotonya ndogera na mato*. *Ndogera,* i.e. piercing of the outer edge of the ears, is done when the child is about four or five years. *Gotonya mato,* namely, piercing of the lobe of the ears, is done when the girl is between six and ten, but the boy's ears are not pierced until he is ten or twelve. At the time when this is done the maternal uncle claims five animals (four sheep or goats and one lamb) before giving his permission. When a boy's ears are pierced he advances

from childhood to boyhood, he can now accompany his
father to a case as witness so that he will be able to
speak of it after his father is dead. But the biggest and
most drastic step in the latter is circumcision, which
admits a boy or girl to the full membership of the community. This used to be done only when a youth could
be expected to prove himself as a warrior. The customary age was thus eighteen or twenty. But nowadays
a boy goes through this ceremony between twelve and
sixteen. Then the youth "comes of age," he is "born
again." The difference in standing of the circumcised
and the uncircumcised is tremendous. Father Buget
points out that the uncircumcised, *kehee,* has no rights
of possession. He cannot build a homestead of his own.
In the days of tribal war he could not go to the battle-
field; he could only stay at home with the women and
defend the homestead. He cannot boast or brag or
even appear to do so. He is not allowed to wear the
long hair of the *mwanake,* circumcised youth; it is taboo
for him to have sexual intercourse with circumcised
girls. In meat feasts, he is not allowed to eat certain
joints; he cannot have a circumcised man as an intimate
friend. In contrast with all this, the circumcised youth
is a warrior, a dandy, a dancer, an eater of good food.
He is full-grown, a proper man, a full member of the
tribe. He is now eligible to inherit property, he can
think seriously of marriage and of putting up his own
homestead. But he has now undertaken new responsibilities; if he errs in any way he is liable to punishment,
he will be told: "You have passed the period of childhood and you cannot behave like this; you are circumcised and you are a man to know right and wrong."
(*We mondo morome wa komenya ooru na wega.*)

The next stage in educational advancement is marriage. It is a superior status and has rights and duties
corresponding. Then follows the birth of the first child;
this allows the parents to take part in the religious cere-

monies. The father is not yet an elder; that is reserved for a higher stage when he has a child circumcised and ready for marriage. He now becomes an elder of the lowest rank, or *kamatimo,* in Gikuyu society. Every elder of this grade gives one sheep to the *kiama* of his district; the sheep is slaughtered for a ceremonial feast in which the candidates are sworn in. *Kamatimo* are more or less assistants at the elders' courts and cannot judge a case yet, they only listen to cases for their legal training. They fetch wood and water and light fires for their seniors. After two sheep or goats have been offered the senior *kamatimo* elders become elders of the *kiama* or Gikuyu Court of Elders. The elders of this grade have a staff, *motirima* or *mothegi,* of a particular tree, *mongirima* or *motaathi,* and a bunch of leaves, *mataathi,* to designate their office. When the elders have advanced to this status they are known as *kiama kia mataathi.* They have power over others, for they have the prerogative of administering Gikuyu law and justice. Of these elders of the *kiama kia mataathi,* the eldest are called *kiama kia maturanguru,* i.e. dignified elders, who form the inner circle of the *kiama* and settle the knotty points of law and custom. They wear special brass ear-rings, *icohe,* and carry a bunch of ceremonial leaves, *maturanguru,* as a symbol of their authority. They decide the dates of circumcision feasts and the holding of the *itwika* ceremony when the older generation of rulers gives place to another. Only the elders of these two grades can take part in the Gikuyu ceremonies at the sacred fig tree, *mogumo.*

This brief description of the social ladder gives the clue to the Gikuyu educational system. Each step in the ladder is marked by a corresponding standard of manners and behaviour. The uncircumcised boy is taught by hard experience to pay respect to the circumcised youth, and during circumcision proper he has to pay dearly for the gaining of knowledge or initiation

into the secrets proper to full manhood. This is the
"school" most characteristic of many of the African
societies, and its importance in the life of a community
is illustrated by the impressive nature of the mysteries
and methods used at this stage to mark the entrance to
manhood. These initiation ceremonies are described
more fully in the chapter under that head. It is to be
noticed that the education given at initiation does not
concern only sex, but the youth is taught with equal
vividness and dramatic power the great lesson of respect
for elders, manners to superiors of different grades, and
how to help his country. The trials of circumcision
teach the youth how a man must bear pain, meet with
misfortune and bear himself like a warrior. He is
taught to think matters over carefully and not to act on
the impulse of the moment. It is borne in on him that
he must work hard in the garden so that he may get
the wherewithal to marry. He is taught to obey parents
and older people, to help men and women who are old
and enfeebled and destitute, and to obey the leader
elected by the people. He learns in particular how to
behave to certain people of his wife's family, he must
use a special salutation to his mother and sister-in-law.
It is worth while to mention here that the European
educationalists have not realised the importance of this
teaching, and the result has been that the children who
have been taught under European influence have almost
forgotten or disregarded the Gikuyu customary law of
behaviour.

The large place given to sex in the initiation ceremonies is often misunderstood by Europeans, as if sexual indulgence is encouraged for its own sake; the
obscenity of songs and dances and the profligacy associated with many of these ceremonies are held to
prove unusual moral depravity. On the contrary the
Africans look upon these ceremonies as a final stage,
in which boys and girls must be given full knowledge

in the matters relating to sex, to prepare them for future activities in their own homesteads and in the community. In fact all the sex-teaching is given with a social reference. Boys are taught to look forward to marriage as a duty to themselves, to the clan and the tribe. They have to provide for wife or wives and children by working hard and multiplying sheep, goats and cattle. The breeding of children and the breeding of cattle, sheep and goats are regarded in the same moral scheme as natural activities to be encouraged for the public good. We shall see later how this applies to the girls.

At marriage the husband is taught his duties towards a wife; to treat her well, to establish good relations with his parents-in-law and to receive their blessing before he takes their daughter to his home. So when a child is born he is taught his duty to offer a present of a goat or a sheep to his wife for her labour, in order that he may see the child. He is instructed when sexual intercourse may be resumed and how he must respect the child's maternal relatives. Similarly when the child has reached the stage of circumcision the father is taught the manners of the next stage, the offering of a goat or sheep to the elders of *kiama* and so on, that he may have the right to join and speak in the *ndundu ya kerera,* or advisory council. This body is the keeper of the tribal secrets, its membership is limited to a few selected elders who have gone through a severe test and have solemnly sworn not to reveal their secret to anyone outside the group.

The same parallelism of grade privileges and knowledge is seen in the training of girls. When a girl is ready to be circumcised she is taught manners such as how to behave when married. It is understood that she will be married and bring wealth to her family so that a poor brother can find the guarantee necessary for marriage. She will bear many children, bring honour

to her family and to the tribe, and she will provide food
for the poor relation. She is taught to behave like a
gentlewoman, not to raise her eyes or voice talking to
men in public, not to bathe in the open, not to eat in
the presence of men other than those of her own age
or kinsfolk. This teaching is given by her mother and
the older women who are in the women's advisory
council, *ndundu ya atumia*. The women of this rank
deal with all matters concerning circumcision of girls,
births and other religious duties.

The girl is taught to treat strangers with the proper
mixture of courtesy and suspicion. Respect for her
husband's people is inculcated and obedience to him;
she is warned against hasty and impetuous behaviour.
At marriage she is again taught to obey her husband's
father and mother, to address them by those names of
"father" and "mother" and to regard all the children
and property in her husband's homestead as hers and
treat them with the care she would give her most personal belongings. She is also taught her husband's rights
in sexual matters and her rights over against his. When
she has a boy- or a girl-child old enough to be circumcised she learns what she must do in giving presents
to the older women that she may be admitted to enter
in their group.

The fundamental nature of personal relationships in
the scheme of education shows clearly how these things
are valued by the Gikuyu. This is clearly brought out
in the position of parents in the society. In fact, they
might be described as custodians of tradition representing the public teaching on life and duty. They have the
right to the service of their children from earliest years,
for it is said that prosperity depends on the joint
activities of all the members of the family group. This
is demonstrated in the way girls share the duties of the
homestead, cooking, grinding, fetching water and firewood, planting and cultivating, nursing small children.

Both girls and boys accompany their parents to the garden when they are small. Little girls have tiny cultivating-knives or digging-sticks which, when they are five years old, they can handle with amazing skill with their right hand while with their left they clear the soil away and gather the weeds and grass in bundles. Boys go with their fathers to herd cattle, sheep and goats, or to perform other tasks. To begin with, the calves are in their charge, and later they can watch all the animals, water them at noon and bring them home in the evening. In this way they learn good and bad pasture, how to milk, to feed the calves and to flay the skin of the animals. Similarly girls learn to carry babies, to feed, to clean and put them to bed. What is important here is that all the work has this character of family duty. Boys and girls not only learn all that boys and girls could learn through an apprenticeship to some particular calling, but they learn this almost incidentally. The bigger things they learn are the habits of helping their parents and working under the system of reciprocity with other people.

But they are also taught definitely at circumcision the theory, as it were, of respect to their parents and kinsfolk. Under all circumstances they must stay with them and share in their joys and sorrows. It will never do to leave them and go off to see the world whenever they take the notion, especially when their parents are in their old age. They must give them clothes, look after their garden, herd their cattle, sheep and goats, build their grain stores and houses. It thus becomes a part of their outlook on life that their parents shall not suffer want nor continue to labour strenuously in their old age while their children can lend a hand and do things to give them comfort.

This respect and duty to parents is further emphasised by the fact that the youth or girl cannot advance from one stage to another without the parent's

will and active assistance. The satisfaction of all a boy's
longings and ambitions depends on the father's and
family's consent. Without it he cannot be circumcised.
Without it he cannot be married, for he has no property
of his own, and marriage involves gifts or exchanges
which only the two families concerned can arrange. He
cannot even join in a meat feast, *keruugu,* or a beer-
drinking party without his father's permission. He must
bring beer for his father and mother and also for uncles
and aunts before he can take his share. Even in snuff-
taking the same respect must be shown. This custom is
regarded as a boy's demonstration of his gratitude and
appreciation for his parents' careful duty and tender-
ness rendered him during his childhood.

A disobedient or careless son or daughter is told:
"If you carry on like this you will never get married,
you will disgrace your parents and the clan." The
obedient son is always well rewarded when his father
dies and the inheritance comes to be divided. Among
other things, natural or supernatural, the curse of a
dying father or mother is the most dreadful thing that
can befall a son or daughter. The disobedient or careless son or daughter lives under the fear of it every day.
"Orokanyararwo ne ciana ciaku otogwo onyarareete"
—"May your children treat you with disrespect as you
have treated me." This is the worst form of sin or uncleanness and is the only one from which deliverance
cannot be gained by purification. It is even transmitted
to a man's children. The father's or mother's position is
thus strengthened by religious sanctions. In the same
way he is the proper means of communication and fellowship with his ancestors. As the nearest relation on
earth, he is the priest of the household, and is alone entitled to offer the family sacrifices. In doing this he is
supported by the will of the ancestral spirits, if there is
strife or dissension in the family the spirits can intervene and punish the wrong-doer. These kinds of spirits

are known as *ngoma cia rohuho,* i.e. spirits of the wind. If after a quarrel one party or his child falls ill, it is said that his ancestors are angry with him and that they have sent the "spirits of wind" to punish him. In this case a medicine man, *mondo mogo,* is called in to find out what will appease the offended spirits. He diagnoses the offence and prescribes a suitable offering according to the nature of the case. If it is serious, beer and a lamb have to be offered, otherwise beer alone is sufficient. At once beer is prepared, and next morning, when the beer is ready, the family gather, the officiating elder pours some of the beer on the ground and calls aloud: "Spirits of our ancestors, do not be angry, we give you back the words we spoke."

This is interesting as an illustration of the statement that the family consists of all the members both living and dead. Anything that disturbs that fellowship is evil, and nothing disturbs the dead more than an offence against family unity and loyalty. So by any harshness or indifference to family claims the youth brings, so we might say, divine vengeance on the whole family group of which he is a member. Thus early and late, by rules of conduct in individual instances, by the sentiment of the group in which he lives, by rewards and punishments and fears of ceremonial uncleanness, the younger generation learns the respect and obedience due to parents. The older generation does likewise.

The teaching of social obligations is again emphasised by the classification of age-groups to which we have already referred. This binds together those of the same status in ties of closest loyalty and devotion. Men circumcised at the same time stand in the very closest relationship to each other. When a man of the same age-group injures another it is a serious magico-religious offence. They are like blood brothers; they must not do any wrong to each other. It ranks with an injury done to a member of one's own family. The age-group (*riika*) is thus a powerful instrument for securing conformity with tribal usage. The selfish or reckless youth is taught by the opinion of his gang that it does not pay to incur displeasure. He will not be called to eat with the others when food is going. He may be put out of their dances, fined, or even ostracised for a time. If he does not change his ways he will find his old companions have deserted him.

The fellowship and unity of these age-groups is rather a remarkable thing. It binds men from all parts of the country, and though they may have been circumcised at places hundreds of miles apart, it is of no consequence. They are like old boys of the same school, though I question whether the Europeans have any association with the same high standards of mutual obligation except perhaps in time of national emergency. The age-groups do more than bind men of equal standing together. They further emphasise the social grades of junior and senior, inferior and superior. We see the same principle in evidence all through the various grades. When an uncircumcised youth is travelling in the same company as a circumcised youth, he may not drink water until his superior has drunk, nor bathe in the river above the spot where the latter is bathing. So in the distribution of food the order of precedence is observed. What is true of uncircumcised and circumcised is true as between the various circumcised groups. The older group takes precedence over the younger and has rights to service and courtesy which the younger must acknowledge. For instance, before a circumcised youth can take part in the dance or wear long hair he must pay a goat or sheep, *mbori ya ihaki,* which is eaten by the *riika* age-group a year or two senior to his own. The whole organisation of the community again enforces the lesson that behaviour to other persons is what matters most.

Owing to the strength and numbers of the social ties

existing between members of the same family, clan and age-group, and between different families and clans through which the tribe is unified and solidified as one organic whole, the community can be mobilised very easily for corporate activity. House-building, cultivation, harvesting, digging trap-pits, putting up fences around cultivated fields, and building bridges, are usually done by the group; hence the Gikuyu saying: *"Kamoinge koyaga ndere,"* which means collective activities make heavy tasks easier. In the old days sacrifices were offered and wars were waged by the tribe as a whole or by the clan. Marriage contracts and ceremonies are the affairs of families and not of individuals. Sometimes even cattle are bought by joint effort. Thus the individual boy or girl soon learns to work with and for other people. An old man who has no children of his own is helped by his neighbour's children in almost everything. His hut is built, his garden dug, firewood is cut and water is fetched for him. If his cattle, sheep or goats are lost or in difficulties the children of his neighbour will help to bring them back, at great pains and often at considerable risk. The old man reciprocates by treating the children as though they were his own. Children learn this habit of communal work like others, not by verbal exhortations so much as by joining with older people in such social services. They see the household and friends building a house for somebody, when everyone brings poles for the uprights or grass for thatching. They go with their relatives to help in another man's garden, building his house or his cattle-pens or granary. They help in provision of his marriage feasts or brewing beer for a kinship ceremonial party. All help given in this way is voluntary, and kinsfolk are proud to help one another. There is no payment or expectation of payment. They are well feasted, of course. This is not regarded as payment, but as hospitality. The whole thing rests on the principle of reciprocal obliga-

tions. It is taken for granted that the neighbour whom
you assist in difficulty or whose house you help to build
will do the same for you when in similar need. Those
who do not reciprocate these sentiments of neighbourli-
ness are not in favour, but there is a saying that even a
bad man will not lack labour in the time of emergency,
especially if he needs to build a hut; though in actual
practice such a man may find it difficult to obtain help.
Just as the public opinion of the age-group enjoins certain obligations of loyalty to fellow-members, and just
as the family edict may call for a sheep or goat from
every household for a sacrifice or a patch of sugar-cane
from every garden, so the public opinion of the tribe
fosters the sentiment of communal labour on a reciprocal basis. As they work in the garden of a man too old
to work for himself, or help a widow with no children
of her own to call in, so they pay off a grudge in common and combine to pay off the fine levied on one of
their number. For example, if one member of an age-
group is insulted and is physically unable to avenge the
injury, the other members of his age-group will co-
operate with him in attaining satisfaction. For an insult to one member of an age-group is regarded as an
insult to the entire age-group. Again, in the matter of
paying off a fine imposed by a senior warriors' age-group
or by elders, members of the particular age-group, *riika,*
will contribute toward the payment of the fine on their
fellow-member.

Naturally the tendency to adopt the habitual behaviour of the age-group grows with the pride of sentiment in belonging to it. Every clan and family has its
heroes, *njamba,* past and present. Their heroic deeds are
related and their praises sung round the fire of an evening. This is one of the methods of instilling ambition
and a sense of duty into the hearts of the growing
generation. The child or youth who does not give the
service demanded of his position will be told "you are

not one of the family of So-and-so" (*ndore wa mbari ya ng'ania*) or (*ndotoketie mbari ya ng'ania*). The good old days before the advent of the Europeans are lauded to the skies. These were the days of wars and national pride of heroes and great leaders of the dance, days when men went together to plunder, when they were all brave, and no man deserted his friend; their motto was "*Njamba egoaga na erea enge,*" which means together we fight and together we win or die. Of course, since the Gikuyu are not a society of angels, adherence to these social rules depends on the morale and courage of individuals.

The selfish or self-regarding man has no name or reputation in the Gikuyu community. An individualist is looked upon with suspicion and is given a nickname of *mwebongia,* one who works only for himself and is likely to end up as a wizard. He may lack assistance when he needs it. He cannot expect that everything he does will prosper, for the weight of opinion makes him feel his crime against society. Religious sanction works against him, too, for Gikuyu religion is always on the side of solidarity. The aged and weak are under the special protection of the ancestral spirits, and they are never far away from home. Thus the labour of the hands, the begetting of children, the amassing of wealth in the form of land, cattle, sheep and goats are, just as much as religious ceremonies, matters of family and clan sentiment.

In the Gikuyu community there is no really individual affair, for every thing has a moral and social reference. The habit of corporate effort is but the other side of corporate ownership; and corporate responsibility is illustrated in corporate work no less than in corporate sacrifice and prayer.

In spite of the foreign elements which work against many of the Gikuyu institutions and the desire to implant the system of wholesale Westernisation, this system of mutual help and the tribal solidarity in social services, political and economic activities are still maintained by the large majority of the Gikuyu people. It is less practised among those Gikuyu who have been Europeanised or detribalised. The rest of the community look upon these people as mischief-makers and breakers of the tribal traditions, and the general disgusted cry is heard: *"Mothongo ne athogonjire borori,"* i.e. the white man had spoiled and disgraced our country.

The rising generation is trained in beliefs and customs necessary to the self-maintenance of the tribe and interrelation with the neighbouring tribes. The fundamental needs of reproduction, extraction of food from the environment, and social solidarity are recognised and met. The tribal society not only maintains its existence, but secures the continuity of its distinctive features over against other tribes. We have therefore to ask ourselves whether a system of education which proves so successful in realising its particular objectives may not have some valuable suggestion to offer or advice to give to the European whose assumed task it is in these days to provide Western education for the African.

The first and most obvious principle of educational value which we see in the Gikuyu system of education is that the instruction is always applied to an individual concrete situation; behaviour is taught in relation to some particular person. Whereas in Europe and America schools provide courses in moral instruction or citizenship, the African is taught how to behave to father or mother, grandparents, and to other members of the kinship group, paternal and maternal. Whereas European schools in Africa provide training in nature study, woodwork, animal husbandry, etc., much of which is taught by general class instruction, the tribal method is to teach the names of particular plants, the use of different trees, or the management of a particular herd of sheep and goats or cattle. After this the child is left free to develop his own initiative by experiments and through trial and error to acquire proficiency.

The striking thing in the Gikuyu system of education, and the feature which most sharply distinguishes it from the European system of education, is the primary place given to personal relations. Each official statement of educational policy repeats this well-worn declaration that the aim of education must be the building of character and not the mere acquisition of knowledge. But European practice falls short of this principle; knowledge is the dominating objective in the European method of teaching in Africa as a whole and, as long as exams rule, it is hard to see how anything else can be given primary importance. While the Westerner asserts that character formation is the chief thing, he forgets that character is formed primarily through relations with other people, and that there is really no other way in which it can grow. Europeans assume that, given the right knowledge and ideas, personal relations can be left largely to take care of themselves, and this is perhaps the most fundamental difference in outlook between Africans and Europeans. It can be safely said that, in the European system of education, school co-ordination, and especially social subordination, marriage, the family, the school, vocation, relation of people to the State, etc., are all regarded as things which have grown up of themselves, as historical forms which, however, are always capable, as such, of change, and over which the free man, namely, the personality, must have authority. For freedom of personality is the highest good, and co-ordination with other people and especially mutual subordination are on the contrary something accidental. Here it is worth while to ask a question which seems very pertinent to our subject: "If it is true that the European system of education aims at individuality, is it then to be wondered at that Europeans educated in this way have some difficulty in finding the right place for the organic tribal relationships of the Africans?" We may sum it up by saying that to the Europeans "Individuality is the ideal of life," to the Africans the ideal is the right relations with, and behaviour to, other people. No doubt educational philosophy can make a higher synthesis in which these two great truths are one, but the fact remains that while the Europeans place the emphasis on one side the Africans place it on the other.

In the European policy for African education it has been suggested that its aim should be that of "conserving as far as possible all sound and healthy elements in the fabric of the African's social life." The Europeans seem, therefore, to be committed to a far greater utilisation of the African's social bonds. The European educational system looks forward to social groupings which are largely determined by economic, professional and religious associations. These are the spheres of social behaviour and the links which bind people together in mutual obligations. With the Africans it is far otherwise. The ties of family and kinship, sex, and age-grouping, as we have seen, form the basis of the whole structure of indigenous education. Unless the Western education in Africa can keep these bonds vital and strong it cannot be expected to mould the African in a way which will make him fit in his community on one hand and to establish good relations with the outside world on the other. If the African is to derive any benefit from Western education, his training should be directed to the strengthening of these basic relationships which are the foundation of moral sentiments and the means of building up character. As Dr. Oldham writes in the course of a review on Dr. Knak's book on African problems: "But whatever change may take place, men will still have fathers, mothers, brothers, sisters, children, blood-relations, neighbours, companions of the same age and fellow-workers, and whatever change may come, the vital thing is that the sense of mutual obligation and responsibility which is found in existing relations should be conserved and express itself in the new conditions."

In one respect the method which we have traced in the Gikuyu system of tribal education bears a remarkable resemblance to one of the features of modern practice in England and America. I refer to the stress now given to learning through experience of life in a community. This is the indirect method which, as we have seen, is the method *par excellence* of the Gikuyu system. By this method instruction is given, as it were, incidentally, as a mere accompaniment to some activity. This is how the Gikuyu boys and girls acquire most of their knowledge and learn most of the rules of social behaviour. This system is precisely what American educators mean by the process which Professor Kilpatrick defines as "Wholehearted, purposeful activity proceeding in a social environment." Here the motive power is provided by the desire to achieve some purpose for which certain knowledge or certain skills are necessary. But the knowledge is a side-issue, not the aim of the process. Educationalists will testify to the fact that knowledge and skill thus acquired are more likely to be retained, for, as has been aptly stated recently by a prominent educator: "It is the side-issues that matter in learning. The knowledge picked up as a side-issue becomes an assumption, and it is the things that are assumed that are really learned." What is the most impressive about the Gikuyu method of learning is that the knowledge thus acquired is related to a practical need, and, therefore, knowledge is merged into activity and can be recalled when that activity is again required. Behaviour also is learned from doing things together, and is therefore directed to social activities from the outset. Thus the idea of education as participation in the life of the community is most clearly realised in Gikuyu society untouched by Western civilisation.

It is worth while to devote some attention to the European educationalist in Africa and his approach to the problem. As a teacher his first concern should be to establish a good understanding with the people amongst whom he works, and to learn how to appreciate what is good in the tribal law and custom of that particular community. The importance of this point is that such an attitude would serve as a connecting-link between the pupils in the schools and the rest of the community.

In the past there has been too much of "civilising and uplifting poor savages." This policy has been based on preconceived ideas that the African cultures are "primitive," and as such, belong to the past and can only be looked upon as antiquarian relics fit only for museums. The European should realise that there is something to learn from the African and a great deal about him to understand, and that the burden could be made easier if a policy of "give and take" could be adopted. We may mention here that the African who is being civilised looks upon this "civilisation" with great fear mingled with suspicion. Above all, he finds that socially and religiously he has been torn away from his family and tribal organisation. The new civilisation he is supposed to acquire neither prepares him for the proper functions of a European mode of life nor for African life; he is left floundering between the two social forces. European educationalists and others, especially those who are guided by racial prejudice and preconceived ideas of what is good for the African, usually fail to take cognisance of this vital fact. This may be due to studied indifference or to an inexcusably meagre knowledge of the functions of African institutions and a lack of intimate contact with the real social life of the people they presume to teach.

The teacher may want to make friends with his pupils, to help them in their difficulties, and to share their thoughts and feelings. Soon he discovers, or should discover, the peculiar difficulties of the African language. It is easy, sometimes, to acquire a sufficient facility for many subjects of instruction, but the teacher needs more than this. If he is really in earnest he will no doubt find that it is impossible with only a superficial knowledge of the language to translate many of the most important terms of social intercourse into African speech. As Professor Malinowski writes: "All words which express religious beliefs, moral values, or specific technical or ritual proceedings, can only be rendered by reference to the social organisation of the tribe, their beliefs, practices, education and economics. The study of a native language must go hand in hand with the study of its culture."

It can be stated definitely here that the study of the above subjects is not so easy as some people may think. The European should devote more time to the study of African language and culture before he starts teaching in Africa, for without a proper knowledge of the functions of African institutions, the more the European tries to influence his pupils in the direction of new habits, standards of life and general Europeanisation, the more he comes up against a social background which he does not understand. Without previous training in African ways of life, the European may get on well enough in the teaching of arithmetic or the imparting of knowledge of geography based on a superficial knowledge of the environment. In doing this the teacher follows the adopted educational policy of educating the Africans in the ways which the Europeans think fit for the "poor savages"; a policy that has been carried out without due regard for the ideals and aspirations of the people concerned. But that would not be the correct approach if, as is so vociferously

proclaimed, the European is out in Africa for the improved health of the African and for the standards of
life and the economic, social, and political status of
the African.

By ignoring the African's point of view and by in-
sisting that pupils should adopt the European methods,
whether the technique fits in with their mode of life or
not, the teacher creates conflicts of ideas in the mental
outlook of his pupils, then he turns to ask himself:
"What sort of homes do the boys or girls come from,
how have they been brought up?" He then jumps into
a paternal conclusion: "The new ideas must be im-
planted to replace the old." This paternal determination
may seem to be working smoothly for a time in the
school, class-room or dormitory, but soon interest flags
and effort decreases, owing to the fact that the new
system of education is not correlated with the African
background; thus it has been very difficult for the
African to comprehend it or to realise from it any
potential benefits that it may have for him.

If then the teacher is given to thinking over his work
and wants an atmosphere of keenness in the school, of
duties voluntarily and cheerfully discharged and responsibilities accepted for house, team, or school, he
is bound to ask himself: "What is it that will maintain
effort and stimulate interest? What motive will keep the
pupils at their best? What system will leave them proud
and satisfied to belong to the school as well as to the
rest of their community?" Even when he has solved
this problem there remains another and a hard one:
"Why do the European standards and habits fail to
carry over into the home life of the pupils? Is it only
the pull of the backward environment or is he up
against something difficult, prejudices, fears, a whole
system of thought deeply entrenched and stubbornly
opposed to progress and change?" Further, the teacher
might wish to see the Western ideas carried by the

pupils into the community. Yet this is precisely the point where the teacher is disappointed. Thus sooner or later he becomes either disillusioned or cynical, feeling that these people are too stupid and obstinate to learn anything else.

What the teacher has failed to see is not that the old social structure cannot adapt itself rapidly enough to changed conditions, but that there is a new trend of thought among young Africans in a new environment; that is, their modern ideals of life and aspiration. The European sees, though he may not understand, that African life is changing with alarming rapidity, that there is disruption and discontent in the body politic, and that the most aggressive individuals are often the least desirable. With a better understanding of the African social structure, an educationalist would be able to adopt a practical theory and method to suit the situation, and to satisfy the African aspiration, so that education, instead of creating confusions, might help to promote progress, and at the same time to preserve all that is best in the traditions of the African people and assist them to create a new culture which, though its roots are still in the soil, is yet modified to meet the pressure of modern conditions. A more sympathetic attitude would help the teacher to change from what is called "educating the native along his own lines," to educating the African for leadership in his community and people, and to make him fit to stand by himself under the strenuous conditions of the modern world.

It is important for the European teacher to realise that "he is not pouring new wine into new bottles, but into very old bottles." But how can he discover the exact flavour of the old vintage, and where is the cellar to be seen? He may set out to learn something of family, clan and tribal organisation, the rights and duties of individuals within the society, and the rules that determine the conduct of any individual within the context of the whole. But after a sketchy study of these institutions, he thinks that he knows all about the mental outlook of his pupils, what they believe and what they do not believe, how they regard themselves, and the world of nature and the society of which they form a part. The assumption of knowing the African's mind has been very often heard in the usual phraseology: "I have lived for many years amongst the Africans and I know them very well." Yet this is far from the actual fact, for there is a great difference between "living" among a people and "knowing" them. While a European can learn something of the externals of African life, its system of kinship and classification, its peculiar arts and picturesque ceremonial, he may still have not yet reached the heart of the problem. In the mass of detail presented to him in what is called "authoritative books," he often loses his way as in a maze of knowledge not yet intelligible because not yet related. With his preconceived ideas, mingled with prejudices, he fails to achieve a more sympathetic and imaginative knowledge, a more human and inward appreciation of the living people, the pupils he teaches, the people he meets on the roads and watches in the gardens. In a word he fails to understand the African with his instinctive tendencies (no doubt very like his own), but trained from his earliest days to habitual ideas, inhibitions and forms of self-expression which have been handed down from one generation to another and which are foreign, if not absurd, to the European in Africa.

6

INITIATION
OF BOYS AND GIRLS

THE CUSTOM of clitoridectomy of girls, which we are
going to describe here, has been strongly attacked by
a number of influential European agencies—missionary,
sentimental pro-African, Government, educational and
medical authorities. We think it necessary to give a
short historical background of the method employed
by these bodies in attacking the custom of clitoridectomy
of girls.

In 1929, after several attempts to break down the
custom, the Church of Scotland Mission to Gikuyu
issued an order demanding that all their followers and
those who wish their children to attend schools should
pledge themselves that they will not in any way adhere
to or support this custom, and that they will not let their
children undergo the initiation rite. This raised a great
controversy between the missionaries and the Gikuyu.
The matter was taken up seriously by both educated
and uneducated Gikuyu. Children of those who did
not denounce the custom were debarred from attending
the missionary schools. People petitioned the Government and educational authorities. During the petition-

ing period many of these deserted schools and churches were used for storing maize and potatoes. A "gentlemen's agreement" was reached between the Government and the missionaries. The ban on children attending the schools was lifted, but the missionaries maintained that teachers must be only those who had denounced the custom, for they hoped that teachers with this qualification would be able to mould the children in the way favourable to the missionary attitude. People were indignant about this decision and at once demanded the right to establish their own schools where they could teach their children without interference with the group custom. The cry for schools was raised high, and the result was the foundation of Gikuyu independent schools and Kareng'a schools. These schools are entirely free from missionary influence, both in educational and religious matters.

In 1930 the question of the custom of clitoridectomy was raised in the House of Commons and a committee of Members of Parliament was appointed to investigate the matter. The members of the committee included the Duchess of Atholl, Colonel Josiah Wedgwood, C. R. Buxton and others. The writer was invited to attend the committee meeting and give the Gikuyu's point of view. It was then agreed that the best way to tackle the problem was through education and not by force of an enactment, and that the best way was to leave the people concerned free to choose what custom was best suited to their changing conditions.

In 1931 a conference on African children was held in Geneva under the auspices of the Save the Children Fund. In this conference several European delegates urged that the time was ripe when this "barbarous custom" should be abolished, and that, like all other "heathen" customs, it could be abolished at once by law. That it was the duty of the Conference, for the sake of the African children, to call upon the Governments under which the customs of this nature were practised to pass laws making it a criminal offence for anyone who should be found guilty of practising the custom of clitoridectomy.

However, this urge for abolishing a people's social custom by force of law was not wholeheartedly accepted by the majority of the delegates in the Conference. General opinion was for education which would enable the people to choose what customs to keep and which ones they would like to get rid of.

It should be pointed out here that there is a strong community of educated Gikuyu opinion in defence of this custom. In the matrimonial relation, the *rite de passage* is the deciding factor. No proper Gikuyu would dream of marrying a girl who has not been circumcised, and vice versa. It is taboo for a Gikuyu man or woman to have sexual relations with someone who has not undergone this operation. If it happens, a man or woman must go through a ceremonial purification, *korutwo thahu* or *gotahikio megiro*—namely, ritual vomiting of the evil deeds. A few detribalised Gikuyu, while they are away from home for some years, have thought fit to denounce the custom and to marry uncircumcised girls, especially from coastal tribes, thinking that they could bring them back to their fathers' homes without offending the parents. But to their surprise they found that their fathers, mothers, brothers and sisters, following the tribal custom, are not prepared to welcome as a relative-in-law anyone who has not fulfilled the ritual qualifications for matrimony. Therefore a problem has faced these semi-detribalised Gikuyu when they wanted to return to their homeland. Their parents have demanded that if their sons wished to settle down and have the blessings of the family and the clan, they must divorce the wife married out-

side the rigid tribal custom and then marry a girl with
the approved tribal qualifications. Failing this, they
have been turned out and disinherited.

In our short survey we have mentioned how the
custom of clitoridectomy has been attacked on one side,
and on the other how it has been defended. In view
of these points the important problem is an anthropological one: it is unintelligent to discuss the emotional
attitudes of either side, or to take violent sides in the
question, without understanding the reasons why the
educated, intelligent Gikuyu still cling to this custom.

The real argument lies not in the defence of the
surgical operation or its details, but in the understanding of a very important fact in the tribal psychology of
the Gikuyu—namely, that this operation is still regarded as the very essence of an institution which has
enormous educational, social, moral, and religious implications, quite apart from the operation itself. For the
present it is impossible for a member of the tribe to
imagine an initiation without clitoridectomy. Therefore the abolition of the surgical element in this custom
means to the Gikuyu the abolition of the whole institution.

The real anthropological study, therefore, is to show
that clitoridectomy, like Jewish circumcision, is a mere
bodily mutilation which, however, is regarded as the
conditio sine qua non of the whole teaching of tribal
law, religion, and morality.

The initiation of both sexes is the most important
custom among the Gikuyu. It is looked upon as a
deciding factor in giving a boy or girl the status of
manhood or womanhood in the Gikuyu community.
This custom is adhered to by the vast majority of
African peoples and is found in almost every part of
the continent. It is therefore necessary to examine the
facts attached to this widespread custom in order to
have some idea why the African peoples cling to this

custom which, in the eyes of a good many Europeans, is nothing but a "horrible" and "painful" practice, suitable only to barbarians.

In the first place it is necessary to give the readers a clear picture of why and how this important socio-biological custom is performed.

NAME OF THE CUSTOM

The Gikuyu name for this custom of *rite de passage* from childhood to adulthood is *irua,* i.e. circumcision, or trimming the genital organs of both sexes. The dances and songs connected with the initiation ceremony are called *mambura,* i.e. rituals or divine services. It is important to note that the moral code of the tribe is bound up with this custom and that it symbolises the unification of the whole tribal organisation. This is the principal reason why *irua* plays such an important part in the life of the Gikuyu people.

The *irua* marks the commencement of participation in various governing groups in the tribal administration, because the real age-groups begin from the day of the physical operation. The history and legends of the people are explained and remembered according to the names given to various age-groups at the time of the initiation ceremony. For example, if a devastating famine occurred at the time of the initiation, that particular *irua* group would be known as "famine" (*ng'aragu*). In the same way, the Gikuyu have been able to record the time when the European introduced a number of maladies such as syphilis into Gikuyu country, for those initiated at the time when this disease first showed itself are called *gatego,* i.e. syphilis. Historical events are recorded and remembered in the same manner. Without this custom a tribe which had no written records would not have been able to keep a record of important events and happenings in the life of the Gikuyu nation. Any Gikuyu child who is not corrupted by detribalisation is able to record in his mind the whole history and origin of the Gikuyu people through the medium of such names as Agu, Ndemi and Mathathi, etc., who were initiated hundreds of years ago.

For years there has been much criticism and agitation against *irua* of girls by certain misinformed missionary societies in East Africa, who see only the surgical side of the *irua,* and, without investigating the psychological importance attached to this custom by the Gikuyu, these missionaries draw their conclusion that the *irua* of girls is nothing but a barbarous practice and, as such, should be abolished by law.

On the other hand, the Gikuyu look upon these religious fanatics with great suspicion. The overwhelming majority of them believe that it is the secret aim of those who attack this centuries-old custom to disintegrate their social order and thereby hasten their Europeanisation. The abolition of *irua* will destroy the tribal symbol which identifies the age-groups, and prevent the Gikuyu from perpetuating that spirit of collectivism and national solidarity which they have been able to maintain from time immemorial.

PREPARING FOR INITIATION

About a fortnight before the day of initiation the girl is put on a special diet, namely, *njahi* and *ngima ya ogembe,* composed of a particular kind of Gikuyu bean (*njahe*), and together with a stiff porridge made of a small kind of grain (*ogembe*) ground into flour and mixed with water and oil. This diet is used in order to prevent the loss of blood at the time of initiation (physical operation) and also to ensure immediate healing of the wound, as well as a precaution against blood poisoning. The girl is properly taken care of by her sponsor, *motiiri,* who examines her and gives her all necessary instructions about the initiation ceremony. In this examination attention is directed to ascertaining that the girl is not near maturity and that menstruation is not likely to begin for at least a month after *irua* and the healing of the wound. She is also closely questioned to verify that she never had sexual intercourse or indulged in masturbation. If she has broken any of the prohibitions of the Gikuyu social codes, the girl makes a confession to the *motiiri,* who reports the confession to the girl's parents. The service of a *motahekania,* or a "family purifier," is then engaged to purify (*koruta mogiro*) the girl and prepare her for the *irua.*

Three or four days prior to the actual physical operation the girl is taken to the homestead where the ceremony is to take place. There she meets the rest of the initiates. The initiates are all introduced to the elder of the homestead and his wife, who adopt them as their children for the purpose of the *irua.* On this special day the boys and girls of the *irua* group, together with their relatives and friends, join in singing and dancing the whole night, and at the same time beating sugarcanes in mortars to prepare a special kind of beer for a ceremony called *koraria morungu,* which is supposed to keep the gods awake. This ceremony is considered an act of communion with the ancestral god (*morungu*), whose protection is invoked to guide and protect the initiates through the *irua* ceremony and at the same time to give them the wisdom of their forefathers. During the dancing and singing no girl or boy is allowed to go to bed, as this is regarded as missing the opportunity of direct contact with *morungu,* which would result in misfortune at the time of the *irua.*

On the morning after *koraria morungu* the fathers and mothers of the initiates are gathered together and

partake of a feast at which the specially prepared beer
is freely indulged in. This is done in the yard of the
homestead. They sit in a circle. Then the children are
called, one by one, according to their order of adoption. Now the ceremony called *korathima ciana,* or
blessing the children, is performed. It includes marking
certain symbols upon the forehead, the cheeks, round
the eyes, the nose, the throat and the navel of the
initiates with a sort of white chalk called *ira* (snow)
obtained from Mount Kenya (Kere-Nyaga), the abode
of the gods. One elder, who holds the senior office in
the ceremonial council, or *athuri a kerera,* is entrusted
with this duty of marking. He places the *ira* in the
palm of his left hand and, dipping his right thumb in
it, marks his candidates as they pass, one by one, before him. An old woman who is also a member of the
ceremonial council follows and, with oil carried in a
bottle-shaped calabash (*kinando*), anoints each girl on
the head, round the neck and on the feet. The rest of
the elders join in chorus, uttering blessings as each
child passes by. On this occasion they use ceremonial
language such as this: *"Ciana irogea thaai, Thathayai
Ngai thaaa-ai-ciana irogea thai, thaaai-thai-thai-thaaa-i,"*
which means—"Peace be with the children. Beseech
Ngai (God) peace—peace, peace. Let peace be with
the children—peace."

When this part of the ceremony is completed, the
boys and girls leave the homestead, escorted by their
relatives and friends, for their respective homes, singing festive songs as they go along.

On their arrival home, the girl is met at the entrance
of the homestead by young married and unmarried
women (*ahiki na airetu*) of the clan, who are singing,
dancing and jumping joyously, and at the same time
tossing small calabashes (*thego*) containing a special

kind of gruel known as *kenage*. The girl then takes
sips from each calabash held to her lips by the women.
When this is finished the girl is left to rest until the day
of the great ceremonial dance (*matuumo*).

THE GREAT CEREMONIAL DANCE (MATUUMO)

The day before the physical operation is performed the
girl is called early in the morning to have her head
shaved by the sponsor. All her clothes are removed,
she is given a massage, after which her naked body is
decked with beads lent to her by women relatives and
friends. About ten o'clock in the morning relatives and
friends gather at the girl's homestead. Here a short
ceremony of reunion with the ancestors of the clan is
performed, and a leader is chosen to lead the procession
to the homestead where the *irua* is to take place.

The girl is provided with a bell (*kegamba*) which is
tied on her right leg just above the calf, or sometimes
above the knee, to provide the rhythm to the procession
and also for the dance. The girl is put in the middle of
the procession, which moves slowly, singing ritual songs
until they reach the *irua's* homestead, where the procession is joined by the other initiates who are accompanied by other processions of relatives and friends
dressed in their best.

The *matuumo* dances and songs begin at forenoon
before the sun is overhead and continue the whole day.
It takes place inside the homestead, but if the homestead is not large enough it is held on some convenient
site which must be in close proximity to the homestead.
The site is cleared and carefully examined to make sure
that there is nothing on the ground that can hurt the
feet of candidates while dancing.

The ceremonial doctor (*mondo-mogo wa mambura*)

goes round the site sprinkling a brownish powder called
rothuko on the ground, to counteract any evil design
which might be directed against the candidates. This is
followed by the elders who sprinkle honey beer (*njohi
ya ooke*) on the ground to appease the ancestral spirits
and to bring them into harmony with those of the living.
When the elders have completed their work of purifying
the ground, the initiates enter the ground accompanied
by their sponsors, relatives and friends, adorned
with ceremonial dresses and green leaves; then all of
them begin to dance. The crowd which has gathered
for the great event forms a thick wall round the arena.
While the dancing and singing is going on a ceremonial
horn is blown at intervals, and before it is sounded, a
little medicine (*itwanda*) is rubbed inside; this medicine
is believed to have power of chasing away evil spirits
and preventing them from doing harm to the initiates.

Late in the afternoon an arch of banana trees and
sugar-canes is built at the entrance of the homestead
of the *matuumo*. The arch is decorated with sacred
flowers of many shapes and colours; no unauthorised
person may pass through the arch. The arch is considered as a medium through which the ancestral spirits
can be harmonised with the *irua* and appeased, so
as not to bring any misfortune on the ceremony in
which the ceremonial council offers sacrifices to the god
Ngai.

When the decoration of the arch is finished the dance
is stopped. The *irua* candidates are lined up ready for
the sacrifice which marks the end of *matuumo*. This
consists of the boys running a race of about two miles
to a sacred tree called *mogumo* or *motamayo,* which
they have to climb and break top branches, while the
girls gather round singing, and at the same time gathering the leaves and the twigs dropped by the boys.

To start the race a ceremonial horn is blown. At this

point the girls, who are not allowed to participate in the race, start out walking to the tree, escorted by a group of senior warriors and women singing ritual and heroic songs. When the girls are near the tree, the ceremonial horn is again sounded, this time indicating that it is time for the boys to start the race. The boys then start running in a great excitement, as though they were going to a battle. The truth is, it is really considered a sort of fight between the spirit of childhood and that of adulthood.

The crowd which has already gathered round the tree await the arrival of the boys in order to judge the winner of the race. They shout and cheer merrily as the excited boys arrive, raising their wooden spears, ready to throw them over the sacred tree. The significance of this ceremonial racing is the fact that it determines the leader of that particular age-group. The one who reaches the tree first and throws his wooden spear over the tree is elected there and then as the leader and the spokesman of the age-group for life. It is believed that such a one is chosen by the will of the ancestral spirits in communication with Ngai, and is therefore highly respected.

The girl who arrives at the sacred tree first is also regarded in the same way. She becomes the favourite, and all try to win her affections with the hope of marrying her.

The *mogumo* ceremony occupies only a short time. As stated above, the boys climb the tree, break the top branches, while the girls collect leaves and twigs dropped on the ground. These are later tied into bunches and carried back to the homestead to keep the sacred fire burning the whole night and also to be used in other rituals, especially in making the initiates' beds. The songs rendered by the relatives and friends round the foot of the tree generally pertain to sexual knowledge. This is to give the initiates an opportunity of ac-

quainting themselves with all necessary rules and regulations governing social relationship between men and
women.

At the completion of *kuuna mogumo* (breaking of
the sacred tree), the boys and girls are lined up according to the order of their adoption. Here a ceremony of
taking the tribal oath (*muuma wa anake*) is conducted
by the elders of the ceremonial council. The initiates
promise by this oath that from this day onward they will
in every respect deport themselves like adults and take
all responsibilities in the welfare of the community, and
that they will not lag behind whenever called upon to
perform any service or duty in the protection and advancement of the tribe as a whole. Furthermore, they
are made to promise never to reveal the tribal secrets,
even to a member of the tribe who has not yet been
initiated.

At the conclusion of the oath ceremony a group of
senior warriors form at the head of the procession, followed by the initiates. Then the crowd flanks both sides
of the procession as a bodyguard. They march slowly
towards the homestead of the *matuumo,* carrying the
leaves and twigs gathered from the sacred tree, *mogumo.*
The initiates are warned never to look behind as they
move along, for to do so would bring misfortune to
them at the time of *irua,* and, furthermore, the childhood misdeeds which they have thrown over the sacred
tree, *mogumo,* would come back to them. The songs
they sing on the homeward march are directed towards
denouncing all things that are not fit and proper for
any adult member of the community to do. Moreover,
the phrases embodied in these songs are to encourage
the initiates to become worthy and honourable members
of the adult community into which they are to be
graduated.

When they arrive at the homestead, a ceremony of
parting is performed, *gotiihera ciana,* that is, spraying

the candidates with honey dews. The ceremonial council forms a circle in the courtyard; the leader of the ceremonial council holds a calabash containing honey juice mixed with milk, and a special Gikuyu medicine called *oomo,* which is supposed to impart bravery or endurance. He takes a mouthful of this liquid and, as the initiates pass through the arch, he sprays them with it. An elderly woman follows and does the same with another kind of liquid called *gethambio.* This is done in order to protect the initiates against fear, bad temptations and attacks of evil spirits. While this is going on, the initiates answer in unison: *"Togotiherwo rerea rea njoke tweriturageria,"* that is: "We have been sprayed with the stings of the bees which we have been longing for. We shall follow the wisdom and the energy of the bees."

At the end of the ceremony the boys and girls are free to go to their respective homes to rest until next morning. Care is taken to protect them from anything that might inflict wounds upon them, as the shedding of blood is regarded as an omen of ill-luck. The initiates are guarded the whole night by senior warriors against outside interference. In every home a ceremonial doctor (*mondo-mogo wa mambura*) is assigned by the traditional council (*njama ya kirera*) to protect the initiates against any possible attacks from witchcraft and also against any temptation or enticement to indulge in sexual intercourse.

HOW THE GIRL IS OPERATED ON

Early in the morning of the day of the physical operation the girl is called at cock-crow. She is fed with a special food (*kemere kia oomo*), eaten only on this occasion, after which she is undressed, leaving only one string of beads across her shoulder, known as *mogathe wa mwenji* (present for the barber). This is given to her sponsor as a symbol of lasting friendship and as a bond of mutual help in all matters. It also signifies that henceforth the girl is supposed to hide nothing from her sponsor nor deny her guardian anything demanded from her, even if it be the last she possesses.

After all necessary arrangements have been made, the girl is escorted to a place appointed for the meeting of all the candidates. From there are led to a special river where they bathe. The boys are assigned to a particular place while the girls bathe at a point below them, singing in unison: *"Togwe-thamba na munja wa ecanake,"* which means: "We have bathed with the cream of youth."

This is done before the sun rises, when the water is very cold. They go up to their waist in the river, dipping themselves to the breast, holding up the ceremonial leaves in their hands; then they begin shaking their wrists, dropping the leaves into the river as a sign of drowning their childhood behaviour and forgetting about it forever. The initiates spend about half an hour in the river, in order to numb their limbs and to prevent pain or loss of blood at the time of operation. The sponsors superintend to see that the initiates bathe in the correct manner, while the mothers, relatives and friends are present, painted with red and white ochre (*therega na moonyo*), singing ritual and encouraging songs. The warriors keep guard to prevent the spectators or strangers from coming too near to the bank.

When the bathing is completed, all the initiates are lined up following their order of adoption. The ceremonial horn is blown to warn the passers-by that the initiates are about to march and that the road must be cleared. No one is allowed to pass across the appointed path, as this is regarded as bad luck (*motino*). A small boy and a girl are chosen, in accordance with what the Gikuyu believe to be a lucky omen (*nyoni-ya-monyaka,* "lucky bird"). Their duty is to carry branches of creepers, called *mokengeria* and *mwambaigoro,* which is believed to have certain antiseptic and healing powers. The boy and the girl, with their branches of creepers, stand at the entrance of the homestead, in order to be the first to meet the initiates on their arrival.

As the candidates approach, a special ceremonial horn is sounded rhythmically. The initiates advance slowly towards the homestead with both hands raised upwards, elbows bent, pressed against their ribs, with the fists closed and thumbs inserted between the first and second fingers, *kuuna thano.* This signifies that they are ready to stand the operation firmly and fearlessly.

Unlike the previous day the songs take on an entirely different form. There is no more dancing and jumping. The singing is of a mournful character, in slow and gentle voices. This is a moment of great excitement and anxiety, especially for the mother and father whose first-born is to be initiated, for not only is their boy or girl passing from childhood to adulthood, but the father and mother are to be promoted to a higher status in the society. They all join in singing songs of anxiety, *"Twahirwoko tondo twagucithio motongoro?"* which means: "Where are we led to in this tedious procession?" In the meanwhile the elders select a place near the homestead where the operation is to be performed. This place is called *iteeri.*

Here a clean cowhide, tanned and polished, is spread on the ground; the ceremonial leaves called *mathakwa* are spread on the hide. The girls sit down on the hide, while their female relatives and friends form a sort of circle, several rows thick, around the girls, silently awaiting the great moment. No male is allowed to go near or even to peep through this cordon. Any man caught doing so would be severely punished.

Each of the girls sits down with her legs wide open on the hide. Her sponsor sits behind her with her legs interwoven with those of the girl, so as to keep the girl's legs in a steady open position. The girl reclines gently against her sponsor or *motiiri,* who holds her slightly on the shoulders to prevent any bodily movement, the girl meanwhile staring skywards. After this an elderly woman, attached to the ceremonial council, comes in with very cold water, which has been preserved through the night with a steel axe in it. This water is called *mae maithanwa* (axe water). The water is thrown on the girl's sexual organ to make it numb and to arrest profuse bleeding as well as to shock the girl's nerves at the time, for she is not supposed to show any fear or make any audible sign of emotion or even to blink. To do 'so would be considered cowardice (*kerogi*) and make her the butt of ridicule among her companions. For this reason she is expected to keep her eyes fixed upwards until the operation is completed.

When this preparation is finished, a woman specialist, known as *moruithia,* who has studied this form of surgery from childhood, dashes out of the crowd, dressed in a very peculiar way, with her face painted with white and black ochre. This disguise tends to make her look rather terrifying, with her rhythmic movement accompanied by the rattles tied to her legs. She takes out from her pocket (*moondo*) the operating Gikuyu razor (*rwenji*), and in quick movements, and with the dexterity of a Harley Street surgeon, proceeds to operate upon the girls. With a stroke she cuts off the tip of the clitoris (*rong'otho*). As no other part of the girl's sexual organ is interfered with, this completes the girl's operation. Immediately the old woman who originally threw the water on the girls comes along with milk mixed with some herbs called *mokengeria* and *ndoga-moki,* which she sprinkles on the fresh wound to reduce the pain and to check bleeding, and prevent festering or blood poisoning. In a moment each girl is covered with a new dress (cloak) by her sponsor. At this juncture the silence is broken and the crowd begins to sing joyously in these words: *"Ciunu ciito ire kooma ee-ho, nea marerire-ee-ho,"* which means: "Our children are brave, ee-ho (hurrah). Did anyone cry? No one cried—hurrah!"

After this the sponsors hold the girls by the arms and slowly walk to a special hut which has been prepared for the girls. Here the girls are put to sleep on beds prepared on the ground with sweet-smelling leaves called *murerecwa, mataathi* and *maturanguru.* The two first mentioned are used for keeping flies away or any other insect, and also to purify the air and counteract any bad smell which may be caused by the wounds, while the last-named is purely a ceremonial herb. The leaves are changed almost daily by the sponsors who are assigned to look after the needs of the initiates (*irui*). For the first few days no visitors are allowed to see the girls, and the sponsors take great care to see that no unauthorised person approaches the hut. It is feared that if someone with evil eyes (*gethemengo*) sees the girls it will result in illness.

HEALING OF THE WOUND

At the time of the surgical operation the girl hardly feels any pain for the simple reason that her limbs have been numbed, and the operation is over before she is conscious of it. It is only when she awakes after three or four hours of rest that she begins to realise that something has been done to her genital organ. The writer has learned this fact from several girls (relatives and close friends) who have gone through the initiation and who belong to the same age-group with the writer.

When the girl wakes up the nurse who is in attendance washes her with some kind of watery herb called *mahoithia* (drainers or dryers). After the washing the wound is attended with antiseptic and healing leaves called *kagutwi* or *matei* (chasers or banishers). The leaves are folded together, about two inches long, half an inch wide and a quarter of an inch thick; then they are dipped in oil, *maguta ma mbariki* (Gikuyu castor oil), to prevent their sticking on the wound and also to prevent the wound from shrinking. The bandage is then placed on the wound between *labia majora* to keep the two lips apart and prevent them from being drawn together while the wound heals.

The girl sits down with her legs closed together so as to keep the bandage in position. Frequently the girl is carefully examined by the nurse, and whenever she urinates, the nurse is there ready to clean the wound and put on a new bandage. The old bandage is hidden away to ensure that no man shall cross over it or put his foot on it, for such an act would bring misfortune to the man or to the girl.

For the first week after her initiation the girl is not allowed to go for a walk or even to touch with her bare hands anything in the way of food. The nurse puts the girl's food on a banana leaf, called *ngoto* or *icoya,* which serves as a plate. The leaf is lifted to the mouth without the girl actually touching its contents with her hands. The food eaten by the invalids is supplied by the parents, relatives and friends. The initiates, both boys and girls, eat collectively all food, irrespective of where it comes from, for all contributions are kept in one place in charge of the nurses and shared in common by the initiates, who refer to one another as sisters and brothers. The invalids are entertained by their sponsors, who sing them encouraging songs, in which they bring out vividly the experience they gained after they were circumcised, that in a few days their wounds will heal and soon they will be able to go out jumping and dancing. These songs have a great psychological effect on the minds of the initiates, for they strongly believe that what has happened to their predecessors will also happen to them. With this in view their thoughts rest not on the operation, but on the day when they will again appear in public as full-fledged members of the community.

On the sixth day the sponsors make a full report to the ceremonial council; if all initiates are well and can walk, a ceremony of *gotonyio* or *gociarwo* (which means to be entered or born) is arranged on the eighth day. If all are not well the ceremony is postponed until the twelfth day, for no ceremony would be arranged on the seventh, ninth or eleventh day after any event has taken place. Uneven days are considered by the Gikuyu to be unlucky for embarking on any important business.

On the day appointed the parents gather at the homestead of the *irua,* bringing with them presents in the way of beer (*njohi* or *ooke*), bananas and vegetables. The ceremony consists of killing a selected sheep, the skin of which is cut into ribbons (*ngwaro*) which are put on the wrists of the boys and girls. The elder who has adopted the children at the time of *irua* stands at one side of the entrance of his wife's hut, while his wife stands on the other side facing him. The rest of the elders with their wives stand in the courtyard in two rows, facing one another. The children are called to appear before the elders. As they pass through between the two rows, the elders utter blessings and at the same time touch them on the head with sacred leaves called *mataathi* and *maturanguru.* At the entrance of the hut the mother and father put the *ngwaro* on the wrists of the boys and girls as they enter the hut. After the initiates have entered the hut the mother and father follow them. The two go to bed while the children remain seated. The door (*riige*) is closed and silence is maintained, both by those inside the hut and those outside.

In a short moment the mother begins to groan as though she were in great pain; the father gets up and opens the door quickly. He calls out for *mociarithania* (a midwife), an elderly woman, who comes in carrying the gut of the sheep which has been killed. It is placed on a hide where the mother is sitting. Another woman comes in and cuts the gut. At this juncture the boy initiates emit a roar as of a lion, *gethamaro,* and the girls join in applauding with *Ngemi-a-ri-ri-ri-i-ri.* After this the gut is cut in a long ribbon, and while the initiates stand in one group close together the ribbon encircles them, being tied so as to cover the navel of those on the outside of the circle. They stand in this position for a few minutes; then the midwife comes along with a razor dipped in sheep's blood and cuts the ribbon in two. This symbolises the cutting of the umbilical cord at birth. This is done to express the rebirth of the initiate. Another woman then comes carrying ceremonial leaves (*mathakwa*) sprinkled with blood, in which she wraps the ribbon which has just been cut. This is similar to the afterbirth, and is put on the *mathakwa* and carried outside to be buried. When the woman appears outside, the parents, who are still seated, give a round of applause, saying: *"Ciana irogea ohoro, thaai—thathayai Ngai thaai"*—"Peace be with the children, peace—beseech ye, Ngai (God) peace."

After this the elder who has adopted the children comes out with his wife, followed by the children. They form a big circle round the fire on which the sheep's meat has been roasted. An elder of the ceremonial council takes the chest of the sheep which has been roasted (*gethori*) and stands up facing Kere-Nyaga, with both hands held aloft. The elder sings a hymn, offering prayers to Ngai. He tears pieces from the meat with his teeth, spits them on the ground, starting from north, east, south, west and ending north. He hands over the meat to the elder of the homestead and his wife, who follow the same example. The two then, holding the meat together, pass it round to each child, who tears the meat in the same manner. The elder and his wife address the children as: "My tribal son" or "my tribal daughter"; the children answer: "My tribal father" or "my tribal mother."

The words used are: Father to son: *"Wanyu-Baba"*; son to father: *"Wanyu-Baba."* Mother to son: *"Wakia-wa";* son to mother: *"Wakia-Maito."* Mother to daughter: *"Wakeri";* daughter to mother: *"Wakeri."* Father to daughter: *"Wakia-mwari";* daughter to father: *"Wakia-Baba."*

This signifies that the children have now been born again, not as the children of an individual, but of the whole tribe. The initiates address one another as *"Wanyu-Wakine,"* which means "My tribal brother or sister." When the ceremony is completed all burst into ritual song. They bid farewell to one another and then leave the homestead under the escort of their relatives. On the arrival at their respective homes a sheep or goat is killed by the parents to welcome them home again and anoint them as new members of the community (*koinokai na kohaka mwanake* or *moiretu maguta*). At this ceremony the parents are provided with brass ear-rings, as a sign of seniority. This is done when the first-born is initiated.

For a period of three or four months, according to the rules of various clans, the initiates do not participate in any work. They devote most of their time to going around the district singing the initiates' song called *waine*. In this several groups take part. The song takes place in the field and is performed only in daytime. The initiates stand in a big circle holding several sticks (*micee*) in their hands. A bunch of *micee* is held in the left hand while one stick is held in the right hand. In this manner the initiates beat the *micee* according to the rhythm of the song. The inner circle is kept clear for the favourites from various groups—namely those who were the first to reach the sacred tree. They enter the circle two by two, a boy and a girl. As they appear in the arena the sticks are beaten rhythmically by all, while at the same time they utter compliments. These meetings afford the initiated boys and girls opportunities of coming into contact with and knowing one another intimately.

At the end of the holiday period, a day is fixed for the initiates to return to the homestead where the *irua* took place. Here the final ceremony of cleansing or purification is performed. This is called *menjo* or *gothiga*. Up to this time the initiates have been regarded as children (*ciana*) or new-comers (*ciumeri*), and, as such, they cannot hold any responsibility in the community, for they are in their transitional period. Neither juvenile nor adult laws can be applied to them, and thus they form a sort of free community of "merry-go-round."

On the day appointed for the ceremony, people gather from far and near to join in the festival dance in which the "new-comers" are introduced into the community. The ceremony consists of shaving the heads (*kwenja*) of the boys and girls. The clothes and ornaments worn during the transitional period are discarded; their bodies are painted with red ochre mixed with oil, after which they are dressed in new clothes. The boys are provided with warriors' equipment; the girls are adorned with beads, armlets and other adornments. Then they are led to the dance, where they are introduced to the assembly as full-fledged members of the community. While the dance is going on, mothers and fathers partake of a feast of beer-drinking (*njohi*), which usually takes place during all solemn functions.

The wound normally requires a week to heal, but, of course, there are some cases which take longer, generally due to negligence on the part of the girl or the nurse in applying the healing leaves in the proper way. Such cases are few, but result in a septic condition, and the formation of much scar tissue on the area of the *labia majora,* which may make childbirth difficult. Cases of this nature sometimes find their way to hospitals and attract the attention of both the missionary and official doctors, who then and there, without careful investigation of the system of female circumcision, attack the custom of clitoridectomy in general, asserting that it is barbaric and a menace to the life of the mothers. To strengthen their attacks on this custom, these "wellwishers" have gone so far as to state that almost every first child dies as a result of this operation at the time of initiation, and that the operation is more severe today than it was formerly. Irresponsible statements of this kind are not to be taken too seriously, for it must not be forgotten that very few of the normal cases of childbirth ever come to the notice of European doctors. The theory that "every first child dies as a result of the operation" has no foundation at all. There are hundreds of first-born children among the Gikuyu who are still living, and the writer is one of them.

The missionaries who attack the *irua* of girls are more to be pitied than condemned, for most of their information is derived from Gikuyu converts who have been taught by these same Christians to regard the custom of female circumcision as something savage and barbaric, worthy only of heathens who live in perpetual sin under the influence of the Devil. Because of this prejudiced attitude, the missionaries are at a disadvantage in knowing the true state of affairs. Even the few scientifically minded ones are themselves so obsessed with prejudice against the custom that their objectivity is blurred in trying to unravel the mystery of the *irua.*

With such limited knowledge as they are able to acquire from their converts or from others, who invariably distort the reality of the *irua* in order to please them, these same missionaries pose as authorities on African customs. How often have we not heard such people saying: "We have lived in Africa for a number of years and we know the African mind well."? This, however, does not qualify them or entitle them to claim authority on sociological or anthropological questions. The African is in the best position properly to discuss and disclose the psychological background of tribal customs, such as *irua,* etc., and he should be given the opportunity to acquire the scientific training which will enable him to do so. This is a point which should be appreciated by well-meaning anthropologists who have had experience in the difficulties of field-work in various parts of the world.

7

SEX LIFE AMONG YOUNG PEOPLE

THE PHYSICAL OPERATION on the genital organs of both sexes is regarded as a starting-point for various activities in the tribal organisation. It signifies that the individual operated upon has been given, during the course of the pre-initiation ceremonial dances and songs, all the essential information on the laws and customs of the tribe.

Among the things taught during this period are the matters relating to rules and regulations governing sexual indulgence. In order not to suppress entirely the normal sex instinct, the boys and girls are told that in order to keep good health they must acquire the technique of practising a certain restricted form of intercourse, called *ombani na ngweko* (platonic love and fondling). This form of intimate contact between young people is considered right and proper and the very foundation stone upon which to build a race morally, physically and mentally sound. For it safeguards the youth from nervous and psychic maladjustments.

The social life of Gikuyu youths covers a wide field of activities. They organise numerous night and day dances for recreation and enjoyment. At these socials young men and women mix freely. It is generally at these social gatherings that friendship begins. A young man may attract the attention of a young girl, or girls, by his appearance, his smartness in dancing or dressing his hair, or by his charming and graceful carriage. Similarly a young girl may attract the attention of a young man, or men. The man who has several girl friends is known as *getharia* or *keombani* (heart-breaker). A Beau Brummel may attract as many as forty girls. A girl may win the admiration of several young men, but they would have to compete for her. The word *ngweko* (fondling) is used in its real Gikuyu sense and not as the loose term *ngweko ya gecomba*, employed by missionaries and detribalised Gikuyu, which means full sexual intercourse.

In a dance a *getharia* can easily be recognised, for he dances with several girls around him, but in order that he will not have a monopoly, a kind of Gikuyu "Paul Jones" dance, *gothombacana*, is repeated very often so as to allow the less attractive young men an opportunity of dancing with nice girls. Girls visit their boy-friends frequently, especially during the dancing seasons. The boys also visit the girls in their homes and take them to dances and escort them home afterwards.

Ngweko, or fondling, is looked upon as a sacred act and one which must be done in a systematic, well-organised manner. The Gikuyu do not kiss girls on the lips as Europeans do; therefore, *ngweko* takes the place of lip kissing, but, unlike the Europeans, who are fond of kissing in public places, the Gikuyu consider such public display of affection vulgar. All matters relating to sex are done according to a well-regulated code of convention.

HOW NGWEKO IS ORGANISED

The girls visit their boy-friends at a special hut, *thingira,*
used as a rendezvous by the young men and women.
They bring with them their favourite food and drinks
as a token of affection. These are shared among the
age-group in the *thingira,* who eat their food collectively.
No boy can eat or drink by himself what has been
brought to him by his sweetheart; such an act would be
severely punished. In this way the boys who have no
girl-friends are included in all entertainment, because
the good-looking young man of the age-group does not
act for himself; his popularity is considered the popularity of the group as a whole, and his girl-friends are
also regarded as friends of the members of the age-
group. So no matter how ugly a boy may be, his ugliness
is compensated for by the more attractive members of
his age-group. There is a saying in Gikuyu: *"Mogekumia
thaka, kumagiai ndoti ya riika ee hinya. Riika retire
gucii"*—(When ye praise the handsome man, first praise
an ugly and strong man of the age-group. There is no
small or despised inferior man in the age-group).

Girls may visit the *thingira* at any time, day or night.
After eating, while engaged in conversation with the
boys, one of the boys turns the talk dramatically to the
subject of *ngweko.* If there are more boys than girls,
the girls are asked to select (*kuoha nyeki*) whom they
want to have as their companion. The selection is done
in the most liberal way. The language used is either in
proverbs or indirectly as, for instance, the phrase
"Kuoha nyeki"—to tie the grass—which is equivalent
to "Choose your partner." In such a case it is not necessary for the girls to select their own intimate friends, as
this would be considered selfish and unsociable. Of
course, this does not mean that the girls do not sometimes have *ngweko* with those whom they are specially
fond of, but generally they follow the rules of exchanging

partners. The same freedom of social contact exists even among married people and for this reason youths are encouraged to cultivate the spirit of comradeship and group solidarity before marriage.

After the partners have been arranged, one of the boys gets up, saying: *"Ndathie kwenogora"* (I am going to stretch myself). His girl partner follows him to the bed. The boy removes all his clothing. The girl removes her upper garment, *nguo ya ngoro,* and retains her skirt, *mothuru,* and her soft leather apron, *mwengo,* which she pulls back between her legs and tucks in together with her leather skirt, *mothuru.* The two V-shaped tails of her *mothuru* are pulled forward between her legs from behind and fastened to the waist, thus keeping *mwengo* in position and forming an effective protection of her private parts. In this position the lovers lie together facing each other, with their legs interwoven to prevent any movement of their hips. They then begin to fondle each other, rubbing their breasts together, whilst at the same time they engage in love-making conversation until they gradually fall asleep. Sometimes the partners experience sexual relief, but this is not an essential feature of the *ngweko.*

The chief concern in this relationship is the enjoyment of the warmth of the breast, *orugare wa nyondo,* and not the full experience of sexual intercourse.

It has been said several times by Europeans, especially missionaries, that it is unbelievable that a young man and a young woman could sleep in one room, let alone in one bed, without copulating. Many Gikuyu have been punished and regarded as "sinners" by missionaries simply for having been found sleeping in the same room with a girl, for in their eyes such an act is sinful.

The Gikuyu who have not been brought up under the missionaries' influence find it difficult to understand this sort of European puritanism, for a Gikuyu man has been taught from childhood to develop the technique of self-control in the matter of sex, which enables him to sleep in the same bed with a girl without necessarily having sexual intercourse; while the missionaries' idea is, that since a white man would not be able to restrain himself under similar circumstances, so the African would not be able to, and so must be forbidden to sleep with a woman-friend in the Gikuyu fashion.

THE RULES GOVERNING NGWEKO

The tribal law prohibits a young man from pulling out a girl's garment (*kogucia mwengo wa moiretu*) while having *ngweko*. He must put his sexual organ between his thighs so as to prevent touching the girl with it. The custom also prevents a girl from touching the male sexual organ with her hands. Of course, it sometimes happens that in the case of a long-standing friendship a girl may allow a boy to put his sexual organ between her thighs and hold it tight in that position without penetrating; or by mutual arrangement a girl may allow her lover to have fuller intercourse, trusting that incomplete penetration would safeguard against the risk of conception. But such behaviour is absolutely against the tribal law and never takes place between casual lovers. If it does happen, which is rare, the law punishes it by imposing social stigma upon the offenders. Neither the man nor the girl can sleep with the back turned against the partner. The girl may not lie on top of the boy or across him (*gotagarara*); to do so, or to touch the man's penis, is "unclean" (*mogiro* or *thahu*), and both must be purified by a *mondo-mogo* (purifier).

The girl is expected to be a virgin in the sense of having an unperforated hymenal membrane when she marries. Any intercourse which may result in pregnancy before marriage is strictly forbidden. Any young man who may render a girl pregnant (*kohira moiretu ihu*) is severely punished by the *kiama* (tribal council). The fine for this is nine sheep or goats and three big, fat sheep (*ndorome*) as the *kiama* fees. Besides this, the man is made a social outcast or "sent to Coventry (*kohingwo*) by all the young men and girls of his own age-group. Punishment is also extended to the girl. She pays a fine by providing a feast to the men and the girls of her age-group. She is also liable to ridicule (*kohingwo* and *gocambio*).

If a man is detected by a girl trying to loosen her garments during the night of *ngweko* she generally reports the matter to all her friends in the district. The matter is taken to the age-group meeting (*getongano kia riika*). Such a man would be ostracised by his friends and would be debarred from having *ngweko* with other girls, as they would not trust or have confidence in him. These guiding principles, ingrained in the very souls of the young men and women, serve as checks to sexual promiscuity, for, unless a man knows a girl very well, he would not run the risk of suggesting copulation to her lest she should not only refuse, but tell other girls and have him *kohingwo* ("sent to Coventry").

SEXUAL TABOOS

Between members of the same family all forms of erotic connection are considered a great sin. Although there is great freedom among young people in their courtship and amorous experiments, brothers and sisters would not dare to indulge in these activities in one another's presence. In bachelor huts, where young people meet freely, brother and sister cannot be present together at the same time, except on purely social occasions when there is no sex-play. For example, if a brother knows that his sister has a lover in a particular bachelor-hut, he makes a point of not visiting the hut during the times when she is frequenting it. The same thing applies to the sister. This rule is also observed in dances and other ceremonies. No brother could take his sister, or any close female relative, as a partner on such occasions. During festival dances, where people from various districts meet and dance together, it is not always possible to recognize a relative who comes from far away, and a man may sometimes be seen dancing with his cousin by mistake. When this happens, people who know will start laughing and joking to warn the young man of his error. At once the two separate and find other partners, and sometimes a present is given to the girl by way of apology from the man.

All sexual familiarity between parents and their children is strictly forbidden. This applies to all children of the members of one's own age-grade, and breach of this rule is considered a great crime. This, of course, does not restrict parents from teaching their children about sex. During early childhood parents talk freely to their children, explaining all matters connected with sexual taboos.

In the Gikuyu community any form of sexual intercourse other than the natural form, between men and women acting in a normal way, is out of the question. It is considered taboo even to have sexual intercourse with a woman in any position except the regular one, face to face.

Before initiation it is considered right and proper for boys to practise masturbation as a preparation for their future sexual activities. Sometimes two or more boys compete in this, to see which can show himself more active than the rest. This practice takes place outside the homestead, under a tree or bush, where the boys are not visible to their elders. It is considered an indecency to be seen doing it, except by boys of the same age-grade. The practice is given up after the initiation ceremony, and anyone seen doing it after that would be looked upon as clinging to a babyish habit, and be laughed at, because owing to the free sex-play which is permitted among young people, there is now no need to indulge in it.

Masturbation among girls is considered wrong, and if a girl is seen by her mother even so much as touching that part of her body she is at once told that she is doing wrong. It may be said that this, among other reasons, is probably the motive of trimming the clitoris, to prevent girls from developing sexual feelings around that point.

Owing to these restrictions, the practice of homosexuality is unknown among the Gikuyu. The freedom of intercourse allowed between young people of opposite sex makes it unnecessary, and encourages them to acquire experience which will be useful in married life.

8

MARRIAGE SYSTEM

IN THE GIKUYU COMMUNITY marriage and its obligations occupy a position of great importance. One of the outstanding features in the Gikuyu system of marriage is the desire of every member of the tribe to build up his own family group, and by this means to extend and prolong his father's *mbari* (clan). This results in the strengthening of the tribe as a whole.

We may mention here that the Gikuyu system of courtship is based on mutual love and gratification of sexual instinct between two individuals. And, therefore, a family is constituted by a permanent union between one man and one woman or several women. Through the marriage ceremony a man acquires sole right to sexual intercourse with the woman or women whom he marries. On signing the matrimonial contract the marriage ceases to be merely a personal matter, for the contract binds not only the bride and bridegroom, but also their kinsfolk. It becomes a duty to produce children, and sexual intercourse between a man and his wife or wives is looked upon as an act of production and not merely as the gratification of a bodily desire. The Gikuyu tribal custom requires that a married couple should have at least four children, two male and two female. The first male is regarded as perpetuating the existence of the man's father, the second as perpetuating that of the woman's father. The first and second female children fulfil the same ritual duty to the souls of their grandmothers on both sides. The children are given names of the persons whose souls they represent.

The desire to have children is deep-rooted in the hearts of both man and woman, and on entering into matrimonial union they regard the procreation of children as their first and most sacred duty. A childless marriage in a Gikuyu community is practically a failure, for children bring joy not only to their parents, but to the *mbari* (clan) as a whole. In Gikuyu society the rearing of a family brings with it a rise in social status. The social position of a married man and woman who have children is of greater importance and dignity than that of a bachelor or spinster. After the birth of the first child the married pair become the object of higher regard on the part of their fellows than they were before.

Marriage is one of the most powerful means of maintaining the cohesion of Gikuyu society and of enforcing that conformity to the kinship system and to tribal organisation without which social life is impossible.

The most interesting feature in the Gikuyu marriage system is the way in which marriages are solemnised, for the validity of marriage and the social position of women in the community is determined by the fulfilment of communal duties regulated by the marriage custom. We will give here a full description of the Gikuyu marriage ceremonies as they are performed to-day.

There has been some confusion in the minds of many writers who have tried to explain the system of marriage and the position of women in the African community. Some, especially missionaries, have gone so far as to say that African women are regarded as mere chattels of the men. Well-informed anthropologists agree that this is erroneous and a misconception of the African's social custom. From the following account of the institution of marriage among the Gikuyu, the reader may judge further as to whether "purchase" is or is not a feature of the Gikuyu marriage system.

CHOICE OF MATES

In the Gikuyu community boys and girls are left free to choose their mates, without any interference on the part of the parents on either side. From earliest infancy there is close social intercourse between the sexes, which provides them with an opportunity of becoming acquainted with one another for a considerable time before courtship begins. Thus, hasty judgment in choosing one's husband or wife is almost out of the question.

FIRST STAGE

When a boy falls in love with a girl he cannot tell her directly that he loves her or display his devotion to her in public, as this would be regarded by the Gikuyu as impolite and uncultured. He therefore discusses the matter with one or two of his best friends in the age-group to which he belongs. They then all pay a visit to the girl's home. On their arrival at the girl's homestead they enter her mother's hut. The girl and her mother exchange greetings with them. The mother then offers them refreshment and immediately goes away. Now the boys and the girl are left alone. At this stage the conversation may start in the following manner: One of the boys addresses the girl: *"Mware wa Njuguna?"* (Daughter of Njuguna), "Wouldn't you like to ask us why we have come here to-night?"

The girl answers: "No, it is not necessary to ask you that. Gikuyu custom provides that anyone passing by can come and have a meal with us."

The boy: "That is right, *Mware wa Njuguna,* but we

are looking for a homestead where we could be adopted and be given food and shelter not only when we are passing by, but as children of the homestead."

At this remark the girl at once knows their object, and she asks them to state definitely which one of them is looking for the adoption. The boy then points out his friend who is in love with the girl. If she accepts him as her future husband she tells them to go away and come back some other time. Sometimes two or three visits of this kind are made. When she gives her final answer, she says to them: "I am willing that the son of So-and-so should be adopted into our homestead, but the ceremonial side of it is a matter for my parents. You had better talk to them about it yourselves."

If she does not accept him, she says: "Our house is not big enough to adopt anyone at present," and they go away.

SECOND STAGE

If accepted, her lover goes home and reports the matter to his parents. They then prepare honey or sugar-cane beer, which they take to the girl's parents. It is carried in two calabashes, one big and the other small. This beer is known as *njohi ya njoorio,* i.e. "The beer of asking the girl's hand." When the parents of the two parties meet, the first thing the girl's parents do is to provide the visitors with food before they go into the question of matrimony. After this they state the object of their visit, but most of the conversation regarding their future son- or daughter-in-law is carried on in proverbs. The girl is called and, after being introduced, she is asked if she has agreed to become engaged. As she cannot answer directly yes or no, a little ceremony is necessary. Therefore, she is asked gently to fetch a particular horn used for beer-drinking; then to fill it with beer and hand it to her father who, after sipping a little and spitting it out, sprinkles some on his chest. He then hands it over to his wife who does the same. The horn is filled a second time and is handed to the boy's parents who repeat the same procedure. In each case the girl takes a sip first as a sign of consent.

If the lover has been refused he reports to his parents who, if they would like their son to marry the girl, may visit the girl's parents. The same ceremony takes place, but if the girl disapproves of it she will not pour out the beer or take the first sip. The visiting parents then go away.

When the parents' initial ceremony is concluded and the girl is willing to be engaged, close friends are invited and the beer is shared among them. At the conclusion of this friendly gathering they all join in a prayer, *korathimithia*, uttering blessings for the future unity and progress of the two families.

THIRD STAGE

When the boy's parents return home they begin to collect sheep and goats, or cattle if they are rich, for the first instalment of the dowry, *roracio;* these would be taken by the lover to the girl's homestead and led to the hut of the girl's mother. This visit is followed by another in which some beer is brought, and the girl is consulted as in the first visit. This beer is called *njohi ya gothugumitheria mbori,* i.e. the beer for blessing the *roracio* sheep and goats. This instalment is followed by another in a few days, and so on until the number of animals amounts to about thirty or forty. Beer is not necessarily brought each time. Even if a man is rich it is considered ill-luck to bring all the *roracio* at once. When, according to the custom of the clan, the amount required for sealing the engagement has been sent, a day is fixed for the actual engagement ceremony, called *ngurario,* i.e. pouring out the blood of unity. In this all the relatives are called to the girl's homestead, where a sumptuous feast is provided, which includes the slaughtering of one fat sheep (*ngoima ya ngurario*) which has been sent from the boy's homestead specially for this purpose.

The significance of this ceremony is in the first place to announce publicly that the girl is engaged; secondly, to provide the relatives on both sides with an opportunity of meeting and getting to know one another; and, thirdly, to decide on how much the *roracio* should be. The amount varies from one clan to another and from district to district, although the amount required by the Gikuyu law is thirty sheep and goats. Sometimes, however, it runs to between thirty and eighty sheep and goats, apart from numerous presents exchanged on both sides. When a cow is included in the *roracio* it is valued at ten sheep and goats, while an ox is valued at five sheep and goats.

The main feature of this ceremony consists in the killing of a fat sheep kept for this purpose. The sheep must be of a certain colour—black, white or brown— in keeping with the symbolism adhered to for ritual purposes by the particular clan concerned. The blood is sprinkled along the gateway and towards Mount Kenya (Kere-Nyaga); the contents of the stomach are also sprinkled in the same way, and also on the sheep and goats or cattle which have been brought in for the *roracio*. This signifies that they are now purified and protected from any evils, and that the boy's parents have presented them to the girl's parents as a sign of good faith. From this time on the interests of the two clans are closely linked.

FOURTH STAGE

After all the arrangements are made in regard to *roracio,* the maturity of the girl is discussed. The boy's short while ago were engaged in a mock fight, join together and start dancing, singing and cheering hilariously. In the evening the bride is visited by her age-group of both sexes, who bring presents in way of food and ornaments. The bride entertains them with songs called *kerero*, i.e. "weeping," in which girls only take part while the boys listen. The *kerero* songs are mostly connected with the collective activities of the girl's age-group, and the part played by the girl. It is considered as the age-group mourning for the loss of the services and companionship of one of their number who, by marriage, has passed to another age-group.

The mourning songs are continued for eight days, during which time the bride is frequently visited by her friends and age-group of both sexes.

During this period the bride may not go out publicly or do any work. She has a special back path which she may use when she leaves the hut during the day to sit under a tree for fresh air. Her girl-friends keep her company, together with the children of the family. The *kerero* goes on the whole day and a part of the evening, except for a few intervals between the arrival and departure of the visitors. About ten o'clock in the evening the bride and bridegroom are left to themselves until the neighbourhood of nine o'clock next morning, when the visitors begin to pour in.

The question of physical virginity (as stated in the chapter dealing with the female circumcision) is very important, and parents expect their daughter to go to their husbands as physical virgins. This must be reported to the parents of both sides. The boy has to show by certain signs that the girl was a virgin; the girl, too, has to do the same to show that the boy is physically fit to be a husband. In case of impotency on either side, the matter is put before the families' council and the marriage is annulled at once.

On the eighth day, when the *kerero* ceases, a sheep is parents say to the girl's parents: "Is your daughter grown-up?"—meaning: "Has she menstruated yet?" At the end of the discussion a final day is fixed on which to sign the marriage contract. On the day in question all representatives of the two clans and friends are invited. They bring with them plenty of food and drink for the feast. The ceremony, which is called *gothenja ngoima*, consists of slaughtering six fat sheep, and in the case of a rich man, an ox and five sheep. In doing this the girl's consent must be obtained. She is asked to provide the knife for skinning the sheep and to take a leading part in slaughtering the first animal. The kidneys of the first sheep are roasted and served to the bride-to-be, who eats them, indicating in this way that the engagement still holds good and that the families can proceed with the formality of signing the marriage contract.

When this is done, the people assemble and take part in the feast. This is followed by a big dance and the singing of songs. The boy, with his age-group, comes in procession, carrying special presents for the girl's mother and for the members of her clan. Any property, such as an axe, basket or large leather strap, which the girl may have lost as a child, will be made up to her parents by these presents. At about sunset, after the casual visitors have gone, the women representatives of the clan are called into the yard where baskets are kept containing their presents. These presents are distributed by one of the elders, while the womenfolk cheer every recipient with great excitement. This is followed by a dance and song, called *getiro*, for women only, which marks the end of the *ngoima* ceremony.

If the boy's homestead is in the neighbourhood, a short visit is paid by a group of women, taking with them presents for the boy's relatives, but if the homestead is far away the visit is left to a later date. From this time onward the girl is regarded as having been blessed and given away to the boy's clan by her parents in agreement with the whole clan. She can now go and weed gardens with the boy's mother and other relatives in company with her girl-friends. The function of the *ngoima* ceremony is to furnish a public wedding celebration in which all marriage agreements are concluded and in which the girl is betrothed to her fiancé, not only by her parents, but by the representative body of the clan acting collectively. She can now be taken to the boy's home as his wife at any time, without any further ceremony being performed at her parents' homestead.

WEDDING DAY

When the boy has provided himself with a hut and made the necessary preparation for housekeeping, he approaches his parents, especially his mother, and asks them to arrange a special day suitable for bringing his wife home. The arrangement is made according to certain propitious days of the moon, in accordance with the clan's history and traditions. For instance, many clans may not hold any wedding between the old and new moon, since this period is regarded as a "dark period" (*mweri we nduma*). The period preferable for embarking on any important project is the interval between the new moon and the full moon.

A Gikuyu wedding is a thing which baffles many outsiders and terrifies many Europeans who may have an opportunity of witnessing the events. This wedding drama misleads foreign onlookers, who do not understand the Gikuyu custom, into thinking that the girls are forced to marry, and even that they are treated as chattels.

In response to the boy's request, the family meets in council; the day is fixed for the wedding and kept secret from the girl—thus adding a dramatic touch to the

proceedings. On the wedding day the boy's female relatives set out to watch the girl's movements. She might be in a garden, weeding, or in a forest collecting firewood, etc. When they have obtained the necessary information as to where she is working they search for her. On finding her they return with her, carrying her shoulder-high. This is a moment of real theatrical acting. The girl struggles and refuses to go with them, protesting loudly and even seeming to shed tears, while the women giggle joyously and cheer her with songs and dances. The cries and cheers can be heard for miles around, and the Gikuyu people will know that the son of So-and-so has taken the daughter of So-and-so in marriage—while foreigners may imagine that the girl has been forcibly seized. It is probable that any person who is not well acquainted with the Gikuyu customs may easily mistake the drama for reality.

In some cases, where the families are large, a counterfeit fight is staged between the women of both sides. This provides great entertainment for the women and is followed by a liberal feast at the bridegroom's homestead. The girl's cries, which are uttered theatrically in a singing manner, include such phrases as: "I do not want to get married! I will kill myself if you take me away from my parents! Oh! How foolish I was to leave my home alone and put myself into the hands of merciless people! Where are my relatives? Cannot they come and release me and prevent my being taken to a man whom I do not love?" and so on. This goes on until the girl reaches the boy's homestead, where she is led into her new hut, while children greet her, singing praises for their new bride. On her way home the bride is cheered by passers-by, who utter blessings for the bride and bridegroom and for their future homestead.

After the bride is comfortably settled in her new hut, the whole party of women from both clans, who a

killed, the fat of which is fried and the oil is used to anoint the bride in a ceremony of adoption into the new clan. After she has been admitted as a full member of the husband's family, she is free to mingle with its members and take an active part in the general work of the homestead. When the adoption ceremony is concluded, a day is fixed immediately for her to pay a visit to her own parents. Care is taken in appointing the day, for she must not travel or cook during her menstrual period. On this particular visit she carries a small calabash with beer in it for the use of her parents in blessing her. On her way she is led by a small girl, who goes before her holding one end of a stick, the other end of which is held by the bride, who follows as though she were blind. She is supposed to be unable to see, and may not speak with any stranger she may meet during her journey. She goes all the way with bent head, hiding her face shyly, especially when somebody passes by her. She returns back in the evening (if the parents are in the neighbourhood) with presents from her parents. Sometimes when parents are rich she is given two or three sheep or goats. Her father-in-law also gives her presents; these vary in some cases from five sheep and goats to ten or a cow and a piece of fertile land. These presents are regarded as an act of "warming" the bride's hut, and they end the marriage ceremonial.

THE GIKUYU SYSTEM OF POLYGAMY

The Gikuyu customary law of marriage provides that a man may have as many wives as he can support, and that the larger one's family the better it is for him and the tribe. The love of children is also an encouraging factor of desiring to have more than one wife. The custom also provides that all women must be under the protection of men; and that in order to avoid prostitution (no word exists for "prostitution" in the Gikuyu language) all women must be married in their 'teens, i.e. fifteen to twenty. Thus there is no term in the Gikuyu language for "unmarried" or "old maids."

Before the advent of the white man the institution of serfdom and wage-workers was unknown to the Gikuyu people. The tribal customary law recognised the freedom and independence of every member of the tribe. At the same time all were bound up together socially, politically, economically, and religiously by a system of collective activities and mutual help, extending from the family group to the tribe. The Weltanschauung of Gikuyu people is: *"Kanya gatuune ne mwamokanero"* ("Give and take").

For economic and political reasons every family was expected to be able to protect its own interests and at the same time help to protect the common interests of the tribe from outside attack. To do this effectively and to command the respect of the tribe, it was necessary for every family to have a number of male children who could be called up for military services in time of crises and alien aggression. It was also necessary to have a number of female children who could also render assistance by cultivating the land and looking after the general welfare of the tribe while the men were fighting to defend their homesteads. Furthermore, the society cannot do without them, for they are the salt of the earth; they have the most sacred duty of creating and rearing future generations. Female children are therefore looked upon as the connecting-link between one generation and another and one clan and another, through marriage, which binds the interests of clans close together and makes them share in common the responsibilities of family life. For this reason, say the Gikuyu: *"Keimba kea mothoni na mothoni igoaga hamwe"* (literally, "Corpses of relations-in-law fall together"), meaning "Together let us live and if need be together let us die."

There is a fundamental idea among the Gikuyu that the larger the family is the happier it will be. In Gikuyu the qualification for a status to hold a high office in the tribal organisation is based on family and not on property as is the case in European society. It is held that if a man can control and manage effectively the affairs of a large family, this is an excellent testimonial of his capacity to look after the interests of the tribe whom he will also treat with fatherly love and affection as though it were all part of his own family. Thus the saying: *"Weega uumaga na mocie"* ("A good leader begins in his own homestead").

After a man has had the first wife, *nyakiambi,* a year or so generally passes, and then his wife starts to question him about getting a second wife, especially if she is expecting a child or immediately after she has had one. "My husband, don't you think it is wise for you to get me a companion (*moiru*)? Look at our position now. I am sure you will realise how God has been good to us to give us a nice and healthy baby. For the first few days I must devote all my attention to nursing our baby. I am weak . . . I can't go to the river to bring water nor to the field to bring some food, nor to weed our gardens. You have no one to cook for you. When strangers come you have no one to entertain them. I have no doubt that you realise the seriousness of the matter. What do you think of the daughter of So-and-so? She is beautiful and industrious and people speak highly about her and her family. Do not fail me, my husband. Try and win her love. I have spoken to her and found that she is very interested in our homestead. In anything that I can do to help you I am at your service, my husband.

"Even if we have not enough sheep and goats for the

dowry our relatives and friends will help you so that you can get her into our family. You are young and healthy and this is the best time for us to have healthy children and so enlarge our family group, and thereby perpetuate our family name after you and I have gone. My husband please act quickly as you know the Gikuyu saying: *'Mae megotherera matietagerera mondo onyotie'* ('The flowing water of the river does not wait for a thirsty man')."

The husband, following his wife's advice, starts to act. He approaches his parents, and after consultation with them, arrangements are made to visit the girl and her parents. If accepted, he proceeds to pay the dowry and other gifts connected with marriages. When all arrangements are completed, he builds a hut next to that of the first wife and then brings the second wife home.

If the family in question is prosperous, after some time another companion is sought, and so the number of wives increase from one to fifty, and sometimes more. There is no limit. Of course, this does not mean that every Gikuyu man has many wives. There are a large number of Gikuyu men who have only one wife, simply because their economic position would not allow them to have as many wives as they and society would like. Taking the Gikuyu population as a whole, it can be said that there is an average of two wives per head, owing to the number of women who attain the marriageable age. Women generally marry between the ages of fifteen and twenty, while the majority of men start marrying from the age of twenty-five. Thus in every generation there are more women of marriageable age than men, which helps to balance the system of polygamy.

THE MANAGEMENT OF A POLYGAMOUS HOUSEHOLD

In a polygamous homestead the husband has his own hut (*thingira*), in which friends and casual visitors are entertained. Each wife has her own hut where she keeps her personal belongings. The cooking also is done in it. While collective ownership is a fundamental principle of the family group, the hut is considered as the private property of the wife and it is entirely under her control. Each wife is provided with several lots of land located in different places within the boundary of the family's land (allotment). The women usually cultivate banana, sugar-cane, sweet potatoes, maize, millet, yams, several varieties of beans and other crops on these holdings.

The working of the land is collective, men doing the clearing of the virgin soil, such as cutting big trees and hoeing, while women come behind them turning the soil to prepare it for planting. The planting is also divided between men and women; the men take the responsibility of planting banana, sugar-cane, yams and sometimes sweet potatoes. The women plant millet, maize, various kinds of beans and potatoes; the last are planted by both sexes.

Each wife is held responsible for what she produces from the land, and can distribute it as she pleases, provided that she has reserved enough food for the use of herself and family until the next harvest. She can sell any surplus stock in the market and buy what she likes, or keep the proceeds for family purposes. Nowadays the majority of women obtain money for their hut taxes in this way. Sometimes, when the harvest is good and there is an abundant supply of products, some are handed over to the husband who buys sheep, goats or a cow for the betterment of the homestead.

While the division of personal property exists between the wives, the husband is the head of the family and the one who contributes his labour power to all equally; he belongs to all and all belong to him. This brings the division to one collective ownership under his guidance.

Having described the division and distribution of labour, it is necessary to mention something about the distribution of love. No doubt some people wonder how one man is able to love many women. This is a very vital question, especially among those whose religious beliefs have taught them that to love more than one woman is a crime, and furthermore a sin against heavenly gods. On the contrary, the Gikuyu are taught from childhood that to be a man is to be able to love and keep a homestead with as many wives as possible. With this in view, Gikuyu male children are brought up to cultivate the idea and technique of extending their love to several women and to look upon them as companions and as members of one big family. The girls, too, are taught how to share a husband's love and to look upon him as the father of one big family. The idea of sharing everything is strongly emphasised in the upbringing of children, so when they grow up they find it natural to share love and affection with others, for it is said that: "To live with others is to share and to have mercy for one another," and: "It is witch-doctors who live and eat alone."

In order to avoid jealousy (*oiru*) among the wives, Gikuyu custom provides that each wife must be visited by her husband on certain days of the moon, particularly the three days following menstruation. Each wife has this special privilege. The wives, knowing that this is the best time to have children, see to it that the husband does not neglect his duty of distributing his love equally among them. Such conjugal relation is the only way in which a polygamous homestead could be kept in harmony. The three days immediately after menstruation are considered as the most likely for a woman to conceive. For this reason the husband does not generally cohabit with her again until after the next menstruation. If by then she has conceived, the husband allows a period of three months to elapse before having intercourse again, in order not to cause an abortion. After this time the husband may cohabit with her, but only in a special way. That is, he must not have full penetration; he may use only about two inches of his penis. The limit is indicated by a process in the *irua* operation, when the operator gathers back the foreskin into a tassel, called *ngwati* (the 'brush,') which is arranged to hang at the right distance below the head of the penis. Its use is to increase sexual excitement, but it can also serve as a catch to check penetration. Fuller penetration is believed to result in destroying the womb.

DUTY OF THE WIVES

The women are essentially the home makers, as without them there is no home in the Gikuyu sense of social life. Each wife has a special duty assigned to her in the general affairs of the homestead. She is responsible for looking after her hut and her household utensils, granary, and her garden. But the duty of looking after the husband, such as cleaning his hut, supplying him with firewood, water, food, etc., is shared by all, in turn. For example, every morning one of them cleans the husband's hut (*thingira*) and lights the fire, while others sweep the yard and do other work connected with the cleanliness of the homestead. At the same time sheep and goats are fed, cows (if they have any) are milked. Calves and kids are tended. The husband is served with food according to what they have prepared. Each wife provides food for her children. When the morning work in the homestead is over, each wife is supposed to prepare a plan of activities for the day. Some go to the forest to collect firewood, others go to cultivate their gardens in the company of their friends, relatives, or individually. During the day-time everyone is engaged in some sort of activity or another. No one stays at home except the small children who are unable to accompany the adult members of the family to the fields, or those grownups who are engaged in some homework, especially that of grinding or beating grain in mortars.

In the evening the wives return home carrying various things: firewood, water, bananas, sweet potatoes, yams and other foodstuffs. Immediately they set about preparing food for the evening meal. The wife whose turn it is provides the firewood and lights the fire in her husband's hut; no cooking is done in that hut except when meat is roasted. Otherwise each wife cooks in her own hut. When the food is ready, each wife takes the husband's share to his hut, where he entertains his friends and casual visitors. When the meal is over and utensils cleaned, the wives may go and spend the rest of the evening in the company of their husbands or remain in their huts. But whenever special visitors, particularly members of the husband's age-group, call, the wives are expected to join the company in the husband's hut. The reason for this is to show the solidarity of the age-group. If the visitors come from far away and they are to spend the night in the homestead, the arrangements for their accommodation are made according to the rules and customs governing the social affairs among the age-group.

On these occasions the wives exercise their freedom, which amounts to something like polyandry. Each wife is free to choose anyone among the age-group and give him accommodation for the night. This is looked upon as purely social intercourse, and no feeling of jealousy or evil is attached to it on the part of the husband or wife. And, having all been brought up and educated in the idea of sharing, especially at the time when they indulged in *ngweko* (love-making), their hearts are saturated with ideas of collective enjoyment, without which there could not be strong unity among the members of the age-group. When this choice is freely exercised, it is an offence for a wife to invite a man secretly to her hut, even a member of the age-group. To do so would be regarded as committing adultery. In order to guard oneself against matrimonial injuries this custom is strictly adhered to. Any man who is caught breaking this rule is punished heavily by the *kiama,* and sometimes the husband takes the law into his own hands, and before the *kiama* punishes the offender he is given a good beating by the outraged husband. There is a saying in Gikuyu which says that "Before a man embarks upon such an adventure of visiting another man's wife, it is advisable for him to arm himself, for there is no mercy for one who entices another man's wife or steals his cow." (*Ng'ombe na aka itire ndogo.*) The wife, too, is punished. She is taken back to her parents who, in order to establish good relationships, have to pay a fine of one or two he-goats to the husband. The fine is followed by a feast of beer-drinking between the two families. Sometimes if this offence is repeated the wife is divorced, and the husband is entitled to get back all his *roracio,* with the interests and custody of his offspring. The divorce is preferred especially in a case where there are no children, but in the case of partners who have children, conciliation is considered as the best procedure, for in this case the matter has already ceased to be between individuals and has moved into the clan through the children, for children are regarded as the pledges of love and unity. It is only when the matter becomes really bad that divorce action is taken. We will deal with the divorce question later under that heading.

Owing to the many taboos (*megiro*) attached to the cohabitation of a married woman, and the social stigma which follows an offence, the breaking of this law is very rare. This is due to the fact that both wife and husband have ample opportunity of meeting their friends in a more open and legalised way, approved by the moral code of the community.

It is worth our while to mention a few of these taboos, *megiro,* which control the relationship between a married woman and an outsider and even the husband. For example, it is *megiro* for a wife to have sexual intercourse outside the homestead; this is considered as bringing evil and bad luck to the homestead; no wife may have sexual intercourse while her husband is away on a journey, on war or other activities, for to do so is to cause misfortune to the husband. No sexual intercourse while food is being cooked, for this will make the food impure and the result to those who would eat such food would be uncleanliness. Children must be put to bed before this; sexual intercourse is not held to be right if the children are away in the fields, for it is considered as a ritual shutting out of the children (*kohingereria ciana*). Sexual intercourse is practised ritually and these and many other *megiro* are considered important, and in order to maintain the harmony and prosperity of a homestead and to guard themselves against matrimonial injuries in the community, these *megiro* (taboos) must be rigidly observed.

DIVORCE

Among the Gikuyu divorce is very rare, because of the fact that a wife is regarded as the foundation-rock on which the homestead is built. Without her the homestead is broken, therefore it is only when all efforts to keep the husband and wife together have failed that an action for divorce can be taken.

According to the Gikuyu customary law, a husband

may divorce his wife on the grounds of (1) barrenness; (2) refusal to render conjugal rights without reason; (3) practising witchcraft; (4) being an habitual thief; (5) wilful desertion; (6) continual gross misconduct. A wife has the same right to divorce her husband on these grounds, except (6) owing perhaps to the system of polygamy. Besides the above-mentioned grounds, she can divorce her husband for cruelty, ill-treatment, drunkenness and impotence.

In the case of barrenness or impotence, both husband and wife go through a practical test to prove who is to blame. The husband would allow his wife to have sexual intercourse with one or more of his age-grade. If this fails to bring fruitful result, a medicine man of repute (*mondo mogo*) is consulted with the hope of finding a successful solution. At the same time ceremonial blessing from parents on the both sides is considered essential to fertilise the womb. Sometimes the wife succeeds in having a child in this way, and is saved from the embarrassing situation of being given a nickname of *thaata* (barren). But when all efforts fail, the case is considered as one above the power of man, and is attributed to the will of Ngai, the Great God. If there is no other disagreement between the husband and wife, the two can live together and perhaps have an adopted son or daughter, provided that the man is not in a position to marry another wife.

In case of impotence the man is given the same trial as the woman. If he can afford it, it is necessary to marry another wife, and in case he succeeds in having children by her, then it is said that the failure to have children by his first wife is due to the fact that their blood does not agree. But if a man knows that he is naturally impotent, and wishes to keep his homestead in harmony, he allows his wife or wives to have sexual companions or friends to fulfil the duty of procreation.

The children of such a union are regarded exactly in the same way as if the real husband had been physically fit to function sexually.

When a wife is ill-treated by her husband she has the right to return to her father for protection. If the ill-treatment is proved, the father may keep his daughter in his homestead until such time as the husband pays a fine and promises not to ill-treat his wife again. If a wife has borne a child, the husband cannot claim his property which he had given as *roracio,* but in case of divorce the child is always left with the father. If the woman marries again her former husband has the right to claim at least half of his sheep and goats or cattle. But if she remains in her father's homestead and perhaps has friends, no property can be claimed. On the other hand, if she happens to have a child during that time, the former husband can claim that child as his, for as long as *roracio* is not returned, the union is not completely dissolved.

When there are no children in a matrimonial union the separation or divorce is much simpler than otherwise. In the Gikuyu system of marriage the presence of children is a sure sign of keeping the two coupled together in harmony.

9

THE GIKUYU SYSTEM OF GOVERNMENT

THE GIKUYU SYSTEM of government prior to the advent of the Europeans was based on true democratic principles. But according to the tribal legend, once upon a time there was a king in Gikuyuland, named Gikuyu, a grandchild of the elder daughter of the founder of the tribe. He ruled many moons and his method of governing was tyrannical. People were prevented from cultivating the land, as he commanded that all able-bodied men should join his army and be ready to move with their families at any time and to wherever he chose. Thus the population lived a sort of nomadic life and suffered many hardships from lack of food. At last they grew tired of wandering from place to place and finally decided to settle down. They approached the King and implored him to let them cultivate the land and establish permanent homes, but owing to his autocratic power he refused to hear or consider their plea. The people were very indignant with him for turning a deaf ear to their appeal, and in desperation they revolted against him. The generation which carried out the re-

volt was called *iregi*[1] (revolter), and the next generation which started cultivation was given the name
ndemi[2] (cutters) in remembrance of the period when
the Gikuyu people began to cut down the forests and
established themselves as agriculturalists.

After King Gikuyu was dethroned, the government
of the country was at once changed from a despotism
to a democracy which was in keeping with the wishes
of the majority of the people. This revolution is known
as *itwika,* derived from the word *twika,* which means
to break away from and signified the breaking away
from autocracy to democracy. This achievement was
celebrated all over the country; feasting, dancing and
singing went on at intervals for a period of six moons
which preceded the new era of government by the
people and for the people. In order to run the new
government successfully, it was necessary to have a
constitution, so during this time of festivities a revolutionary council, *njama ya itwika,* was formed to draft
the constitution. "In fact it seems probable that the
reason why kingly government was the rule in early
times is that it was rare to find persons of extremely
eminent virtue, especially as the States of those times
were small. And further, kingly power was then conferred upon individuals as reward of services rendered
to the State. But it is the function of good men to
render such services, and if they were rewarded with
kingly power, the number of good men must have been
very small. In process of time, however, there came
to be a number of persons equally virtuous, and then
they no longer submitted to kingly rule, but sought to
establish a sort of commune or constitutional government. From Oligarchies they passed in the first instance

---

[1] The word *iregi* is derived from *rega,* which means refuse, or
revolt. It is the name of the age-group that revolted.

[2] The word *ndemi* is derived from *tema,* cut. So the age-group
was called cutters.

to Tyrannies and from Tyrannies again to Democracy." [1]

Every village appointed a representative to the Council, which took the responsibility of drafting the new constitution. The first Council meeting was held at a place called Mokorwe wa Gathanga, situated in the centre of the Gikuyu country, where the tribe is believed to have originated. At the first meeting of the *njama ya itwika* it was decided that in order to maintain harmony in the government of the country, it was necessary to make a few rules which would act as the guiding principles in the new government; and the following rules, which afterwards became law, were made:

1. Freedom for the people to acquire and develop land under a system of family ownership.

2. Universal tribal membership, as the unification of the whole tribe, the qualification for it to be based on maturity, and not on property. For this reason it was then decided that every member of the community, after passing through the circumcision ceremony as a sign of adulthood, should take an active part in the government; and that males should go through this initiation between the ages of sixteen and eighteen, and females between the ages of ten and fourteen.

3. Socially and politically all circumcised men and women should be equally full members of the tribe, and thereby the status of a king or nobleman should be abolished.

4. The government should be in the hands of councils of elders (*kiama*) chosen from all members of the community, who had reached the age of eldership, having retired from warriorhood. And the position of elders should be determined by a system of age-grading.

5. All young men between the ages of eighteen and

[1] *The Politics of Aristotle*, Book 3, Chapter 15, p. 151.

forty should form a warrior class (*anake*), and be ready to defend the country, and that the country should respect them and have pride in them.

6. In times of need, the Government should ask the people to contribute in rotation sheep, goats, or cattle, for national sacrifices or other ceremonies performed for the welfare of the whole people.

7. In order to keep up the spirit of the *itwika*, and to prevent any tendency to return to the system of despotic government, the change of, and the election for, the government offices should be based on a rotation system of generations. The community was divided into two categories: (a) *mwangi*, (b) *maina* or *irungu*. Membership was to be determined by birth, namely, if one generation is *mwangi*, their sons shall be called *maina*, and their grandsons be called *mwangi*, and so on. It was further decided that one generation should hold the office of government for a period of thirty to forty years, at the end of which the ceremony of *itwika* should take place to declare that the old generation had completed its term of governing, and that the young generation was ready to take over the administration of the country.

8. All men and women must get married, and that no man should be allowed to hold a responsible position other than warrior, or become a member of the council of elders (*kiama*) unless he was married and had established his own homestead. And that women should be given the same social status as their husbands.

9. Criminal and civil laws were established and procedure clearly defined. Rules and regulations governing the behaviour between individuals and groups within the Government were laid down.

NDAMATHIA AND ITWIKA CEREMONY

Besides my general knowledge of the subject, I learnt the details of this ceremony from my late grandfather,

Kongo wa Magana, who took an important part in the last *itwika* ceremony, performed between 1890–1898, and also from my relative-in-law, Kaambo wa Gethuku, who sounded the ceremonial horn during the same celebration in Ng'enda, a section of the Kiambu district.

When the *njama ya itwika* had completed the work of drafting the constitution, a big ceremony was arranged to set a seal upon the laws and regulations of the new Government. Great magicians were summoned to use their oracular powers to find ways and means through which the *itwika* ceremony could be made sacred. At once the council of these wise men and prophets met at their secret oracle-place in a cave by the river. After consultation it was decided that in order to make the *itwika* inviolable, it was necessary to get the tail hair of a mysterious monster known as *ndamathia,* which lived in rivers. With confidence in their powers the magicians set to work enthusiastically to prepare medicine which would stupefy the monster and induce him to come out of the river without being dangerous to the people.

When the medicine was ready, the magicians went to the *njama ya itwika* and asked for a little innocent girl who had not yet reached the age of puberty. One of the ceremonial elders offered with grief his only daughter for the national ceremony. The magicians comforted him by saying that the child would be returned safely, for they were sure of their magical power against the great monster (*ndamathia*).

The child, her body covered with beads on which the medicine was smeared, was taken to the river, where the magicians had located the *ndamathia,* or the mysterious monster. There the child was given a small magical gourd to draw water from the river. At the same time one of the magicians began to blow a ceremonial horn rhythmically to induce the *ndamathia* to come out of the river. Soon they saw the mysterious monster splashing the water and coming towards the ford where the child was standing with her magical gourd. The ceremonial trumpeter was instructed to sound the horn vigorously and to walk slowly on the hill. The child was asked to draw the water and to follow steadily behind sprinkling the water on the ground as she walked along. The rest of the magicians, with a few warriors, hid themselves in the bush along the path, ready to pluck the tail hair of the *ndamathia*.

In a short time the *ndamathia* protruded its long neck, the sounds of the ceremonial horn enticed the big creature and it started to follow the man and the child. At the same time it began to lick the ground on which the medicine-water had been sprinkled by the child. It took some hours before the tail of the *ndamathia* came out of the water, for the creature was very long (its length is compared with that of the rainbow, and the people believed that it was the *ndamathia* which caused the rainbow to appear on the sky). The magicians and the warriors waited patiently to fulfil their sacred mission. At last the tail came out of the water, they sprung at it and each of them plucked as many tail hairs as he could lay his hands on. Then immediately they returned to the bush and ran as fast as they could to avoid being followed by the angry monster. Because when the hair was plucked, the pain drove the great monster mad, and made it return back to the river at a great speed to see who it was that dared to interfere with its sacred tail hair. But finding no one at the ford, and owing to the stupefaction caused by the work of the magicians, it did not bother to return to the villages, but went straight back into the water.

The sacred tail hair of the *ndamathia* was taken to the ceremonial place where the *njama ya itwika* were waiting anxiously for the return of the magicians with their sacred objects. The elders received the magicians with great rejoicing for having fulfilled their mission of national importance. The ceremonial elder who had offered his only daughter was rewarded and his child returned with a title of national heroine. She was also given an important place in the ceremony, and the same thing was done for the man who sounded the ceremonial horn and for the magicians.

Having received the sacred tail hair, the *njama ya itwika* killed a bull, a male goat, and a fat ewe; they also fermented beer of pure honey (*moruru wa ooke*), for the *itwika* ceremonial feast. The skins of the goat and the ewe were cut into ribbons (*ngwaro*) and dipped in the contents of the stomach mixed with the blood of the animals. The skin-ribbons were slit and the tail-hairs of the *ndamathia* tied on to them and then every elder of the council put one of these on the wrist like a bracelet, and another on the ankle; all on the right hand side. This acted as a seal of their deliberation and at the same time bound them together in their national duty. Under the leadership of the president of the *njama ya itwika*, the ceremonial elders started to sing the constitutional songs. All the words of the drafted constitution were put into song-phrases, for as there was no system of writing, the songs served the same purpose as the newspapers do in the Western world.

After the *njama ya itwika* had concluded its preliminary ritual and feasting, which was limited to the members of the council of the *itwika,* a public proclamation of the new government under democratic leadership was arranged to take place at Mokorwe wa Gathanga, the headquarters of the *itwika* revolution, and similar arrangements were made in all districts.

It was considered that the effective way of proclaiming the new government was to call for war dances to be held in every district, in order to give the population an opportunity of hearing the announcement of the new constitution. This suggestion was carried unanimously, for it was the only way through which the words, phrases and rhythmic movements of the new songs and dances, in which the laws and regulations of the new democratic government were embodied, could be introduced effectively into the life of the community. On the day appointed, war horns were sounded in all districts, calling the population to come out and hear the decision of the *njama ya itwika*. From early in the morning people, old and young, gathered at the appointed place in their particular district and started to dance joyously.

At about midday, when the sun was overhead, the ceremonial leader entered the circle which the dancers and spectators had made. The master of the ceremony called upon the people to sit down and listen to the ceremonial leader. At this juncture silence was maintained, and the ceremonial leader began to recite the constitution in the form of a song; the assembly answered in chorus after each phrase. This went on until the whole version was gone through. Then the people rose and started to sing and dance hilariously, for they were overcome with joy. The warriors jumped, brandishing their spears and shields enthusiastically, as a sign of welcoming the new system of government which gave freedom and equality to all the members of the community on the one condition only that all should have to go through the same form of circumcision ceremony, irrespective of the condition of their birth.

After the proclamation ceremony and feasts were finished, and the new government started to function, the revolutionary council, *njama ya itwika,* was dissolved, and delegates returned to their respective villages, leaving the officiating elder to take care of the ceremonial objects which were necessary for the perpetuation of the *itwika*.

The *ndemi* generation was very much devoted to the communal cause for which it had dethroned King

Gikuyu. The great desire was to give the country a new order where every section of the community would have some practical part to play in the people's government. The first step in this direction was the organisation of the people into several groups linked up with the function of the government.

The starting-point was the family unit. From the governmental point of view members of one family group were considered as forming a family council (*ndundu ya mocie*), with the father as the president. The father represented the family group in the government. The next group was the village council (*kiama kia itora*), composed of the heads of several families in the village. The senior elder acted as the president of the council and this group represented the villagers in the government. Another wider group was formed and named the district council (*kiama kia rogongo*), in which all the elders of the district participated; this council was presided over by a committee (*kiama kia ndundu*), composed of the senior elders of the villages. Among these elders the one most advanced in age and wisdom was elected as a judge and president (*mothamaki* or *mociiri*) of the *ndundu*. From the district council a national council was formed, composed of several *ndundu,* representing the whole population. Among the judges, a president was elected at the meetings of the national council. All these councils were composed of men from the age of about thirty onwards.[1] But there was a very important council of young men known as *njama ya ita* (council of war). Its members were between the ages of twenty and forty. This council, apart from its military activities, represented the interests of the young people in the government. In the whole governmental organisation there was no inheritable position, everything depending on personal merit. Elevation to high office was based entirely upon the behaviour

[1] See *Eldership*, p. 193.

of an individual to his group and to the community at large. The group had the right to recall and dismiss or suspend any of its representatives whose behaviour was contrary to the well-established rules of conduct. In fact, it was the voice of the people or public opinion that ruled the country. Individualism and self-seeking were ruled out, for every representative spoke in the name of his particular group or in the name of the tribe. The personal pronoun "I" was used very rarely in public assemblies. The spirit of collectivism was so much ingrained in the mind of the people that even eating, drinking, working and sleeping were done collectively. This may sound like Utopia to those who are not acquainted with the Gikuyu tribal organisation, but the fact remains that the system is still functioning in those parts of the country where the people have not yet been saturated with the Western individualistic ways of life.

From the *ndemi* generation onwards the principles of democratic government, as laid down by the first *itwika,* continued to function favourably until it was smashed by the British Government, who introduced a system of government very similar to the autocratic government which the Gikuyu people had discarded many centuries ago. The present system of rule by the Government Officials supported by appointed chiefs, and even what is called "indirect rule," are incompatible with the democratic spirit of the Gikuyu people. It has been said that the Gikuyu do not respect their chiefs, namely, the "appointed ones." This is perfectly true, and the reason is not far to seek. The Gikuyu people do not regard those who have been appointed over their heads as the true representatives of the interests of the community. No one knows this better than the chiefs themselves, because many of them are only able to continue in their position through the fact that might is over right. The Gikuyu knows perfectly well that these chiefs are appointed to represent a particular interest, namely, the interest of the British Government, and as such they cannot expect popularity from the people whom they help to oppress and exploit. In the eyes of the Gikuyu people, the submission to a despotic rule of any particular man or a group, white or black, is the greatest humiliation to mankind.

The spirit of *itwika,* namely, the changing of government in rotation through a peaceful and constitutional revolution, is still ingrained in the minds of the Gikuyu people. About 1925–28 was the time when the *itwika* ceremony was to take place corresponding to the last great *itwika* ceremony which was celebrated about 1890–98.

The *irungu* or *maina* generation, whose turn it was to take over the government from the *mwangi* generation, organised in 1925 and began singing and dancing *itwika* ceremonial songs and dances to mark the termination of rule by the *mwangi* generation. But after a short time the *itwika* ceremonial dances and songs were declared illegal, or in other words, "seditious," by the British Government. In this way the present generation, *irungu,* has been denied the birthright of perpetuating the national pride and enjoyment in the peaceful institution which afforded their forebears the most harmonious participation in the social, political, economic, and religious organisations of the tribe.

In the Kenya White Paper of July, 1923 (cmd. 1922), it was declared that: "It is the mission of Great Britain to work continuously for the training and education of the Africans towards a higher intellectual, moral, and economic level than that which they had reached when the Crown assumed the responsibility for the administration of this territory." It is beyond our comprehension to see how a people can reach a so-called "higher level" while they are denied the most elementary human rights of self-expression, freedom of speech, the right to form social organisations to improve their condition, and above all, the right to move freely in their own country. These are the rights which the Gikuyu people had enjoyed from time immemorial until the arrival of the "mission of Great Britain." Instead of advancing "towards a higher intellectual, moral, and economic level," the African has been reduced to a state of serfdom; his initiative in social, economic and political structure has been denied, his spirit of manhood has been killed and he has been subjected to the most inferior position in human society. If he dares to express his opinion on any point, other than what is dictated to him, he is shouted at and black-listed as an "agitator." The tribal democratic institutions which were the boast of the country, and the proof of tribal good sense, have been suppressed. Oppressive laws and ordinances, which alone engross the monopoly of thought, of will, and of judgment, have been imposed on the African people.

In our opinion, the African can only advance to a "higher level" if he is free to express himself, to organise economically, politically, and socially, and to take part in the government of his own country. In this way he will be able to develop his creative mind, initiative, and personality, which hitherto have been hindered by the multiplicity of incomprehensible laws and ordinances.

To return to our analysis of the Gikuyu system of government. We have seen that the circumcision ceremony was the only qualification which gave a man the recognition of manhood and the full right of citizenship. It is therefore necessary to take the circumcision ceremony as our starting-point. Before a boy goes through this ceremony he is considered as a mere child, and as such has no responsibility in the tribal organisation; his parents are responsible for all his actions. If he commits any crime he cannot be prosecuted personally, it is his parents' duty to answer for him. But this liberty ceases immediately he is circumcised, because he is now "full grown," and has assumed the title of *mundo-morome* (a he-man), and as such he must share the responsibility with other "he-men" (*arome*). As soon as his circumcision wound heals he joins in the national council of junior warriors, *njama ya anake a mumo*. At this stage his father provides him with necessary weapons, namely, spear, shield,[1] and sword; then a sheep or a male goat is given to the senior warriors of the district, who receive it in the name of the whole national council of senior warriors. The animal is killed for a ceremony of introducing the young warrior into the general activities and the etiquette of the warrior class.

In former days the ceremony was more elaborate. The weapons of the young warrior were sprinkled with the blood of the ceremonial animal, then the leading warrior shouted a war cry (*rohio*), his companions stood up brandishing their spears and lifting their shields upwards; and in a ritual tone they chanted in unison the following warrior's resolution (*mwehetwa wa anake*): "We brandish our spears, which is the symbol of our courageous and fighting spirit, never to retreat or abandon our hope, or run away from our comrades. If ever we shall make a decision, nothing will change us; and even if the heaven should hold over us a threat to fall and crush us, we shall take our spears and prop it. And if there seems to be a unity between the heaven and the earth to destroy us, we shall sink the bottom part of our spear on the earth, preventing them from uniting; thus keeping the two entities, the earth and the sky, though together, apart. Our faith and our decision never changing shall act as balance." After this

[1] The shields are slowly disappearing. There is no chance of a new supply being made, owing to the fact that they are made of buffalo-hide, and buffalo-hunting is now a monopoly of European big-game hunters.

ceremony all joined in the meat feasting, and a mock fight was arranged to test the skill of the young warrior. This initiation gave the young warrior the privilege of participating in all warriors' dances and songs; but he was not yet allowed to perform or to appear inside the circle, this being reserved for the senior warriors.

The second stage in warriorhood was celebrated about eighty-two moons or twelve rain seasons following the circumcision ceremony. At this juncture the junior warrior was promoted to the council of senior warriors, *njama ya ita* (war council). The initiation fee to this rank was two sheep or goats. There was no ritual performed at this stage, but the animals were slaughtered and eaten in a general meat feast. Immediately after this, the candidate was taken to a big dance, and introduced to the higher rank inside the circle of the dance. There he was proclaimed as having reached the status of senior warriors.

From the governmental point of view the whole of the warrior class, composed of several age-groups, was divided into two sections, from which the two councils of senior and junior warriors were formed. Each group had its village, district and national leaders (*athamaki a riika*), who acted as spokesmen in all matters concerning the welfare of the groups and the tribe. These leaders were chosen by their particular groups at general or public assembly. They were men who had proved by their own actions, their capability of leadership; had shown bravery in wars, impartiality in justice, self-sacrifice, and above all, discipline in the group. A man with these qualities was able to attain a high position and esteem in the community, especially when he had retired from the activities of a warrior. Judges and responsible elders, as we shall see later, were chosen from such men.

The principles of the warriors' organisation, such as age-grading and the etiquette of general behaviour, are still adhered to inside the Gikuyu country, but owing to the liquidation of military exercises, which were the main function of the warrior class as the defence force of the country, the warriors' organisation has lost the significance which it used to have in former days.

ELDERSHIP

The third stage in manhood is marriage. When a man has married and has established his own homestead, he is required to join the council of elders (*kiama*); he pays one male goat or sheep and then he is initiated into a first grade of eldership (*kiama kia kamatimo*). The word *matimu,* which means spears, signifies the carriers of spears, which denotes the warriors who have joined the *kiama* while still functioning as warriors, and who are carrying spears because they have not yet been given the staff of office. They are not yet elders; they are learners of the *kiama's* procedures. The *kamatimo* act as messengers to the *kiama,* and help to skin animals, to light fires, to bring firewood, to roast meat for the senior elders, and to carry ceremonial articles to and from the *kiama* assemblies. They must not eat kidneys, spleen, or loin, for these are reserved for the senior elders. Any *kamatimo* who dares eat one of these portions from a ceremonial animal is fined a ram, which is killed to purify the offender and at the same time to initiate him into the secret of the higher grade of eldership.

Next to *kamatimo* comes *kiama kia mataathi,* i.e. the council of peace. This stage is reached when a man has a son or daughter old enough to be circumcised. Before the child enters in the circumcision ceremony, the father is called upon by the *kiama kia mataathi* of his village, and asked to prepare himself for a ceremony called *gotonyio kerera,* that is, to be initiated into the core of the tribal tradition and custom. The initiate then consults a diviner or a seer to predict a suitable date for the ritual; finally, a day is fixed according to the prediction. The senior elders of the district are invited to attend the ceremony at the candidate's homestead.

On the day appointed, the elders of ceremonial rank assemble and sit down in a circle outside the hut, or huts; here they are welcomed by the candidate and his wife, or wives. After exchanging greetings, food and drink are brought to them, for they must first satisfy their hunger before entering into ritual acts. Two of the elders are appointed to act as officiating priests.

The chosen elders, carrying their staff of office, *mothegi,* and sacred leaves, *mataathi,* enter the hut, where they are welcomed by the candidate and his senior wife, whose child is about to be circumcised. A small calabash filled with honey or sugar-cane beer is handed to them by the man, while his wife gives them a small drinking-horn. Four of them sit round the fireplace in the centre of the hut. One of the elders fills the horn with the beer, he takes a sip and spits over his right and left shoulders; then he pours out the beer over the three stones which support a cooking-pot over the fire; at the same time the officiating elder calls upon the ancestral spirits to commune with them. The horn is filled a second time and, after the leading elders have taken a sip each, the horn is handed over to the man who sips and then passes it to his wife. In a low and ritual tone, all four join in chanting a prayer, saying: "May our child grow well and live to pass this ceremony with joy and prosperity; may our child live to be father (or mother) of many healthy children and thereby perpetuate our family group."

When the preliminary ceremony is completed, the candidate and his wife are sworn to keep the secret of the *kiama,* and never to reveal it to anyone who is not ritually initiated into the age-grade of the *kiama kia mataathi*. It is only when they have taken this solemn oath that the secret matters and the procedure, including the etiquettes of the Peace Council, are revealed to them. This done, the candidate is led outside to be introduced to the assembled elders. He walks between the two officiating elders, his wife following behind them carrying a big calabash of beer. The small procession enters into the circle. Here the candidate is greeted ceremonially. To the elders he says: *"Wanyuwakine"* ("my equals"); the elders answer: *"Wanyuwakine"* ("our equal"). This form of greeting is only exchanged by those who are politically, religiously, and socially equals. The salutation signifies that the candidate has been accepted as a full member of the peace council. He now sits in the circle in that capacity.

Immediately one of the elders takes the beer and fills a drinking horn with it. He stands facing Kere-Nyaga (Mount Kenya), and calls upon *Ngai* (God) to give them peace, wisdom and prosperity, and to bless the candidate and his homestead. The rest of the elders lift up their staffs (*methegi*), and answer in chorus, saying: "Peace, peace, beseech *Ngai,* peace be with us, peace." After this the candidate is invested with his staff of office (*mothegi*) and a bunch of sacred leaves (*mataathi*). This signifies that he is now a peaceful man, that he is no longer a carrier of spear and shield, or a pursuer of the vanity of war and plunder. That he has now attained a stage where he has to take the responsibility of carrying the symbols of peace and to assume the duty of peace-maker in the community.

At the end of the ceremony of installing the candidate in the status of the *kiama kia mataathi,* a male goat is slaughtered, its blood is poured at the entrance of the homestead, the contents of the stomach are sprinkled at the entrance of the hut and in the compound to keep the evil spirits away. Finally, the sexual organ of the goat is dipped in the contents of the stomach, then it is slit and worn as a bracelet on the right wrist of the candidate. This is a pledge of calmness, for the sexual organ is considered as the driving factor in fierceness, and having been symbolically cut away and placed on the wrist, the man is thereby expected to be guided by reason and wisdom, and not by emotion. The ceremony is concluded with a big feast of beer and meat and other edibles—at this feast elders and their wives join in singing ceremonial songs.

RELIGIOUS SACRIFICIAL COUNCIL (KIAMA KIA MATURANGURU)

The last and most honoured status in the man's life history is the *kiama kia maturanguru* (religious and sacrificial council). This stage is reached when a man has had practically all his children circumcised, and his wife (or wives) has passed the child-bearing age. At this stage the man has passed through all age-grades, has been initiated to them all. Apart from his staff of office, he wears brass rings (*icohe*) in his ears, but he is not yet invested with the power to lead a sacrificial ceremony at the sacred tree (*mogumo mote wa Igongona*). To acquire this privilege he has to pay a ewe. This is taken to the sacred tree where the animal is slaughtered by the elders of the sacrificial council. This ceremony is performed in secrecy and only by the selected few who are fortunate enough to live to that esteemed age. No one outside the members of the sacrificial council is allowed anywhere near the sacred tree when this ceremony is in progress. Half of the animal is eaten by the elders and the other half is burnt in the sacrificial fire. The main feature of this ceremony is dedication of the man's life to *Ngai* (God) and to the welfare of the community. What actually happens at the sacred tree with regard to preparation of the ceremony is very hard to say, for the writer has not had the opportunity of attending the ceremony, having not yet reached the required age. But he had the privilege of watching the elders going to and from the sacred tree while herding sheep and goats near the ceremonial grove called *mogumo wa Njathi.*

On coming out from the sacred tree the elders carry bunches of sacred leaves called *maturanguru.* The elders of this grade assume a role of "holy men." They are the high priests. All religious and ethical ceremonies are in their hands.

In the previous pages we have described how the Gikuyu tribal government was originally organised and how the political, ethical or religious, and social groups and ranks within it were formed. We have also seen that there were five principal councils, namely: (1) the council of junior warriors; (2) the council of senior warriors; (3) the council of junior elders (*kamatimo*); (4) the council of peace (*kiama kia mataathi*); and (5) the religious or sacrificial council (*kiama kia maturanguru*). Having these in mind, we will now proceed to analyse the functions of these councils.

MILITARY ORGANIZATION

The whole of the warrior class was divided into several regimental groups, according to the system of age-grades (*riika*). Every *riika* had its leader (*mothamaki wa riika*) who was responsible for the activities of his group. His main duty was to keep harmony and discipline in the group, and to settle minor disputes and quarrels between the members of his regiment; he also acted as spokesman of the group in general matters. He was the chief composer and organiser of songs and dances of his *riika,* and sometimes arranged competitions between his group and other groups. The warrior dances and songs served two main purposes, namely, enjoyment and drill for physical development. In jumping and running, warriors developed the power of endurance and the art of battle. In time of war these regiments were united under the leadership of *njama ya ita* (council of war) composed of several *athamaki* (leaders) of the various age-grades. At the head of this council was a *mondo mogo wa ita* (war magician or priest), whose duty was to advise the council as to the best time of waging war. He blessed the warriors and gave them war medicine to protect them against the enemy.

Every regiment or *riika* had its regimental songs and war-cry (*ndoogo ya ita*). There were distinctive designs on shields and on the head-gear to distinguish each regiment. There was no particular uniform, for warriors went to war practically naked except for a small apron (*corori*), which was worn at the back, and the head-gear (*thombe ya ita*). On the outbreak of a war, a war-horn was sounded as a signal of readiness. The warriors immediately took arms and started shouting their particular war-cry. This brought together all regimental units in the district and they formed a procession towards the enemy. Each regiment followed different directions, all leading to the battle-field. The senior warriors formed front lines (*ngerewani*), while the junior warriors formed the rear-lines (*gitungati*). The council of war went in between the two forces giving the advice and directions to both sections. The motive of fighting was merely to capture the livestock of the enemy and to kill those who offered resistance. In other words, it was a form of stealing by force of arms. Women were rarely killed, for it was a disgrace for a warrior to kill a woman unless it was unavoidable.

If the warriors succeeded in a war and captured the enemy's livestock, they returned home as quickly as possible to avoid the recapture of their loot by the enemy. Before reaching home, after the crossing of the enemy's boundary, they halted and counted the cattle they had captured. The council of war then divided the

loot among the regiments. In the first place, brave warriors (*njamba*) were rewarded according to the task
performed in fighting the enemy. Then a small number
of cattle were set aside for the *mothamaki wa borori*
(the high councillor or the chief of the country), the
medicine man was given his share, and the other members of the council of war. If there was any surplus
left, and not enough to go round equally, it was settled
by drawing lots.

When this was done the warriors returned to their
respective districts singing songs of praise of their own
bravery (*koina kaare*). In these every warrior described
his action in the war and the number of men he had
killed in the battle, and also the position his victims
held in their regiments. A warrior who had not killed
an enemy could not participate in the singing of *kaare*
songs. These brave warriors, as they were called, went
round in their districts singing ceremonially the *kaare*
songs. They paid visits to their relatives and friends,
who gave them presents in the form of sheep or goats
and ornaments as the recognition of their bravery in
the battle. The animals thus given were used for peri-
odical meat feasts (*keruugu*), in which the warriors
spent several days eating meat and drinking soup mixed
with various herbs and roots which served as a stimulating tonic to keep the warriors in good and healthy condition. After *kaare* songs were ended, the warriors' long
hair was shaved off, and a purification ceremony performed to remove any curse that might have been
uttered by the dying enemies who were killed in the
battle. During this ritual cleansing the warriors were
dressed in long garments (*nguo ya maribe*) usually
worn by the women. They stayed in seclusion for some
days, at the end of which the long garments were discarded and the warriors resumed their activities in
normal life.

In time of peace the warriors were occupied in gen-

eral work of the tribe. They took active part in cultivation, in building cattle-pens and huts, herding sheep
and goats and cattle, and above all, did their physical
exercises which kept them fit for defence or attack.
These activities were organised according to seasons.
When there was plenty of work in the fields, the warriors
took their full share in it and arranged their dances and
songs to take place in the evenings, but when there was
less work in the fields, then numerous day dances and
songs were arranged. Different age-groups competed in
dances, and in dexterity in throwing spears and fencing,
as well as high and long jumps.

THE CAUSE OF TRIBAL WARFARE

Let us consider for a moment the reason why the tribal
wars were fought. The main cause of friction between
tribes, especially in Kenya, was economic. There was
no war of annexation of territory or subjection of one
tribe to another. The fights which were carried on from
time to time between various tribes, such as the Masai,
the Gikuyu and the Wakamba, can hardly be called
"wars," because all fights were in the nature of armed
raids. For example, when cattle disease invaded the
Masai country and reduced their livestock below mini-
mum, the Masai, whose lives depended entirely on meat,
milk, and blood of the animals, were forced by necessity
to raid the stock of their neighbours or die of hunger
and starvation. In order to save their livelihood, spies
were sent out to investigate how a successful raid could
be carried out, and in what district in the neighbouring
tribes the stock were abundant and least protected.

After the spies had reported, a raid was at once organised, and the warriors set out to get food for the tribe.
Sometimes it took days to cover a short distance, for
the raiding party or parties travelled mostly during the

night and spent the daytime in hiding, eating and preparing for the attack. After they located the cattle-pens they slept in a forest nearby until the dead of night, when they stealthily crept through the darkness and took the few herdsmen by surprise. The cattle-pens were surrounded and a few of the herdsmen killed to avoid any cry that would give the signal to the warriors of the enemy's tribe. The cattle were captured in this way and led away as quickly as possible, in a zigzag way, and at the same time some of the warriors were left behind to cover the trail and also to await the enemy who might follow; so that while they were engaged in fighting, the cattle would reach the starving families in Masailand. Sometimes it took some days before the raid was discovered, especially when the cattle were grazing far away from the homesteads.

In this way the stock was lost and the lives of a few herdsmen. We can therefore compare the "tribal warfare" with the "smash-and-grab" practised in civilised Europe and in America. The only difference between the two systems is that smash-and-grab is a frequent practice, whereas the tribal warfare was an occasional raid, with long intervals in between. In some parts of the Gikuyu country, especially in the centre of the country, a generation passed without experiencing any raid at all.

Apart from the fighting strength of, say, the Gikuyu or the Masai, there were natural features dividing the two tribes, such as huge forests full of all kinds of dangerous wild animals and snakes, which made the forests a very effective blockade. Sometimes, it is said, a party of warriors entered the forests and never came back again; not that they fell into the hands of the enemy, but they lost their way and were either devoured by the animals or perished by starvation, thus feeding vultures and hungry hyenas. In places where there were no such natural barriers, and where the two tribes came into contact frequently, peace treaties were signed and friendly relations established. In this case intermarriages were one form of peace-making.

To take a concrete case, my grandmother, on my father's side, was a Masai woman called Mosana, and in reciprocity for this friendly feeling, my aunt (i.e. elder sister of my father) was married to a Masai chief called Sendeu, and was treated as the head-wife. Exchange visits were made on both sides, and I had the opportunity of visiting her and staying there for some months as a member of the family.

In territories where this friendly relationship was established, especially between the Kaptei Masai and the Southern Gikuyu, the warriors of the two tribes joined together to invade another section of Masai, like Loita, or a section of Gikuyu, like Mbeere or Tharaka. This information was given to me by my grandfather, Kongo wa Magana, who led several of these attacks as a fighting warrior and later as a magician of war.

It can be said that the relation between one tribe and another was no more or less than the relations existing in the present day between various tribes of Europe and America. The only difference is that the relations between European countries involve great suffering for the majority of the people, either through economic fights, tariff barriers and distribution of wealth, etc., or through actual fights in battle-fields. The case of the Spanish Civil War, where one tribe fought within itself, or the case of Japan and China, where strong tribes have tried to dominate weaker ones, are illustrations.

The raids in the tribal warfare affected only a few villages, probably those along the frontiers, with the loss only of a few hundred of their livestock which they recovered in one way or another by a counter raid. But generally speaking, the tribal organisation as a whole was very little disturbed. Cultivation, which was, and still is, the source of food supply, was carried on with little or no interference at all, for the raiding parties did not concern themselves with land or what grew thereon, but with the movable property in the way of cattle, and only a small number of sheep and goats were taken by the raiders to provide them with food on the journey and to avoid killing cattle which they valued highly.

Apart from the loss of livestock, chiefly cattle, we can add the burning of a few huts which were immediately rebuilt after the raiders had gone. The actual fighting did not take more than six days at the most, and it took the form of hide and seek, like an armed gang of thieves being caught and in their desperation trying to fight their way out. Generally the fighting was a matter of a few hours or a day, and the raiders were either victorious or they were defeated and the cattle restored, or in some other way they managed to take away the cattle without any resistance, especially in a case where the warriors of the invaded country were away raiding another tribe. For the work of spies was to enable the raiders to get away with cattle without any fighting which would result in heavy loss of life. And this was only possible at a time when the villages were not properly protected.

Since the coming of the Europeans the warrior organisation has been rendered powerless, for although the system of age-grading still exists (except the formation of *njama ya ita*) the spirit of manhood in the youth has been almost killed by the imposition of imperialistic rule which restricts people from moving and functioning freely in their own country. The European prides himself on having done a great service to the Africans by stopping the "tribal warfares," and says that the Africans ought to thank the strong power that has liberated them from their "constant fear" of being attacked by the neighbouring warlike tribes. But consider the difference between the method and motive employed in

the so-called savage tribal warfares, and those employed
in the modern warfare waged by the "civilised" tribes
of Europe, and in which the Africans who have no part
in the quarrels are forced to fight to defend so-called
democracy. Take the case of the Great War, 1914–18,
in which tens of thousands of Africans lost their lives.
The reward for this was taking away the best lands from
the Africans, the introduction of *kipande* with its diabolical system of finger-prints as though the Africans
were criminals, imposition of heavy taxation and denial
of freedom of speech, of the press, and of forming
political or social organisations. This is what "democratic Britain" did in recognition of the services rendered by the Kenya Africans during 1914–18. Another
example is the Italian invasion of Ethiopia, where the
wholesale massacre of the defenceless population took
place to demonstrate European civilisation. With these
glaring facts in view can the Europeans boast of having
stopped the "tribal warfare" and having established
"perpetual peace" in Africa? It would have been much
better for the Africans to continue with their tribal
warfare, which they fought with pride and with the loss
of a few warriors, rather than to receive the so-called
civilising missions which means the subjugation of the
African races to a perpetual state of serfdom.

In the old order of the African society, with all the
evils that are supposed to be connected with it, a man
was a man, and as such he had the rights of a man
and liberty to exercise his will and thought in a direction which suited his purposes as well as those of his
fellow-man; but to-day an African, no matter what his
station in life, is like a horse which moves only in the
direction that the rider pulls the rein. The harmony
and stability of the African's mode of life, in political,
social, religious and economic organisations, was based
on the land which was, and still is, the soul of the
people. The first step which the European civilising

missions took to disorganise the Africans in order to exploit and oppress them, especially in South and East Africa, was to take away the best African lands. This is one of the evils of European civilisation that has found its way to the great African continent, and one which the past, present, and future African generations will never forget.

The land not only unites the living members of the tribe but also the dead ancestors and the unborn posterity. This fact is obvious, because it is in the ancestral lands that the ancestors lie buried, in the land which they once occupied. In this way the dead are able to keep direct communication with the living, and the sanctions which control behaviour in both the collective life of the tribe and private lives of its individual members are the approval or disapproval of the ancestral spirits. Through incarnation the future generation is linked up with the past, thus bringing spiritually the three groups, i.e. dead, living and unborn, into one organic whole. The annexation of the ancestral lands by the Europeans has robbed the African of the use of the productive asset on which his entire economic life depended. It has also interfered with the whole tribal organisation whose genuine co-operation is based on constant communion with the ancestral spirits through which tribal law and custom, morality, and religion are maintained.

We have discussed at length the activities of the warriors in the old Gikuyu system of government, and the present condition under which the warriors as well as others find themselves. We will now enter into an analysis of the old system of judicial procedure, how it was conducted and who took part in it.

PROCEDURE

In every homestead the father acted as judge; he settled all minor disputes between the members of his family.

If there was a big dispute it was necessary to call together the heads of families within a *mbari* (kinfolk),
who acted not only as the heads of their particular immediate families but also in their capacity as elders of
the *kiama*. All such matters were treated as a family
concern, and as such it was the privilege of the family
council (*ndundu ya mocie*) to deal with the cases within
the precincts of their homesteads. These elders acted as
arbitrators rather than judges. Their duty was to point
out the recognised tradition and custom of the family
to be followed. The chief object in their deliberations
was to find ways and means by which they could bring
the disputing parties into a mutual agreement, and to
avoid any act of vengeance which might result in breaking up the family group. No case could go before general
assembly or public court of the elders before it had
been first tried by the family council. When two relatives
had a dispute, the offended party brewed a sugar-cane
beer as a sign of taking action. The night when the beer
was being fermented he went or sent round for the elders
of his family council and informed them that there was
a dispute to be settled between himself and another
member of the group. He therefore invited the elders to
come on the following morning and bring with them the
offender.

On the next morning the beer was strained into two or
three calabashes. After the sheep and goats were taken
to pastures, the elders arrived one by one; the offender,
who had been informed about the meeting, came all by
himself or in company of his friends. The beer was presented to the assembled elders as a sign of peaceful and
friendly discussion. They were informed why the beer
had been brewed, then the senior elder among those
present took a ceremonial drinking-horn (*rohea rwa
goitanga*) and filled it with the beer. This was poured
on the ground, and in a loud and ritual tone he invoked
the ancestral spirits to join them in their deliberation.

When he had done this, he stood up holding his staff of office (*motheegi*), and facing Kere-Nyaga, uttered a prayer in the following words: *"Athuuri, ugai nyomba eroiguana"* (i.e. "Elders, say let there be agreement and peace in the family group"). The elders answered in chorus: *"Nyomba eroiguana, thaai thathayai Ngai thaai"* (i.e. "Let there be peace in the family group, beseech Ngai, peace be with us"). He then proceeded to utter curses for anyone who might disobey the impartial decision of the *kiama*: *"Ugai mondo orea okararagia kiama arwaga na mocie wake na mogonda"* (i.e. "Elders, say let curses be upon him who disobeys *kiama's* decision; let curses lie upon his homestead and his fields"). The elders answer in chorus: "Let curses be upon him and his homestead and fields."

After this ceremony was completed the elders sat in council to hear the case. The plaintiff was called upon to state his case. He entered in the circle holding a bunch of twigs as a record of his statement, or in other words as notes for reference. At the end of each concrete statement of a complaint or claim he handed over to the elders one twig. The twigs thus handed were held by the presiding elder. The defendant was then called to defend himself or plead guilty. He stated his case and handed over twigs which were held by another elder.

To make this clear let us suppose that a man whom we will call A was claiming two sheep, three goats, and one heifer from his relative who we shall call B. Mr. A would stand up and begin to describe the colour and size of his two sheep. He would hold one of the twigs and tell the elders that one of his sheep was big and black, then he would hand over a long twig; then he would say that the other sheep was brown and small, for that he would hand over a shorter twig. He would then pass on to his three goats and describe them in the same manner, and then on to his heifer. When he had finished, Mr. B would be given the twigs which represented the claim of Mr. A and asked to admit or deny the charge. The twigs then were returned to the presiding elder.

When both had finished making their statements, the case was open for discussion. In this all the elders joined and each expressed his opinion either for or against one of the party, the twigs serving as the reference in the matter. After the whole case was reviewed and witnesses examined and cross-examined, the elders appointed a committee (*ndundu*) to give judgment for the case. The *ndundu* retired alone in a private place where no one could hear them. Immediate relatives such as father, uncle or brother of either party were excluded from the *ndundu*.

After discussing the merit and demerit of the case, and having agreed as to what was a proper and impartial judgment of the case, the *ndundu* returned to the council with the twigs arranged according to their decision. The twigs were handed over to the senior elder who announced the decision. The two men in the dispute were called before the elders and asked if they agreed with the judgment given or if either of them wanted to appeal. If both agreed, then all the elders stood up beating their staves together and at the same time reciting some ritual words which indicated that the case was settled for good. Two of the senior elders were then appointed to see that the judgment was carried out.

Having described the way in which a family dispute was settled, we will now pass on to analyse the type of case which was sent to a public court or elders' assembly, and how they were settled.

In the Gikuyu country there was no special courthouse, but there were several recognised meeting-places (*keharo,* pl. *iharo*) where the *kiama* or the council of elders met in the open air under a tree. All big cases and other matters of national importance were settled there. The majority of cases which were heard in the *kiama* general assemblies were those dealing with debts resulting from transactions of sheep and goats or cattle which were exchanged in buying land or paying marriage insurances (*roracio*). There were also a few criminal cases, such as murder (which was rare), theft, trespass, assault, and witchcraft.

CIVIL PROCEDURE

According to the Gikuyu law and custom, if Mr. A bought something from Mr. B for which he paid him four sheep or goats, should any of the animals die before it had a kid, Mr. B had to return the carcass to Mr. A who would replace the dead animal. On the other hand, if Mr. B failed to fulfil the contract for which Mr. A had paid the four sheep, then Mr. A had the right to claim back the original number with their offspring and without paying any compensation to Mr. B for looking after the animals. But in case of a land transaction where sheep, goats or cattle had been exchanged, if after a year or so the bargain was broken, the return of the animals' offspring could not be claimed, for the land also gave fruits which were equal to the offspring of the animal.

Another example of how an individual or a family group got into debt is a case of unsuccessful marriage. Sometimes this involved a rather complicated proceeding in the *kiama* assembly. For instance, when a man had paid forty sheep and goats to his father-in-law as *roracio* ("bride price") and if after two or three years' time his wife ran away with another man or divorced him without a good reason, the husband was entitled to claim the return of all the animals and the offspring thereof, especially if there were no children of the marriage. This type of case involved a lot of investigations on the part of the elders who tried it. For each sheep or goat or cow was traced from the time it left the homestead of the first owner to the time of dispute. If the parents-in-law had sold or exchanged one of the animals, they must redeem it from the person it had passed to. Sometimes a case of this nature involved several persons who had either bought or had been given the animal during the celebration of the marriage ceremony or after the marriage contract was signed.

The proper procedure adopted in recovering a debt was that a man brewed sugar-cane beer and took it to his debtor. He took with him also one of the elders of his village. The beer was presented to the debtor as a reminder and as a sign of friendship and of the wish to settle the matter peacefully. In this way the debtor might be moved by the friendly approach and perhaps make full settlement of the debt or promise to pay it in instalments. If the debt was not paid, another beer was prepared and presented to the debtor, and this time two elders accompanied the creditor. If this failed to bring any successful arrangement towards settlement of the debt, a third visit was made, taking the beer as before, and three elders as witnesses. Now the creditor had full right to take the matter before the *kiama,* because he had tried his best to persuade his debtor to settle the matter mutually out of court and had failed.

The next step was that the creditor or claimant went to the elders of his village and laid his case before them. He asked them to call on the elders of the neighbouring villages and arrange for the hearing of his case. After the elders had consulted together, a date was fixed for the case to be heard. As there was no system of writing, notices were sent verbally by the *kiama's* messengers to all those concerned in the case.

On the day appointed the elders gathered at their open-air court, under a shady tree, where they squatted in a semi-circle. Then a ceremonial elder rose and recited a prayer asking for peaceful deliberation of the *kiama* and prosperity for the country. At the end of this the two parties in the case were called before the assembly to state the nature of their case. After the number of sheep, goats or cattle involved was specified, both parties were asked to pay court fees before the case was heard. Fees were paid in kind, namely, sheep or male goats. In big cases such as inheritance or land cases a bull was paid, especially where cattle were involved. The fees paid to the elders depended on the number of animals connected with the case. For instance, if the plaintiff was claiming five sheep or goats, his court fees would be two or three gourds of beer. If the number of animals claimed was between ten and twenty, the court fees would be one fat ram or a male goat.

Both plaintiff and defendant brought their court fees in form of a ram or a male goat and handed them to the elders; if accepted, the animals were tied to a tree nearby ready to be slaughtered. The elders then sat in the council according to their grades. In the inner semi-circle were the *kiama kia maturanguru,* behind them came the *kiama kia mataathi,* then followed the *kiama kia kamatimo* and the general public who came to listen to the case.

The two contesting parties were invited into the circle to state their case to the assembly. Among the judges (*athamaki*) two elders were appointed to conduct the proceedings on behalf of the whole council. In giving the evidence twigs were used in the same way as already stated in dealing with the family dispute. The two appointed elders took charge of the twigs and conducted the examination and cross-examination. Any other member of the council had the right to intervene and ask questions or make a statement, but generally this was done through the conducting elders. After all the evidence was heard from both sides, the case was open for discussion in general assembly. Anyone in the assembly could stand up and express his opinion. In this way the young people were given an opportunity to develop and improve their talent in legal matters; for with no special school for this, the assemblies served two purposes, for deciding cases or settling disputes, and at the same time giving practical legal education to the youth.

At the conclusion of the general discussion a committee of judges (*ndundu ya athamaki*) was appointed; both parties were allowed to choose two elders each to represent them in the committee. The rest were chosen by the assembly, for the committee was composed of ten or twelve elders. Anyone known to have direct or indirect interest in the case was excluded from the committee so as to avoid any biased judgment. Before the committee retired to consider the case, the ceremonial elder stood and uttered curses on anyone who might try to force wrong judgment through the influence of bribery and corruption. This form of curse acted as a check against the evils of bribery and corruption, for no one would agree to sit on the committee knowing that he had been bribed to pervert the course of justice.

After receiving the caution, the committee (*ndundu ya athamaki*) retired alone to discuss the matter in private, taking with them for reference the twigs from both parties. While the *ndundu ya athamaki* was discussing the case, the animal which had been given as court fees was being slaughtered and the meat roasted over a fire. This duty fell on the *kamatimo* elders who at this time sat in a separate group. The galls of the animals were taken out and handed over to the *ndundu ya athamaki* (committee of judges). The galls were then broken with a piece of stick from a shrub called *mogere*. In doing so the elders shouted in one voice, saying: "Let evil be upon him who disobeys our decision, may his galls be broken in the same way as we have broken these of the animal." Then the *ndundu,* having agreed as to the judgment of the case, cut twigs and arranged them according to their finding. The presiding elder of the *ndundu* recited what each twig represented in a ritual tone; the rest answered in chorus as a sign of their agreement.

After the *ndundu* had concluded their discussion, the meat which had been roasted was distributed according to the ranks of the *kiama*. Certain joints went to the *kiama kia maturanguru, mataathi, kamatimo,* and the rest to the nonmembers of the *kiama*. Skins, heads and the fat tails of rams went to privileged senior elders who took them home to their wives.

After the meat was eaten, the court reassembled and the committee of the judges gave their decision. The presiding elder stood and invoked poverty, sickness and calamity upon anyone who unreasonably refused to obey the *kiama's* decision. He then uttered a blessing for the assembly and for the general welfare of the community. In each case all those present answered in unison.

At the end of this judicial ceremony the two parties in the dispute were called and asked if they had confidence in the elders. To this they answered in the affirmative; then came the official announcer of judgments who had been told privately the finding of the *ndundu*. He stood in the circle surrounded by the elders. After telling one or two stories of ancient times and court procedures of the days gone by, as a grand climax, he pronounced the judgment on the present case. The whole assembly rose and gave a yell as the sign of their agreement.

Two elders were appointed to see that the judgment was carried out. The property involved in the judgment was not given to the plaintiff directly, but was passed through the hands of the appointed elders who acted on behalf of the whole *kiama*. If the claim was not settled the plaintiff could not go directly to the defendant, his proper channel was through the elders in charge of the case. *Kiama* judgment was invariably carried out, the curses acting as a police force. The fear of public opinion expressed in the way of curses was the chief preventative of mischief and crimes, because there was no police organisation in the Gikuyu society.

If one of the parties did not agree with the *kiama* decision he was given an ample opportunity to appeal and had his case re-heard. In this case he had to take a strong oath to prove that there was ground for his appeal, and that he was not playing tricks with the *kiama*.

In the Gikuyu society, oath or ordeal was the most important factor controlling the court procedures. It served two purposes. On the one hand, the fear of it prevented people from giving false evidence, and helped to bring the offenders to justice through guilty conscience and confession. On the other hand, it ruled out bribery and corruption and ensured impartial or unbiased judgment. For not only the parties in a case were subjected to take oath of one kind or another, but also the elders of the *kiama* were sworn in before being allowed to try a case. In this oath the elders promised that they would not accept bribery or any private gift from those concerned in the case or from anyone else acting on their behalf.

Among the Gikuyu there were three important forms of oaths which were so terribly feared, morally and religiously, that no one dared to take them unless he was perfectly sure and beyond any doubt that he was innocent or that his claim was genuine.

For the interest of our readers we will here give a short description of the three kinds of oaths and their symbols. First, there was *muuma*. This was taken generally on minor disputes. The symbol of the oath consisted of a lamb which was killed and the contents of the stomach mixed with herbs, water, and a little of the blood of the animal. The compound was put into a wild banana leaf (*icoya rea ihendu*) and then placed in a small hole dug in the ground. The medicine man (*mondo mogo*) tied a brush of twigs and leaves from a ceremonial shrub called *mogere*. Then the party concerned in the case knelt down towards the hole. The *mondo mogo* dipped the brush into the mixture and lifted it to the mouth of the kneeling man, who took the oath by licking the brush, saying: "If I tell a lie, let this symbol of truth kill me. If I falsely accuse anyone, let this symbol of truth kill me. If the property I am now claiming is not mine, let this symbol of truth kill me."

The symbol of the second oath was *koringa thenge* (to swear by killing a male goat). This form of oath was administered in a big case with a lot of property, involving more than one or two persons. A small male goat was brought before the *kiama* and the parties concerned were asked to take an oath by breaking all the limbs of the animal. The male goat was spread on a rock in a lonely and uncultivated field, then a ceremonial stone (*ngangae*) was handed in turn to each individual who proceeded to break the bones of the male goat, saying: "If the property I am now claiming is not mine, let my limbs be smashed to smithereens like the bones of this male goat. If I am claiming more than what is due to me, let my family group be crushed like the bones of this male goat."

The third form of oath was *gethathi;* this was taken mostly in criminal cases such as murder or stealing. The symbol of this oath consisted of a small red stone with seven natural holes on it. The stone was put on a small stick which was planted on the ground. The elders stood at a little distance facing the spot where the oath ceremony was being prepared. The place had to be a barren ground not likely to be cultivated, for no one would allow the ceremony to be performed on or near his cultivation. It was feared that the evil of the oath symbol might spread to a cultivated crop and destroy it.

When the preparation was done, the accused persons were asked to pass several grass stalks (*ngoonda*) through each hole seven times, at the same time swearing to the validity of their statement which they had made or were about to make. While this was taking place all the elders present put a piece of creeper (*mokengeria*) on their ears to protect themselves against the evil of the symbol of the oath. Women were excluded from taking any of these oaths. Their husbands or sons took the responsibility, for the women were not considered fit mentally and bodily to stand the ordeal which involved not only the individual going through it but the whole family group.

Nowadays these oaths and ordeals are neglected and discouraged by the European administration who regard them as mere superstition. Instead, the Europeans have adopted a form of raising hands or kissing the Bible as symbols of oath. It can be definitely said that this form of oath has no meaning at all to the Africans. It has no binding force, moral or religious. The result has been fabrication of evidence in courts of justice, and furthermore, bribery and corruption is the order of the day in many cases that come before a magistrate or a court of elders. It would not be exaggeration to say that in most cases judgment depends entirely on who pays most. I speak here with experience in both European and *kiama* courts, where bribery and corruption are prevalent.

The reason for this miscarriage of justice is that the chiefs and elders who are entrusted with the administration of justice are very poorly paid by the British Government. Their wages or salary runs from ten shillings to about £5 per month. With this they are expected to display their power and wealth. However, in spite of the small salary which these chiefs receive, the moment a man is appointed a chief or a headman, immediately he starts to accumulate large herds of sheep, goats and cattle, and also a number of wives. It cannot, therefore, be denied that the Government is aware of the diabolical state of bribery and corruption existing and displayed under their very eyes. The above remark is strictly directed to the chiefs who are appointed over the heads of the majority of the people, and who, like their masters, want to get rich quick at the expense of the poor Africans who have no voice at all in the administration of their country. This state of affairs can be stopped if the Government is willing by letting the people have power to choose their chiefs under a democratic system, and power to dismiss them when they abuse their position.

We have now seen how the judicial procedure in civil cases was conducted. Let us for a moment turn to personal injuries or assaults. Redress for insults was settled out of court. No man with any dignity would take another to court for an insult. A man was considered responsible and capable of taking care of his dignity and seeing that it was not abused. The proper procedure was duelling or fencing. If a man insulted another an apology was asked, and made by paying a small tribute of banana or a calabash of beer or gruel to the age-group of the insulted man. If this was refused he was asked to be ready for a duel. There and then the two men, in the presence of their friends, settled the quarrel by duelling. After this the two men shook hands and became friends again.

CRIMINAL PROCEDURE

In the Gikuyu society all criminal cases were treated almost in the same way as civil cases. The chief aim in proceeding was to get compensation for the individual or the group against whom the crime was committed. Since there was no system of imprisonment, the offenders were punished by being made to pay heavy fines to the *kiama* and compensation to right the wrong done.

Murder and manslaughter were treated in the same way, for the *kiama* was not chiefly concerned with the motive of the crime or the way in which the crime was committed, but with the fact that one man had taken another man's life. Premeditated murders were very rare among the Gikuyu, for it was a crime against society for a man to strike another without warning him, unless he was a foreign enemy. If a man killed another in cold blood the murderer was treated with the greatest contempt, because not only had he disgraced himself but also his age-group. But if it happened that two men were engaged in a fight and one of them was killed or died of the wound, in such a case the murderer had the sympathy and respect of the community, because he acted in a manly fashion and in self-defence. For this reason the murderer was treated leniently in his trial.

The first step in a murder case was that the family group of the murdered man took up arms and invaded the murderer's homestead with the object of killing the murderer or one of his close relatives, and letting them realise that the murdered man had a family group capable of inflicting retribution on behalf of one of its members. If the invaders succeeded in killing the murderer or one of his kinsfolk, the case was settled there and then, for the two lives were considered equal. But if this failed, the family group of the dead man invaded the cultivated fields of the murderer's family group. The crops thereon, such as bananas, sugarcane and yams, were razed to the ground by the swords of the invaders as a sign of indignation and mourning for the death of one of their kinsmen. Whenever there was a conflict between one family group and another as stated above, it was the duty of the elders of the peace council to intervene and bring the quarrelling parties to conciliation. In this way private revenge and blood feud was checked by settling the matter peacefully once and for all before the court of elders.

Universal rules were made fixing the amount payable as compensation for loss of life, according to sex. The rules aimed at punishing a murderer, irrespective of whether he killed a man instantly or caused him to die of the wound inflicted in a fight. If a man wounded another seriously he was asked to provide a male goat, which was killed to supply nourishment for the wounded man. If the wound healed the matter ended there, but if sooner or later he died, the man was charged with murder, because the providing of a male goat was considered as pleading guilty to the charge.

The compensation for loss of life of a man was fixed at one hundred sheep or goats or ten cows. For a woman's life thirty sheep or goats or three cows. The only exception to these rules was when a man or a woman was killed by poisoning or witchcraft. This was looked upon as a crime against the whole community, and the penalty was death by burning as stated in the chapter dealing with Magical Practices.

Apart from the fact that there was inequality of sex in the Gikuyu society (as in most of the early human societies), which was responsible for the great difference between the value of a man's life and that of a woman's, as shown in the above rules, the only other explanation would be that the Gikuyu conception of value of life was according to services which a man or a woman would have rendered to his family group during lifetime. And, therefore, it was considered right and proper to fix the compensation for loss of a woman's life to thirty sheep or goats or three cows, the same number as that which was given for the marriage ceremony, after which the girl entered into the activities of another family unit and ceased to serve her own parents or family group. But a man was considered as permanently part and parcel of his family group, and as

such his services were continuously rendered for the
benefit of his family group during his lifetime. And
therefore the number of one hundred sheep or goats or
ten cows was assessed on the assumption that the man
would have been able, had he lived, to bring property
to his group equal in value to that fixed for compensation for the loss of his life. The rule applied to all
males and females in the community from the time of
birth to the time of death. There was no distinction.
Whether it was a male or female baby murdered or a
rich man or woman, the compensation was the same
as stated above.

Next to murder cases came personal injury inflicted
on a man or woman. Any bodily hurt or cut without loss
of a limb was not considered as a serious crime, for it
was a common happening, especially in a community
like Gikuyu or Masai, where quarrels between two
individuals or groups were always settled by a fight or
a duel. In case of loss of a limb or part of it, there was
a payment for compensation fixed for each limb. For
example, loss of a finger was compensated by ten sheep
or goats. For loss of hand or arm thirty sheep or goats.
For one ear ten sheep or goats. For a tooth one sheep
or goat, and so on. These rules varied according to
the wealth of the various districts.

The punishment for adultery or rape was that the
man paid a fine of three fat rams to the *kiama* and nine
sheep or goats to the husband or parents. In some cases
the offender was ostracised. The stigma attached to the
ostracism was far greater and very much worse than
that attached to the European form of imprisonment.
Many Gikuyu would prefer to go to jail rather than to
be ostracised. The fear of this was one of the chief factors which prevented the people from committing
crimes.

Next came theft; this depended on what was stolen,
and the fines were fixed according to the article or the

animal the thief had taken. For instance, if a man had stolen a sheep, he was required to return the original sheep with another one to "purify" it. If the stolen sheep was killed and eaten, the crime became serious and the thief, with all those who participated in eating the meat, were fined ten sheep or goats each. If a man had stolen honey from another man's bee-hive, the fine was thirty sheep or goats. In spite of these fines, if a man found a thief stealing his property, he had the right to take the law into his own hands and beat the thief to his satisfaction and then bring him before the *kiama* to be fined. In every one of these cases the offender had to give one fat ram to the *kiama* as court fees. If a man became a habitual thief, he was looked upon as a public danger and was put to death publicly, sometimes by being beaten to death or burnt in the same way as a witch or wizard. In the Gikuyu society theft and witchcraft were considered as very serious criminal offences.

10

RELIGION
AND
ANCESTOR WORSHIP

THE GIKUYU PEOPLE, it is certain, maintain a close and vital relationship with spiritual entities. Their daily lives, both as individuals and groups, are influenced at all points by belief in the supernatural. It is then of the very first importance to know the nature of the beliefs themselves and of the Beings in whom they are reposed. Is there a belief in a single High God? If so, is it a vital belief or a mere formalism? Who and what is the High God? Is He a mere abstraction, easily forgotten, or a real entity, visible both in picturesque dwelling-places and in His awful or beneficent works?

These and many such questions must be asked and answered before we begin to appreciate the religious life of the Gikuyu people, as of any other people. Further, are there any other spiritual creatures besides the Deity, and, if so, how do they function in the day-to-day, year-to-year life of the people? We shall assume that there are such beings, the spirits of our ancestors. With them we constantly commune. Hence the first two elements in the title of this chapter. Further, sacrificial practices are of such importance in establishing connections with both the High God and the other supernatural Beings that I have given them a third place in the title. Our work is to bring out the functioning mode of these two great departments of Gikuyu religion and of the main means of their formal expression in the sacrificial ceremonies which everywhere define and punctuate them. To do this adequately it is necessary to describe various forms of religious ceremonies and sacrifices. In this way we shall make clear the differences among the three parts of our subject-matter: Deity worship, communion with ancestors, and sacrificial practices.

The ideas underlying these three expressions may best be brought out by means of linguistic analysis. First, we have *gothaithaya Ngai,* which may clearly be translated: "To beseech Ngai," or "To worship Ngai." The essential difference between Deity worship, in the true sense, and what is known as "ancestor worship," is demonstrated by the fact that *gothaithaya* is never used in connection with ancestral spirits. The term used for what I shall call "communion with ancestors" is *goitangera ngoma njohi*—literally, "to pour out or to sprinkle beer for spirits." This refers to the pouring out of a little of whatever you are drinking on to the ground for the ancestors, and, in a special sense, to a larger offering of a similar nature made on the occasion of communion ceremonies, when a special quantity of beer is brewed for presentation to the ancestral spirits. At the same time a beast will be sacrificed. Generally on special occasions these two elements are necessary.

When both the beer and the animal are offered, an additional term has to be used: *gothenjera na goitangera ngoma njohi*—literally, "to slaughter and pour out beer for the spirits." It will be clear from this that the Gikuyu people have a clear idea and understanding of two supernatural elements. On the one hand is the relationship with the one High God, Ngai, which may accurately be termed one of worship. Gikuyu religion has definitely two departments. Both are really vital; they function in unison, but in different spheres. We shall find, for example, that when a sacrifice is made to the High God on an occasion of national (tribal) importance, the ancestors must join in making the sacrifice.

The term for "sacrificial practices" is *koruta magongona,* "to offer or to perform sacrifices or rituals and ceremonies." *Igongona* (sing.) is the only Gikuyu word which can possibly be translated "religion," although *mambura* (lit. "sacred") is practically synonymous with it. These words convey the idea of sacredness in general, so that *koruta magongona* may also be translated "sacred offerings." These are carried out, as we shall see, in connection with both Ngai worship and *ngoma* communion.

It may be worth mentioning at this stage that Christian missionaries in Gikuyu country have ignored both of the Gikuyu words for religion. The reason is probably that they feel them to be associated with "native ideas of spirit worship." Instead, the Swahili term, *dini,* has been imported.

THE CONCEPTION OF A DEITY

The Gikuyu believes in one God, Ngai, the creator and giver of all things. *Ngai moombi wa indo ciothe na mohei kerende indo ciothe.* He has no father, mother, or companion of any kind. His work is done in solitude. *Ngai ndere ithe kana nyina, ndere gethia kana gethethwa.* He loves or hates people according to their behaviour. The creator lives in the sky. *Ngai eikaraga matuine,* but has temporary homes on earth, situated on mountains, where he may rest during his visits. The visits are made with a view to his carrying out a kind of "general inspection," *koroora thi,* and to bring blessings and punishments to the people. *Korehere ando kiguni kana gitei.*

The common name used in speaking of the Supreme Being is Ngai; this name is used by three neighbouring tribes, the Masai, the Gikuyu, and Wakamba. In prayers and sacrifices Ngai is addressed by the Gikuyu as Mwene-Nyaga (possessor of brightness). This name is associated with Kere-Nyaga (the Gikuyu name for Mount Kenya), which means: That which possesses brightness, or mountain of brightness.

The mountain of brightness is believed by the Gikuyu to be Ngai's official resting-place, and in their prayers they turn towards Kere-Nyaga and, with their hands raised towards it, they offer their sacrifices, taking the mountain to be the holy earthly dwelling-place of Ngai. *Kenyororokero na kehuroko kia Mwene-Nyaga*—literally, "descending and resting- or dwelling place of God."

The Being thus described cannot be seen by ordinary mortal eyes. He is a distant Being and takes but little interest in individuals in their daily walks of life. Yet at the crises of their lives he is invariably called upon. At the birth, initiation, marriage, and death of every Gikuyu, communication is established on his behalf with Ngai. The ceremonies for these four events leave no doubt as to the importance of the spiritual assistance which is essential to them.

This assistance is always obtained, however, by the family group. No individual may directly supplicate the Almighty. The group which may do so is very clearly defined; it is the group of mother, father, and children, which thus receives supernatural sanction. The father is the key personality. A group of families or a clan cannot function together except in times of tribal crisis, for each will have its own father. The family may, especially if polygamous, number one or two hundred souls. The "father" may in fact be a great-grandfather, but excepting only those of his children who have settled elsewhere, the family unit thus defined is the religious unit. Although the crises are in the life of the individual, he may not make supplication on his own behalf; his whole family group must pledge their interest in his life.

There are occasions in each man's life, apart from the four main crises, when he requires spiritual assistance. He may have broken a taboo; he may attribute some ill luck to such an infraction. This is reckoned as an individual matter, and Ngai is not approached. The man's purification or absolution is achieved by means of the medicine man, who will work by establishing contact with such of the ancestral spirits as may be thought to be involved. It is possible that only one ancestor will need to be propitiated, and there will be no need for the whole family group to be brought into action to approach him. This is reserved for appeal to Ngai himself. Thus are the four main crises of life marked off from its minor difficulties. Religion deals with the former; communion with the ancestors suffices for the latter. Every other occasion again is transcended by crises involving the whole tribe, such as a threatened drought. Then, of course, Ngai himself must be appealed to, and the appeal must be made by the active participation of the whole people.

To see whether linguistic analysis will help us to emphasise these points: *Ngai eikaraga matuine, na nderoranagia na wera wa mondo omwe mwanya, eroranagia na mawera ma ando oothe, kana ando a nyomba emwe. Ngai ndegiagiagwo;* may literally be translated: "God lives in the heavens and he does not bother with the work or affairs of one man alone. He looks after the affairs of a whole people or a homestead group. There is no one man's religion or sacrifice."

Apart from the official abode of Mwene-Nyaga at Kere-Nyaga on the north, there are minor homes such as Kea-Njahe (the mountain of the Big Rain) on the east; Kea-Mbiroiro (the mountain of Clear Sky) on the south; Kea-Nyandarwa (the mountain of Sleeping Place or Hides) on the west. All these are regarded with reverence as great places and mysteries symbolic of God, *Manage na oriro wa Ngai*. The Gikuyu, who has no "temple made with hands," selects huge trees, generally *mogumo* or *motumayo* and *mokoyo* trees, which symbolise the mountains. Under these trees he worships and makes his sacrifices to Mwene-Nyaga. These sacred trees are regarded in the same manner as most Christians regard churches—as the "House of God."

Ngai, who is not visible to mortal eyes, manifests himself in various ways. The sun, the moon, the stars, rain, rainbow, lightning and thunder are looked upon as manifestations of his powers. *Moriro na mahinya ma Ngai*. Through these signs he can reveal his love or hatred. For instance, when there is thunder and lightning it is taken as a warning to clear the way for Mwene-Nyaga's movements from one sacred place to another. When a man happens to be stricken by the lightning it is generally said that he was so stricken for daring to look upwards to see Mwene-Nyaga stretching himself and cracking his joints in readiness for his active service to chase away or smash his enemies.

It is taboo to look towards the heavens during a thunderstorm. Children are told by their mothers not to look upwards, but to go indoors. If anyone is lying in bed and is not asleep, he is very careful not to lie looking up. He quickly turns to lie upon one side.

In the ordinary way of everyday life there are no organised prayers or religious ceremonies such as "morning and evening prayers." So far as people and

things go well and prosper, it is taken for granted that
God is pleased with the general behaviour of the people
and the welfare of the country. In this happy state there
is no need for prayers. Indeed they are inadvisable, for
Ngai must not needlessly be bothered. It is only when
humans are in real need that they must approach him,
without fear of disturbing him and incurring his wrath.
But when people meet to discuss public affairs or decide
a case, or at public dances, they offer prayers for
protection and guidance.

For linguistic illustrations we may take the following: When a man is stricken by lightning it is said
*Ahehenjetwo ne korothereria Ngai ekenogora egethie
komemenda na koingata tho ciayo,* literally, "He has
been smashed to smithereens for seeing Ngai in the act
of cracking its joints in readiness to go to smash and
chase away its enemies."

The noise of the thunder is believed to be that of
Ngai "cracking" his joints. In the same way it is said
that the lightning is a visible representation of some of
God's weapons which he uses against his enemies.
Ngai has no messengers whom he may, like an earthly
chief, send on ahead to warn people of his coming and
to prepare and clear the way. His approach is foretold
only by the sounds of his own preparations. Thunder
is his cracking of his joints, as a warrior limbering up
for action. It is also the noise of his approach in general, as if drums were being beaten and horns blown to
warn the people of the presence of the heavenly chief.
Further, he uses lightning as a sword to clear his way.
He will strike down anything that dare stand in his way
—trees, men, animals—and blast open land by its
means. The thunder is also the noise of his using, or
preparing to use, this weapon. The lightning is the
actual sword of Ngai. The Gikuyu know this by experience, for they see its works.

Further, in our linguistic illustrations, we have: *Ngai*

ndegiagiagwo, literally, "Ngai must never be pestered."
This is a saying much used in Gikuyu. It has wide
implications. In the first place it implies that even if a
terrible calamity, such as the death of his child, should
befall a man, his attitude must be one of resignation,
for the people know that Ngai gives and has the power
to take away. The man is not left hopeless, for Ngai
may restore his losses—another child may be born to
him.

The following is an example of the kind of prayers
offered up at public assemblies:

Korathimithia

1. *Ugai kiama kiroiguana.*
2. *Thaithayai Ngai thaaai.*
1. *Ugai borori uroagirira, na ando maroingeha.*
2. *Thaithayai Ngai thaaai.*
1. *Ugai ando na mahio marogia uhoro.*
2. *Thaithayai Ngai thaaai.*
1. *Ugai megonda irogia iro, na ithaka irokiria konoru.*
2. *Thaithayai Ngai thaaai.*

The number 1 in this prayer denotes the lines spoken
by an elder, while the number 2 indicates the responses
of an assembly.

Asking for Blessing

1. Say ye, the elders may have wisdom and speak
with one voice.
2. Praise ye Ngai. Peace be with us.
1. Say ye that the country may have tranquillity and
the people may continue to increase.
2. Praise ye Ngai. Peace be with us.
1. Say ye that the people and the flocks and the herds
may prosper and be free from illness.
2. Praise ye Ngai. Peace be with us.
1. Say ye the fields may bear much fruit and the land

may continue to be fertile.

2. Praise ye Ngai. Peace be with us.

These are phrases which are generally used in all public assemblies in the Gikuyu country.

In prayers of this nature no sacrifice is made, for the Gikuyu turn to God and offer sacrifice only in serious matters such as drought or outbreak of an epidemic, and great distress, as with a serious illness. In this case the Gikuyu, who believes in the law of "give and take" (*Kanya gatune ne mwamokaniro*), expect Mwene-Nyaga to answer their prayers favourably in return for the present given him in the way of the animal killed for the sacrifice.

As in the case of other cultures, Gikuyu religious feelings and practice may well be illustrated by reference to health and sickness. If a person falls sick or has an injury it is not, at first, a matter for supernatural treatment. Ordinary medical knowledge is applied. If this does not succeed, the nature of the case is changed. Then the ancestors are communicated with. Perhaps with the aid of a diviner it is found that one of them has been offended. Atonement is made and the invalid recovers.

Yet even when it is certain that no ancestors remain offended, the illness may still not yield to the treatment. Then the father of the family must organise the next appeal—to Ngai himself. He leads his kin in the approach to the almighty through a sacrifice. But the mortals do not go thus alone to Ngai. The living and the dead of the family now together approach the highest Power. This assures Mwene-Nyaga that the occasion is serious and that the whole family is indeed at one, having exhausted all other means, in pleading for his help.

In such a case one of life's greatest crises, death, is either imminent or possible, so that the essentially religious aspect of social behaviour comes into prominence.

And the approach is made by means of a sacrificial ceremony, which is essential to the form of Gikuyu religion. It is further instructive to note the case of a man being injured, but not killed, by lightning. Here is a calamity of a double nature. The treatment also is twofold. The actual physical injuries are treated in a practical medical way. But the man was struck by Ngai, so communication with the High God is at once called for. A sheep is slaughtered in the place where the lightning came to earth. With its stomach contents the man is washed for purification. The beast is then offered to Ngai through sacrifice. The ancestors are not involved, since the lightning was not their weapon. Yet, since the religious act is made by the whole properly constituted family group, they will be present. The living and the dead of the family will together try to propitiate the god who, in his wrath, has struck down one of their members. The sacrifice has to soothe him, so that no more of his anger will come upon that family group.

These two cases, of an ordinary illness and of an injury by lightning, throw some light on the respective parts played in the actual lives of the people by Ngai worship, communion with ancestors, and sacrificial ceremonies.

THE NATURISTIC ASPECT

One aspect of Gikuyu religion remains to be indicated. Inevitably the people are daily and hourly in the most intimate contact with Nature. We have already seen that certain natural phenomena, the thunder and lightning, are regarded as direct manifestations of Ngai and his works. We shall see later that he controls not only the health and lives of men and the beasts on whom men depend, but also the rain and the supply of food which the rain brings from the soil. Hence all these phenomena of Nature are in some degree, like thunder, imbued with the spirit of Ngai. Any description of Gikuyu religion which left these out of account would be incomplete. We cannot speak of "Nature worship" as a department of the religion, but it is a quality that runs through the whole, vitalising it and keeping it in constant touch with daily need and emotions.

PRIESTHOOD

In Gikuyu religion there is no provision for official priesthood, nor is there any religious preaching. Converting campaigns are, of course, a thing unknown. This is due to the fact that the religion is interwoven with traditions and social customs of the people. Thus all members of the community are automatically considered to have acquired, during their childhood teachings, all that it is necessary to know about religion and custom. The duty of imparting this knowledge to the children is entrusted to the parents, who are looked upon as the official ministers of both religious ethics and social customs.

Gikuyu religion can be defined as being based on belief in a supreme being, Ngai, and on constant communication with Nature. To make use of European terminology, it might be said that religion in Gikuyu is "State established," but it would be even more true to say that Church and State are one.

The most solemn religious service is that of sacrificing to Mwene-Nyaga. This duty and privilege belongs to the elders. These may be, and often are, chiefs and sub-chiefs, high political officers; but they perform in the sacrificial ceremonies simply in their role of elders of various gradings. *Athuri a kiama,* i.e. miraculous elders. In this category of sacrificial elders, some of them are "wise men," or seers (*Morathi,* sing.; *Arathi,* pl.). These men are believed to be endowed with powers beyond those of ordinary human beings. They are held to be in direct communication with Mwene-Nyaga who gives them instructions, generally during their sleep. Mwene-Nyaga assists and directs them in executing their sacred duty. The powers so given, it is said, are never to be used for personal purposes, but only for the welfare of the community. For it is feared that if any-one dared to misuse such powers, thus acting contrary to Mwene-Nyaga's instructions, the result would be disaster, not only to himself but to the whole of his family group. *Mondo konyitwo ne ng'oki ohamwe na rociare rwake,* literally, "defilement befalls a man and his children."

A *morathi* (and the writer's grandfather, Kongo wa Magana, was one of them) uses no magic or medicine in interpreting the messages or instructions given him by Mwene-Nyaga. He is commanded not to seek earthly aid in executing his sacred mission. Thus a seer was in a very delicate position, for while he was in direct communication with Mwene-Nyaga on the one hand, on the other hand his life was in danger, especially a beginner's. Unless he had received messages and in-structions from Mwene-Nyaga repeatedly and was quite sure that he had got them accurately, he dared not deliver them to the people, because if his prophecy proved to be false he was taken to be a pretender, and the punishment for an act of this nature was death.

A seer is not in the same category as the witch-doctor or medicine man (*mondo mogo*), whose pro-fessional duty it is to help the elders in carrying out certain rites, such as purification ceremonies, trials by ordeal and healing of various maladies. The medicine man has no power beyond his professional duty, which does not carry him into teaching of morality or religious ethics, as this duty is entrusted to the elders in their capacity as parents. Sacrifices, through which people establish communication with Mwene-Nyaga, play a very important part in Gikuyu religion. It is through these that one can fully understand and appreciate the significance of Gikuyu religion. We have already seen that Gikuyu turn to Ngai (God) only when they are in great need or distress, resulting from such causes as drought or illness of the people or livestock. Having this as our basic principle in religious rites and sacrifices, let us now proceed to describe some of the important sacrifices. In dealing with these it is necessary to show how and where these sacred duties are performed and in whose hands the ritual lies.

SACRIFICE OR PRAYERS FOR RAIN

Sacrifice to Mwene-Nyaga for rain is made if rain fails to fall at the usual time; when people, after preparing their fields for planting, see that the rain has failed and that the drought is prolonged. At this moment of anxiety the elders of fourth grade (*kiama kia maturan-guru*) get together and summon the seers. The seers (*arathi*) are asked if they have received any message or instruction from Mwene-Nyaga in connection with the causes of the drought. If no messages have been received by any of the *arathi,* they are asked to go home and report again in the morning if they have been able to communicate with Mwene-Nyaga. Next morning the elders and the *arathi* meet again to solve the mystery. At this time some of the *arathi* may have received instructions from Ngai describing what has made him angry and to act so unkindly as to refuse to bring rain for his people as usual; and also the message will describe what sort of animal would be acceptable to Ngai and soothe his anger.

The animal thus described may be a lamb of a certain colour—black, brown, red, or white. After the seers have given the elders this information the lamb is sought for. The lamb thus to be sacrificed must be of one colour only; it must not have any spot or blemish, no matter how small. The origin of such a lamb is carefully investigated. Great importance is attached to how the lamb in question was originally acquired by the present possessor. The lambs for sacrifices of this nature must be only those which were acquired by lawful means; either bought by grain cultivated from rightfully owned land or by honey from a beehive made out of a sacred tree. The possessor of such a lamb must be a man who is known to be honest and trustworthy. He must not be a man who has committed murder, theft, rape, or had any connection with poison (witchcraft) or poisoning.

After the lamb is secured the next step is to select participants who are to be entrusted with the offering of the sacrifice. These must be (1) the elders who have outlived their more worldly desires and can now be believed to have only the consideration of the welfare of the community at heart; (2) if women are to be permitted, they must be only those who have passed child-bearing age, for they are considered to be immune from worldly mischief and are now mothers, not of individuals, but of the community; (3) two children, a male and a female. They must not be above eight years of age. Children under that age are considered pure in heart, mind, and body, and are free from worldly sins. (The writer had the privilege of participating in one of these sacrifices for rain, accompanying his grandfather, who was a *morathi*.)

The next step taken in preparation for the sacrifice to Mwene-Nyaga is to select a place suitable for offering the sacrifice. This must be under one of the sacred trees, *mogumo* or *motamayo*. In the writer's district there still remains one of these, a famous one called *mogumo-wa-njathi*, under which generations have offered their sacrifices to Mwene-Nyaga. Many of these trees were cut down when Europeans took possession of Gikuyu lands.

When all the necessary arrangements have been made, a day is appointed on which the sacrifice is to be offered. In this connection a public proclamation is made announcing the date of the ritual ceremony. A notice is given in advance that after five days and nights have passed, the sixth day will be the day of communion with Mwene-Nyaga, and that no one will be allowed to make a journey which will make it necessary for him or her to ford a river or a stream; that no stranger will be permitted to come in or depart on that day of communion. Warriors are not allowed to dance in a warlike manner on that day, for fear of a quarrel which might arise out of a dispute at the dance and result in a fight amongst the warriors, thus defiling the sacrificial ceremony. Precautions are taken in all districts concerned to make the sacrificial day peaceful. The offering is made in all districts and locations simultaneously. Locations are divided by rivers or streams. Thus people between one river and another are considered to constitute a sacrificial unit. They have one sacred tree or grove under which they offer their sacrifice in common.

The elders entrusted with these sacrificial duties are not allowed to have any sexual intercourse or to sleep in their wives' huts during the preparation and performance. This period covers eight nights; six nights before the offering of the sacrifice and two nights after the sacrifice is offered.

On the eve of the sacrificial ceremony all the elders in the sacrificial council gather in the homestead of the leading elder; the lamb and the two children are also brought in. Here a small quantity of honey-beer is prepared and kept near the fire to ferment during the night.

Early in the morning the beer is strained and put into a small ceremonial calabash (*kanya ka igongona*). At the same time a ceremonial cow (*ng'ombe ya igongona*) is milked into another small calabash. When this preparation is completed the elders form a procession; the two children, the boy carrying the milk calabash and the girl the calabash containing the honey-beer, are put at the head of the procession; the lamb, its eyes covered, follows, and then the elders. Now the procession moves slowly towards the sacred tree (*moti wa Ngai* or *moti wa igongona*), which means "God's tree," or "ritual tree."

When the procession reaches the base of the sacred tree the leading elder takes from the children the two calabashes. He raises his hands, holding the calabashes, towards Kere-Nyaga and, standing in this position, he utters prayers to Mwene-Nyaga in these words:

"Gethuuri wee uikaraga iguru ria Kere-Nyaga— wee wenyenyagia irema, na ukaiyuria njuue, togokohukeru igongona reere otuurerie mburu. Ando na ciana ne mekurira; mburi na ng'ombe ne ikurera. Mwene Nyaga togogothaitha na thakame na maguta ma ndorome eno togothenjera; moruru wa ooke na iria netokoreheire. Togogo-kongoera ota oria ndemi na mathathi magokon-goagira o moteine oyo no kamoirerla mbura. Togogothaitha wetekere igongona reere riito na oturerie mbura ya Keguni. Thaai thathaiyai Ngai thaaai."

Literal translation:

"Reverend Elder (God) who lives on Kere-Nyaga. You who make mountains tremble and rivers flood; we offer to you this sacrifice that you may bring us rain. People and children are crying; sheep, goats, and cattle (flocks and herds) are crying. Mwene-Nyaga, we beseech you, with the blood and fat of this lamb which we are going to sacrifice to you. Refined honey and milk we have brought

for you. We praise you in the same way as our
forefathers (*ndemi na mathathi*) used to praise
you under this very same tree, and you heard
them and brought them rain. We beseech you to
accept this, our sacrifice, and bring us rain of
prosperity." (*Chorus or response*): "Peace, we
beseech you, Ngai, peace be with us."

The chorus is chanted by the elders after each sentence.
The tone used in this connection is of a ritual character used only in solemn ceremonies.

After this the leading elder lowers his hands and
sips the liquid from the two calabashes. This is to
prove to Mwene-Nyaga that the calabashes contain
nothing harmful or unworthy, and that the sacrifice is
offered in good faith. For Gikuyu custom requires that
anyone giving food or drink to another should taste
it first to prove his sincerity; and, therefore, when offering sacrifice to God (who is regarded as the Great
Elder) this custom must be adhered to, or else he will
be displeased.

The liquid thus sipped is spat over the right and left
shoulders to feed the ancestral spirits who are the
keepers of the Tree of God, and who are at this moment
in the procession guiding the elders.

When the preliminary ceremony is completed, the
procession goes round the sacred tree seven times,
moving from right to left, and, at the same time,
sprinkling the milk and honey-beer around the trunk
of the sacred tree. On the eighth time round they sit
down in a circle; the lamb is spread on its back, the
head facing Kere-Nyaga. It is then strangled. The
children place their little thumbs on the lamb's throat
while one of the elders does the strangling. The children's thumbs are considered as a symbol to signify
that the lamb has been killed with undefiled hands.

While some of the elders are skinning the carcass

some are collecting sacred leaves and firewood; others are engaged in drilling fire. This fire is made by friction between two sticks cut from the sacred tree. A big fire is made on which the meat is to be roasted. The blood of the lamb is put into the calabash which formerly contained the milk, the mutton-fat is melted and poured into the calabash in which the honey-beer has been carried. After a careful evisceration of the carcass the intestines are taken out and tied round the tree; then the fat and the blood are poured on it. When the meat is roasted it is laid on the leaves and the twigs already collected and, before the feast is begun, small pieces of meat are cut from all joints. The tasting is done in the manner already described. The small pieces of meat are put together in one heap as Mwene-Nyaga's portion; the rest is consumed by the elders and the two children. When they finish feasting, the heap of the small pieces of meat and all the bones are collected together and put on the fire, together with some leaves and twigs of sweet-scented wood. While these are burning and the smoke is going up towards the sky, the elders rise and begin to chant a prayer around the fire. They stand up with their hands held aloft and their heads lifted towards Kere-Nyaga in the north. In a few minutes they turn right, towards Kea-Njahe in the east, and then towards Kea-Mbiroiro in the south, and Kea-Nyandarwa in the west, finishing towards the north where they started. They do this seven times, and on the eighth the procession is formed homeward. On leaving they take with them a small quantity of the contents of the lamb's stomach, to be used in a planting ceremony. This completes the procedure in the ceremony for the sacrifice of rain.

In the case of the ceremony in which I took part I well remember that our prayers were quickly answered, for even before the sacred fires had ceased to burn, torrential rain came upon us. We were soaked, and it will not be easy for me to forget the walk home in the downpour.

When I was older I saw other ceremonies for rain. I remember four distinctly, but there may have been others. I had a good opportunity to see them because although I had, unfortunately, lost the infant purity which enabled me to take part in the first one, I used to herd the cattle on the pasture around the sacred tree of my district.

This tree, whose individual name was *Mogumo-wa-njathi,* was the sole survivor of the sacred trees in my neighbourhood. It was a huge tree, round which a variety of trees grew; thus it was an outstanding landmark. The other sacred trees had been cut down by European planters who were clearing the newly acquired land for cultivation and were cutting down all trees. *Mogumo-wa-njathi* owed its survival to being on un-alienated land. Gikuyu Christians, fired with enthusiasm by their new-found faith, have spoken about cutting it down, to clear away the "influence of Satan," to destroy the abodes of the old gods so as to make room for the new; but the elders have prevented this, and *Mogumo-wa-njathi* will for many years yet be a centre of communion for Ngai and his people. Gikuyu attachments to such a tree are very intense. It is one of the key institutions of their culture. It marks at once their unity as a people, their family integrity (for their fathers sacrificed around it), their close contact with the soil, the rain and the rest of Nature, and, to crown all, their most vital communion with the High God of the tribe.

I wish to put it on record that every rain ceremony that I have witnessed has been very soon followed by rain. It is not believed, however, that the rain ceremony must always be successful. Should it fail, a clearly defined procedure is ready for use. Enquiry would be made into every detail of the ceremonial performance and perhaps some omission found. In any case the whole ritual would be repeated with special care until eventually rain came.

It is an undisputed fact that rainfall is much less in Gikuyu than formerly. I myself remember pools in which a full-grown man could get out of his depth, and in which we all used to bathe, but which are now replaced by dry soil. The chief physical reason is, in all probability, the destruction of the forests. This deforestation followed the alienation of the Gikuyu lands. It is not unnatural that the people should link up such a first-class misfortune with their religious and moral beliefs.

The current explanation heard from the lips of many people is that *Gikuyu harea keari kianoimaho,* which means, "The Gikuyu are no more where they used to be"; that is to say, "All is confusion." Religious rites and hallowed traditions are no longer observed by the whole community. Moral rules are broken with impunity, for in place of unified tribal morality there is now, as anthropological readers will be well aware, a welter of disturbing influences, rules and sanctions, whose net result is only that a Gikuyu does not know what he may or may not, ought or ought not, to do or believe, but which leaves him in no doubt at all about having broken the original morality of his people. The rules of hospitality and kinship are disregarded, commercialisation of tribal mutual assistance institutions is becoming more and more pronounced every day. Hence it is no wonder that Mwene-Nyaga does not bless his people with rain and prosperity as of old. The older generation attribute this lack of blessing to the behaviour of the younger generation who, as they say, have become individualised and selfish and have turned away from Mwene-Nyaga's guidance.

There are two more definite aspects or expressions of this belief. In the first place the tribe has lost its unity; hence it cannot speak with Mwene-Nyaga with its full contingent of voices. That being so, he is not impressed. Further, the people have to some extent lost touch with their ancestral spirits; hence those cannot so effectively join in the appeals to the god. The loss of the tribal unity is perhaps exemplified in the fact that formerly all the Gikuyu, with no exceptions whatever, believed in Mwene-Nyaga. It was a religion of tribal unity and helped to consolidate tribal organisation, both spiritually and materially. Now part of the people are Christians, Moslems, or merely "detribalised," having no religion at all.

In the second place Gikuyu religion was based on the active supplication of the family. Now even a single family may well have members among all the competing religions and sects. The breaking of family ties, kinship, and tribal grouping, has to some extent weakened the material and spiritual forces in the community. Thus their degree of spiritual integration in communion with Mwene-Nyaga on the one hand, and with the ancestral spirits on the other, is rendered somewhat inadequate.

THE PLANTING CEREMONY

When the rain, so anxiously awaited, has fallen, the elders of the sacrificial council (*athuri a igongona*) immediately arrange for a short planting ceremony. This is to bless the seeds in order to ensure good crops.

The first step taken in performing this ceremony is to secure various seeds of prominent crops of the season, namely, millet, tree peas (*njogo*), *njahe* (a very valuable Gikuyu bean, especially for mothers after giving birth), maize, and a variety of beans. These, together with the contents of the stomach of the lamb which has been sacrificed, are put into seed-calabashes (*kegeena,* pl. *igeena*). They are then handed over to one of the women who are qualified for the position of the "Mother" of the community. The woman keeps the seeds in her hut, where they remain for one night before planting.

The next step is to select two sticks amongst those on which the meat for sacrifice was roasted. The way in which the sticks resisted fire determines the ones to be used. They are sharpened at one end only for planting. The sticks, which we will now call *moro,* pl. *mero* (digging-sticks), are given to the children who participated in the sacrifice for rain. The children, with their digging-sticks, spend the night in the hut where the seeds are kept.

Early in the morning the elders, who also spent the night in the hut, call the children to open the door, so as to be the first to go out of the hut, and then re-enter, and thus bring good luck for the planting journey. The custom of selecting who is to enter or go out from a hut first thing in the morning is very strong amongst the Gikuyu. For this is believed to bring good or ill luck. Almost every household has its favourite, *moroki wa mocie,* or *nyoni ya monyuka* ("One who opens the door in the morning," or "A lucky bird"); no one else must call first thing in the morning except the person chosen.

After these preliminary arrangements are completed the leading elder, the woman, and the two children start out to a selected field where the first seeds of the season are to be planted. On their journey there no one is allowed to speak to them or touch them, for fear that someone ritually unclean may put a bad spell or defilement on their sacred undertaking. When they arrive in the field the elder takes the seed calabashes and, standing facing Kere-Nyaga, he raises his hands, holding one of the calabashes, and in this position he recites the following prayer:

*"Mwene-Nyaga, we otuureirie mbura ya kemera,
reu ne hingo tokwanbia mbeo thi, oirathime noreke
iciare ta gikonyi."*

("Mwene-Nyaga, you who have brought us rain
of the season, we are now about to put the seeds in
the ground; bless them and let them bear as many
seeds as those of *gekonyi*.")

The *gekonyi* is a very prolific creeper.

After recitation of this prayer the elder takes out
some seeds and hands them to the woman. She then
gives a few to each child, who plants them, breaking
the ground with the ritually clean digging-stick. The
form of the stick is clearly defined. It is from the sacred
tree; it was used in roasting the sacrifice; it resisted the
fire; it was sharpened with the sacrificial knife used only
for skinning the animals; finally, it was kept overnight
in the care of the pure young children, and is now applied to the earth by one of them. It is not used again
until the first weeding of the sacred seeds. In the meantime it is carefully kept with the other ceremonial objects. In outward appearance it may be exactly like
other digging-sticks, but taken in its full context, it is
completely unlike them, and is adapted very specially
to its unique function. The same procedure of reciting
the prayer and handing over the seeds is repeated till
all the different seeds have been ritually planted.

At the end of the ceremony the party returns to the
homestead. Here a horn of the planting ceremony is
sounded; this announces that the planting ceremony has
been completed, and the people can now proceed in
planting their fields. This ceremony is now becoming
less pronounced in some districts, especially where
Christians are in the majority. Here the system of passing words from mouth to mouth has replaced the sounding of ceremonial horns. This method was adopted when
a large number of Gikuyu people, including my own

father, were prosecuted and punished for being in possession of any ceremonial objects, which the authorities assumed to be "witchcraft." In order to protect themselves from these prosecutions and punishments, the people resorted to the system we have described.

THE CEREMONY OF PURIFYING THE CROPS

The ceremony is performed about two or three moons after the planting of the seeds. During this time there has been weeding and the crops have been tended. Now they have begun to bear fruits. It is now that the elders meet and prepare for the ceremony which purifies the fields. To ensure a good harvest the plants must be protected from insects. The most essential feature of this ceremony is a lamb, in securing which the elders follow the same procedure as that already described in the previous pages dealing with the sacrifice for rain. The elders who participate in the purification ceremony are the same ones who offered the sacrifice to Mwene-Nyaga. Sometimes they are replaced by other elders of the same grade. This time the children do not take part in the actual ceremony.

When all the preliminary preparations have been made, a place is selected in the centre of the district. This must be a place where planted fields are numerous and where a sacred grove is in existence. The articles necessary for this ceremony are: (1) the lamb; (2) *makori* (a herb believed to have a fertilising substance, and whose smell, when burned, acts as a protection against insects); (3) *mokenia* (a herb, the smell of which gives pleasure); (4) *mokengeria* and *mohoroha* (herbs for maintaining peace). Apart from these there is a variety of herbs used in connection with rituals, but the above-mentioned are the central part of the ceremony.

When the arrangements are completed, the elders leave the homestead to go to the place where the ceremony is to be performed. The lamb is killed by strangling. After the carcass is skinned, the stomach and intestines are taken out, for these are very important in this ceremony. The contents of the stomach are carefully emptied into a calabash plate and mixed with herbs which have been cut into small pieces. The fire is made, wood and twigs from sacrificial trees are put on it and allowed to burn down; then the meat, supported by a "grill" of crossed sticks, is roasted over the embers. The elders partake of the feast, reciting ritual songs, but there are no musical instruments or dancing. In all Gikuyu solemn sacrifices, rituals and ceremonies dedicated to Mwene-Nyaga, dancing is ruled out altogether; as we have already seen, the participants in these are old men, women, and small children. No musical instruments are used, excepting a ceremonial horn which is used in some cases. The horn thus used is for making ceremonial announcements and not for any other purposes.

When the elders have finished feasting, wood and herbs are added to the fire, together with the bones, hoofs, a little blood and contents of the lamb's stomach. These cause the fire to produce huge clouds of smoke. At this juncture the elders prepare torches, by tying together twigs of a shrub called *motei*. These torches are lighted from the ceremonial fire. The elders divide themselves into four groups, each carrying a torch and a small quantity of the contents of the stomach (*taatha*), blood and mutton-fat. Then they march in four directions—east, north, west, and south. The sacrificial fire is thus carried by the elders to spread in all districts and locations. The field owners prepare dry grass and twigs in their fields and wait eagerly to receive the purifying flame for their crops. As the elders pass by, they transfer the fire on to those inflammable substances. By these means the purification fire is spread very rapidly, and in a short space of time almost every field has been supplied with the flame.

The fire is carried not only to the fields but to the homesteads as well. The old home fires are extinguished and the new ones lighted from the sacred torches. These new fires are carefully guarded; they must not die until they, in their turn, are replaced by the sacred fire of the next season.

THE HARVESTING CEREMONY

When the crops have ripened and are almost ready for harvest, it is time to offer a sacrifice to Mwene-Nyaga for his generous gift of rain which has now brought prosperity to the community. The elders of the ceremonial council, including seers and diviners, whom we may call high priests, meet to decide what will be most acceptable to the deity. The sacrifice of this nature is practically always a lamb, and its colour is determined by the colour most prevalent in the maize cobs about to be harvested. If in the majority of maize fields it is found that the mixture of white and chocolate, or black and yellow, is most prominent, the elders will decide that a lamb of those colours is the one for the occasion. Much trouble will often be taken to find precisely the animal most desired. Sometimes it will have to have one spot of a certain colour on its forehead or navel, or it may have to have the two desired colours (say black and yellow) equally spread over its body.

When finally the animal decided upon is secured, a day is appointed for the thanksgiving ceremony. Before the day of the ceremony, temporary granaries are erected on the most popular main roads leading to the cultivated fields. These small granaries are of a ritual character and play an important part in the ceremony, as we shall see later.

Early in the morning of the ceremonial day the elders take the lamb and other ritual objects to a tree called *mokoyo* (fig tree), under which the sacrifice is offered. The *mokoyo* tree has a special significance for the Gikuyu people. It might even be suggested that the name of the people is derived from that of the tree, e.g. *mokoyo,* the tree; *mogekoyo,* a Gikuyu person.

When the lamb is ritually killed, the bark of the tree is then pierced and a piece peeled off. Sap comes, and it appears to be reddish and white-cream. The pieces of the bark, and sap, and the contents of the lamb's stomach are now mixed together. The leading elder then proceeds with the ritual of cutting the lamb's skin into small ribbons. These are carefully counted, for they must make an even number. They are then dipped in the mixture. This is divided into small quantities and wrapped in ceremonial leaves (*mathakwa*). After this the elders stand facing Kere-Nyaga and then, in ritual voices, they recite a prayer in the following words:

> *"Mwene-Nyaga, wee otuureerie mbura no gatche kemera keega, reke kerende kerie irio cia kemera geke ngiri. Menya ogatorehere itwanda. Torigitere morimo wa ando kana wa mahio maito. Tumumia tho ciito ciothe, negetha torire kemera geke twe-gangareete. Thaai thathaiyai Ngai thaai."*

Which means:

"Mwene-Nyaga, you who have brought us rain and have given us a good harvest, let people eat grain of this harvest calmly and peacefully. Do not bring us any surprise or depression. Guard us against illness of people or our herds and flocks; so that we may enjoy this season's harvest in tranquillity. (*Chorus*): Peace, praise ye, Ngai, peace be with us."

This chorus is repeated and chanted by the elders after each sentence.

When the prayer is concluded the elders take the parcels containing ceremonial particles and start off to perform their ritual duty of purifying the harvest. On all cross-roads, where many paths cross one another, there a hole is dug and one of these parcels is buried therein. This is to purify the harvester's feet while passing through from his homestead to the fields, and again when coming back carrying the harvested crops. The rest of the ceremonial parcels are distributed among the community to put in their granaries before storing their grains.

Now let us for a moment describe the significance and ritual aspect of the small granaries which are built temporarily on main roads. They are said to belong to Mwene-Nyaga, for, as we have already stated, Mwene-Nyaga is addressed as "Reverend Elder," and as such he must have his own granaries in which his tributes may be deposited. In order to show gratitude to the deity, everyone passing by from harvesting must put into the granaries a few grains of whatever crop he or she has harvested. This symbolises the Gikuyu custom of "give and take," and, as Mwene-Nyaga has given the rain to the people, so he is entitled to be rewarded by a gift of the first crops of the season. For it is said that without his aid the people could not have any crops. Thus for a man to fail to pay tributes to his benefactor would be contrary to the established custom, and would be regarded as shameful and greedy.

The elders of the ceremonial council take a small quantity of each crop thus deposited and then have them prepared in various ways according to the ritual ethics. Some are roasted, some cooked; others, such as millet, are ground and gruel made out of the flour. The preparation is done at the leading elder's homestead, where the rest of the elders of the ceremonial council meet to perform ritual acts and to partake of the feast. The feast is regarded as tasting the food and the drink of the crops of the season which have been given to Mwene-Nyaga; and, in this way, assuring him that there was no defilement in the tributes and that the people have not given the deity anything that the elders would hesitate to eat or drink.

THE CEREMONY OF FIGHTING AND CHASING AWAY EPIDEMIC OR ILLNESS

There is a belief in Gikuyu that illness is carried to the people by some kind of evil spirits. These are believed to conceal themselves in the bushes round the homesteads, and when they want to launch a mass attack on the people they are carried by winds from one homestead to another. On these occasions the evil spirits are said to travel during the day. When a whirlwind is seen in its terrific speed, one can hear people shouting and abusing vigorously what is believed to be the mass of evil spirits gathering their forces for general attack on the people.

On the outbreak of an epidemic or illness, the cause of which people cannot clearly understand nor find any effective remedies for in their wide range of herbal treatments, the elders of various grades meet to consult seers and diviners to find out how they can relieve the people from their suffering. In this consultation it is reported that medical aid has failed and that physical force has to be applied against the enemy. It is then decided that the only way to get rid of such a malady is to prepare a real fight with the evil spirits which have so unkindly brought suffering upon the community. For it is believed that if the evil spirits are defeated in the battle, not only will they run away and take with them the illness, but also that they will be frightened and it will be unlikely that they will in future dare to bring misery to the people.

It is ritually considered that the evening is the best time to wage war against the evil spirits. They are then believed to be round about near the unfortunate homesteads, so as to be able to make records of their victims. After the consultation of the elders, the day is decided upon on the evening of which the fight will start against the unseen creatures. The most favourable moment for the ritual fight is when the moon comes out, about seven o'clock in the evening. Following the elders' decision, notices are sent out by word of mouth announcing the date of the battle. The news is carried out from homestead to homestead, from village to village, and from district to district. In this way the people are told to prepare themselves for the ritual fight and to be in readiness for the signal. The custom in respect to this ceremony requires that all members of the community, old and young, should participate ceremonially in the battle.

On the evening appointed, war horns (*coro wa ita,* sing.; pl. *macoro ma ita*) are sounded from various centres to signal the starting of the battle against the malicious spirits. On hearing the war horns, men, women, and children, armed with sticks, clubs, and other weapons, rush from their huts in great excitement. The elders take great care to see that spears, swords, and knives are not used in this fight, for it is feared that if the spirits' blood is shed on the land its uncleanliness might spread defilement which might cause great calamity in the community. To avoid misery and suffering, people are asked to use only blunt weapons.

As soon as the people are ready they come out of their homesteads and form ceremonial fighting units. They start beating their sticks together in the rhythm characteristic of this ritual, and at the same time they shout and scream furiously, moving slowly towards the river. On the way down they beat bushes along the side of the paths, and examine them carefully to make sure that they do not leave behind any malicious spirit hiding in these bushes.

In all districts, during the time of this ceremony, one hears nothing but human cries and noises of the sticks being beaten together. The echoes of this tumult run from hill to hill, and the whole of the affected district has an atmosphere of great panic. When the people come near the river the inhabitants from both sides of the river shout and beat the sticks vigorously. At this point the war horn is again sounded from central points. This time it is a signal to tell all the people to get ready by the river-sides so as to sink the evil spirits in the river simultaneously.

At the end of the echoes of the first war horns the leader of the ceremonial war unit on the one side of the river talks to the one on the other side, and asks him: "Have you collected together all the evil spirits with their illness from your side?"

The other leader answers: "Yes, we have collected them all, and even those which tried to hide themselves in the bushes we have dragged them out, and now we have them all here with their illness messages. Now get ready and let us throw them into the river."

At this juncture the thunderous cry and the beating of the sticks are intensified. Again the war horns are sounded, this time in rhythmic notes, sharp and short, characteristic of this ceremony. On hearing these, the crowds which have gathered along the river-sides start to throw their sticks and clubs in the river, shouting victoriously and contemptuously, saying: "Evil spirits and your illness, we have crushed you. We now sink you in the river. Let the water drive you far away from us. You will go for ever and never return again."

The sticks thus thrown into the rivers symbolise the evil spirits and epidemic. When this is completed the people then beat off the dust from their garments and dust off their feet to make sure that none of the malicious spirits have been left behind. At the end of the ceremony the crowds scatter in various directions towards their homesteads. They march on, singing merrily, for they are now convinced that the enemies have been banished, and thus the people's minds are free from fear of being attacked by the epidemic.

On the journey homewards the people are requested by the leading elders not to look back, for the psychology of the ritual demands that every vestige of memory of the evil spirits shall now be cast out from the people's minds.

Next day, early in the morning, mothers are engaged in the ceremony of shaving small children who were not able to take part in the battle against the malicious spirits. The children are shaved in a very peculiar fashion; the hair is shaved off in one line running from forehead to the back of the head, and in another line from one side of the head to the other, thus forming a sign of the cross on the centre of the head. It is believed that by so doing, the remnant of the illness is scraped off, and that the sight of the children shaved in this matter will frighten the malicious spirits. After the shaving, the children are washed and then painted with red ochre.

"ANCESTOR WORSHIP" OR COMMUNION WITH ANCESTRAL SPIRITS

The system of age-grouping in connection with the living and the dead plays a very important part in the life of the Gikuyu community. As a man grows old his prestige increases according to the number of age-grades he has passed. It is his seniority that makes an elder almost indispensable in the general life of the people. His presence or advice is sought in all functions.

In religious ceremonies, and in political and social gatherings, the elders hold supreme authority. The custom of the people demands that the elder should be given his due respect and honours, not only when he is present, but when he is absent. For instance, if a young man happens to have a ritual feast or a ceremony during his father's absence, he must invite a member of his father's age-group to act as a ceremonial leader, and treat him in every respect as he would his own father. If a son wrongs his father, he appeases his father's anger by giving him a sheep or a he-goat and two or three calabashes of beer; and in this way he holds a communion with his father and the ancestral spirits who are represented by the father.

On receiving these gifts the father, before partaking of the feast, sprinkles on the ground a hornful of the beer to quench the thirst of the ancestral spirits and at the same time to appease them. He then blesses the son and declares that, in agreement with the ancestral spirits, he has forgiven him. If a son is married and has a homestead of his own, the father and mother always receive a specific portion of whatever the son has prepared. If he kills a sheep or a goat, the tongue and the fleshy portions of the back are reserved for the parents. If it is beer he has brewed, the father and the mother have the right to drink the first horn filled from the fermenting calabash (*ndua*), and a special calabash is reserved for the parents. These gifts are given as tribute and recognition of the parental duties, as advisers and guardians of the family group. The elder, when holding a feast or ceremony in his own homestead, gives these tributes to the ancestral spirits in the same manner and with the same respect as he himself receives them from his living son.

An elder in a community renders his services freely. He receives no remuneration in the way of a salary, but helps the community with his advice and experience in the same way as he directs the management of his own homestead and family group. In recognition of these services he receives public tributes ceremonially, and is regarded specifically as the father and officiating priest of the community.

The function of an elder, both in his own family group and in the community, is one of harmonising the activities of various groups, living and departed. In his capacity of mediator his family group and community in general respect him for his seniority and wisdom, and he, in turn, respects the seniority of the ancestral spirits. This is because he realises that his present elevated position is due to the care and guidance rendered him by his departed ancestors, and whatever he gives them, he gives them not in form of a prayer, but in gratitude and to hold their memory green.

Having this in mind, we can now proceed to discuss what is generally called "ancestor worship." In this account I shall not use that term, because from practical experience I do not believe that the Gikuyu worship their ancestors. They hold communion with them, but their attitude towards them is not at all to be compared with their attitude to the deity who is truly worshipped. To clarify this point I shall therefore use the term "communion with ancestors." The ceremony of communing with ancestral spirits is closely associated with the everyday life of an African, for it brings back to him the memory and glory of his forefathers. It is hard to say whether this can be compared with the ceremony practised in European communities in connection with the graves of their "unknown warriors." There appears to be some such communion with ancestors when a European family, on special occasions, has an empty chair, the seat of a dead member, at table during a meal. This custom might be closely equated with Gikuyu behaviour in this respect.

The Gikuyu, the Masai, and Wakamba, whom the

writer knows best, have clear and definite terms which differentiate the ceremonies of communing with the ancestors' spirits from those directed to the Supreme Being. The words "prayer" and "worship," *gothaithaiya, goikia-mokoigoro,* are never used in dealing with the ancestors' spirits. These words are reserved for solemn rituals and sacrifices directed to the power of the unseen.

The gifts which an elder gives to the ancestors' spirits, as when a sheep is sacrificed to them, and which perhaps seem to an outsider to be prayers directed to the ancestors, are nothing but the tributes symbolising the gifts which the departed elders would have received had they been alive, and which the living elders now receive.

The Gikuyu believe that the spirits of the dead, like living human beings, can be pleased or displeased by the behaviour of an individual or a family group, or an age-group. In order to establish a good relation between the two worlds the ceremony of communing with the ancestral spirits is observed constantly.

The ancestral spirits can act individually or collectively. There are three main recognised groups in the spirit world: (1) The spirits of the father or mother (*ngoma cia aciari*), which communicate directly with the living children and which can advise or reproach the children in the same way as they did during their lifetime; (2) clan spirits (*ngoma cia moherega*), which have an interest in the welfare and prosperity of the clan. They act collectively in accordance with the living clan, administering justice according to the behaviour of the clan or any of its members; (3) age-group spirits (*ngoma cia riika*). These are concerned with the activities of their particular age-groups. This group, in other words, can be called tribal spirits, for it is the age-group which unifies the whole tribe. It is the spirits of this group which enter into tribal affairs.

The three groups of the spirits, composed of young and old men, women, and children in their respective age-groups are joined in a wider group. This grouping corresponds to a tribal organisation of the spirit world. It directs its activities to the more important matters of the tribe; it is not interested in individuals, for the behaviour of an individual is dealt with by the members of the groups which are closely related to that particular individual.

When misfortune or illness befalls a homestead or a member of a family group, the service of a medicine man (*mondo-mogo*) is sought, in order to ascertain the cause, which is almost invariably assumed to be the work of a spirit or spirits. The *mondo-mogo* is asked to make some divination by the casting of lots, so as to find out what spirit or spirits are responsible. When the *mondo-mogo* finds out the particular spirit he proceeds then to find what reason caused it to act in such an unfriendly way; also, what the spirit would accept to appease its anger and thus restore the individual to health. The cause of the anger may be that the family have had a feast in which they forgot the departed by not inviting them or giving them their share. In this case, if the feast in question consisted of a sheep or a goat which was killed for food, and a beer-drinking party, the same feast has to be repeated in a lesser degree to symbolise the one already passed. The spirits so offended would be invited and offered the feast, and asked to communicate with and resume friendly relations with the living family or individuals. The spirits thus invited would generally appear in the form of a mongoose or a hawk and partake of the feast provided for them. The elder concerned with the offering conceals himself near the spot where the spirits' feast has been carefully laid. This is in order to enable him to watch the character and the mood of the spirits which join in the feast. This helps the elder to form some judgment as to whether the spirits have really enjoyed the feast or not. It is like apologising to a friend who has been slighted; the spirits, according to Gikuyu belief, require the same courtesies that are due to living members of the community. The relation between living and dead, established in the manner described, can hardly be called a "worship" or "prayer," but only communion between living and dead.

11

THE NEW RELIGION
IN EAST AFRICA

DURING the last fifty years various religious sects have appeared in many parts of Africa. The most popular and one which conforms with the African secret societies is Ethiopianism, which has a strong hold in South Africa, and which is well known by the name of the "Watch-Tower Movement." The growth of these new religious cults can be attributed to the following facts:

In the early days of European colonisation many white men, especially missionaries, landed in Africa with preconceived ideas of what they would find there and how they would deal with the situation. As far as religion was concerned the African was regarded as a clean slate on which anything could be written. He was supposed to take wholeheartedly all religious dogmas of the white man and keep them sacred and unchallenged, no matter how alien to the African mode of life. The Europeans based their assumption on the conviction that everything that the African did or thought was evil. The missionaries endeavoured to rescue the depraved souls of the Africans from the "eternal fire"; they set out to uproot the African, body

and soul, from his old customs and beliefs, put him in
a class by himself, with all his tribal traditions shattered
and his institutions trampled upon. The African, after
having been detached from his family and tribe, was
expected to follow the white man's religion without
questioning whether it was suited for his condition of
life or not.

Since the coming of the *mzungu* (European) to the
present day the study of African religious customs and
beliefs has not been considered as essential. The *mzungu*
thought that to deal with simple folks of Africa did not
require the selection of men with good social standing
and better qualifications. We will here let one of the
mzungu speak for himself; referring to the early colonisation, he writes: "It was deemed unnecessary for
white men to have any special training before dealing
with and being put in charge of natives. It was a common assumption that work on the colonies required
men of less education than work at home, so the
colonies became a sort of clearing-house for failures
and worse. This unfortunately applied equally to the
missionary[1] as to other callings, and until recently it
was the prevalent opinion that the Gospel could be
better preached and interpreted to ignorant and de-
graded savages by less intellectual and less educated
men. Of course, in this case the whole line of reasoning
was wrong, for the natives were not as savage and de-
graded as was supposed, and anyway, the more difficult
they were to deal with, the better equipped their teachers
should have been." (*Seething African Pot,* by Daniel
Thwaite, p. 3.)

We can see from this that the early teachers of the
Christian religion in Africa did not take into account

[1] ". . . the European women missionaries now engaged in
educational work in Uganda only one-third have any professional
training as teachers. Only 20 have received any kind of training,
and of these about 10 are fully certificated." (*Report on Higher
Education in East Africa,* September 1937, p. 67.)

the difference between the individualistic aspects embodied in Christian religion, and the communal life of the African regulated by customs and traditions handed down from generation to generation. They failed, too, to realise that the welfare of the tribes depended on the rigid observance of these tribal taboos and rights, through which all the members of a tribe, from kings and chiefs down to the lowest and most insignificant individual, were bound up as one organic whole and controlled by an iron-bound code of duties. The agencies of the Western religious bodies, when they arrived in Africa, set about to tackle problems which they were not trained for. They condemned customs and beliefs which they could not understand. Among other things the missionary insisted that the followers of the Christian faith must accept monogamy as the foundation of the true Christian religion, and give up dances, ceremonies, and feasts which are fundamental principles of the African social structure. Faced with this acute problem, the African, whose social organisation was based on polygamy, which harmonised his communal activities in tribal affairs, set about to look for the evidence in the Bible. In the holy book the African failed to find evidence to convince him about the sacredness of monogamy. On the contrary, he found that many of the respected characters in the Book of God, *Ibuku ria Ngai* (as the Bible is translated in Gikuyu), are those who have practised polygamy. On this evidence the African asked for further enlightenment from his missionary teacher, but the missionary ignored all these queries, with the assumption that the African was only suited to receive what was chosen for his simple mind, and not ask questions.

The missionary associated polygamy with sexual excess, and insisted that all those who want salvation of their souls must agree to adopt monogamy. In their attempt to break down the system of polygamy and other African institutions, they imposed monogamy as a condition of baptism, and demanded that even those who had more than one wife must give up all but one. Without complying with this rule they could not be received in church. This caused a great confusion, for the African could not understand how he could drive away his wives and children, especially in a community where motherhood is looked upon as a religious duty; the children are regarded as part and parcel, not only of the father, but of the whole clan (*mbari*), and without them the *mbari* is lost. It was also terribly hard for a woman to be driven away, and to lose her status in the society where she is respected as a wife and a mother. However, the African, having no other choice, superficially agreed to fulfil those conditions in order to get the little education which the missionary schools afforded him. The education, especially reading and writing, was regarded as the white man's magic, and thus the young men were very eager to acquire the new magical power; a fact which undoubtedly had escaped the notice of the Europeans.

The African, faced with these problems and seeing how his institutions have been shattered, looked again in the Book of Books. There he found polygamy sanctioned by the personal practice of great biblical characters. Thereupon he decided that in order to please his Creator, he would select his Christian names for baptism from among those characters who had practised polygamy. Thus names like Solomon, David, Jacob, etc., are most popular, for the African believed that with names such as these he could follow the examples of these ancient teachers without committing any sin. But he was shocked to find the missionary again condemning him as a sinner for fulfilling that which is sanctioned and condoned in the *Ibuku ria Ngai* (the Bible).

Now, having described the cause which is responsible

for the new religion that has appeared in different forms in various parts of Africa, we will give a concrete description of one of these sects which has appeared, and has found followers among the Gikuyu. This new religious sect is known as *Watu wa Mngu* (people of God) or *Arathi* (which means in Gikuyu language prophets or seers).

It was in 1929, when a controversy started between the Gikuyu and the Church of Scotland Mission Gikuyu, which among other things attacked seriously the custom of clitoridectomy. During this upheaval a large section of people broke away from the main Christian body and began to seek other means to satisfy their spiritual hunger without denouncing their social customs. Apart from religious sentiments, there was a general discontentment about political and economic affairs of the country, especially about the land question. At this time people who broke away from the missionary influence, together with the indigenous population, began to form their own religious and educational societies. The most popular of these are the Independent Gikuyu schools and Kareng'a schools, which combine religious and educational activities.

Watu wa Mngu are a group of people who are fundamentally concerned with religious aspects of life. Although they subscribe to the aims and objects of the other independent Gikuyu societies such as those we have mentioned above, nevertheless their outlook in life is entirely different from the rest of the community. *Watu wa Mngu,* as their name signifies, assume the role of holy men; they claim to have direct communication with Mwene-Nyaga (God). They claim, too, that Mwene-Nyaga has given them power to know the past and present, and to interpret his message to the community at large, hence their name, *Arathi*. They travel widely and in groups. As a demonstration of their sacred mission they have given up their property and homes; the members of this sect maintain that: "to own property is a sin." Everything, they say, belongs to Mwene-Nyaga, *"Indo ciothe ne cia Mwene-Nyaga,"* and having been chosen to serve him, they have no need of accumulating wealth. The groups of the *Watu wa Mngu* are harmonious, and consist of men and women. They have their headquarters in various districts where they have built large temporary shrines; here they cook, eat, drink, and sleep in common.

Watu wa Mngu have a special characteristic in their religious ceremonies. Their prayers are a mixture of Gikuyu religion and Christian; in these they add something entirely new to both religions. They perform their religious duties standing in a picturesque manner. In their prayer to Mwene-Nyaga they hold up their arms to the sky facing Mount Kenya; and in this position they recite their prayers, and in doing so they imitate the cries of wild beasts of prey, such as lion and leopard, and at the same time they tremble violently. The trembling, they say, is the sign of the Holy Ghost, *Roho Motheru,* entering in them. While thus possessed with the spirits, they are transformed from ordinary beings and are in communion with Mwene-Nyaga.

In their social intercourse with the rest of the community they have a very special way of hand-shaking; they claim to have physical strength above that of the average man. They demonstrate their bodily supernatural power in hand-shaking. They would hold a man's hand in greeting and in this way they give a jerking pull, saying thus: *Newageithio ne Roho Motheru,* which means: "The Holy Ghost is greeting you." The members of this religious sect strongly believe that they are the chosen people of God to give and interpret his message to the people. They proclaim that they belong to the lost tribes of Israel.

In travelling, they do not carry food, for they believe

that Mwene-Nyaga (the Lord) will provide them with things which are necessary for their sustenance. They sleep generally under trees, on the hills, and on mountain-sides. Caves provide a good place for resting and meditation. They hate money and foreign articles. In their preaching they emphasise the saying that: "Money is the root of all evils." Some of them have burnt foreign articles and thrown away all utensils which are of foreign origin. They preach this doctrine to their followers and tell them that Mwene-Nyaga is the God of Gikuyu: *"Mwene-Nyaga ne Ngai wa Gikuyu,"* and has given the Gikuyu good land with large forests, mountains, hills, and plenty of good water in rivers and in springs. For this reason they must not approach their benefactor with articles which are ritually unclean, for they say emphatically that foreign goods are full of defilements, and as such they are not fit for sacred rituals. Having foreign articles around them, they say, would mean losing their direct communication with Mwene-Nyaga, and their prophetical power. This attitude symbolises their strong nationalistic feeling, and the Bible provides them with many examples, such as: *"Ngatha cia Othamaki ikoima borori wa Afrika, Mbari ya Abaci ne ikirie kwambararia moko igoro hare Mwene-Nyaga,"* namely, "Princes shall come out of Africa, Ethiopia shall soon stretch out her hands to God." This quotation has a deeper meaning and different interpretations among the *Arathi* group, for they claim that Mwene-Nyaga has given them power to interpret the Biblical sayings. As we have seen, the above quotation is the basis for stretching their arms to the sky while praying.

The miracles performed by Jesus and His Apostles are some of the inspiring elements, especially the raising of the dead and the healing of the sick. *Watu wa Mngu,* being the chosen people, naturally believe that they possess these powers, and they go about trying to heal the sick. Sometimes they succeed in doing so, and this gives them more prestige among the indigenous population.

While *Watu wa Mngu* believe in certain parts of the Bible, they also believe in communion with their ancestors. We have already mentioned that the new religion sanctioned polygamy on the ground that several leading personages of the Bible, *Ibuku ria Ngai,* as it is called by the Gikuyu (Book of God), often had many wives without being discredited for it; on the contrary, they are praised for their good deeds and wisdom. *Watu wa Mngu,* therefore, deduced from this fact that the *mzungu,* missionaries, were not interpreting the Bible correctly, and that they only adopted the system of monogamy to suit their own ends, and that they wanted to impose it on the Gikuyu in order to decrease the population (*kohomia rorere*). These words go further to suggest that if the whole tribe were to adopt the system of monogamy the tribe would gradually be wiped out of existence.

As to communion with ancestors, it was argued that since the Church recognises the sacredness of saints, who are but ancestors of the *mzungu,* and if the deity can be addressed by the saints and can listen to their intercessions, it will be the more likely that the spirits of the Gikuyu ancestors will act effectively. The Gikuyu ancestral spirits would have more personal interest in transmitting the prayers and needs of their descendants than mere outsiders who have to deal with requests from different peoples of the world. Furthermore, by following the ancestral line the spirits of the Gikuyu ancestors, who had departed before the coming of Christianity, would thereby profit by the transaction, for in providing for the welfare of their descendants they would find the opportunity of maintaining their contact with the earth.

Watu wa Mngu also include in their new religion

most of the ritualistic points which the missionaries had condemned. By widening the basis of their religious ceremonies they were able to get a large hearing, especially among those who were suffering from spiritual hunger. At first this group was looked upon as simply a bunch of lunatics, and little attention was paid to their activities. However, after some time the Government began to watch the activities of the prophets. Some of them were arrested for agitation and incitement and brought to court. During the hearing of the case the *Arathi* would not defend themselves, they refused to speak on many occasions, and instead, they chanted their prayers. This was a demonstration against the foreign institution. They did this in courts and in gaols. We will give here a short formula of their prayer:

> "*Mwene-Nyaga, hinya waku we mbere ya mahinya mothe.*
> *Totongoretio newe gotire ondo tongetigera.*
> *Newe otoheete hinya wa orathi na uumbori wa maondo mothe.*
> *Totioe motongoria ongi tiga wee wiki.*
> *Togogokaera otorinderere magerio-ini ona mato-ndior-woine ma methemba yothe.*
> *Netooe ate ore o hamwe na ithue, ota oria ware o hamwe na maithe maito ma tene.*
> *Twerigitanetie nawe gotire ondo totangehoota.*
> *Thaaa-i, thathayai Ngai, thaaa-i, thai-tha-a-a-i.*"

This formula can be translated to mean:

> "O Lord, your power is greater than all powers.
> Under your leadership we cannot fear anything.
> It is you who has given us prophetical power and has enabled us to foresee and interpret everything.
> We know no other leader but you alone.

We beseech you to protect us in all trials and
   torments.
We know that you are with us, just as you were
   with our ancient ancestors.
Under your protection there is nothing that we
   cannot overcome.
Peace, praise ye Ngai, peace, peace, peace be with
   us."

Watu wa Mngu do not indulge in politics, nor do
they belong to any political organisation, they devote
their time to religious activities. But the Government
suspected them of having planned to defy authority.
Some of their shrines were closed down by the Government, on the assumption that they were used for secret
meetings of a political character. About the end of
1934 there was a conflict between a group of *Watu wa
Mngu* and the police in a place called Ndarugu Forest.
During this conflict three Gikuyu belonging to this sect
were killed. In the Government report of this incident
it was stated as an excuse for this atrocity that they
were shot by accident, and that they were preparing
for a rebellion. It was also said that *Watu wa Mngu* had
engaged the Wandorobo blacksmiths to manufacture
war-arrows and spears for a future revolt.

This statement was challenged by the Gikuyu, who
knew closely the activities of *Watu wa Mngu,* and the
fact that there was no such preparation. Anyhow, what
could bows and arrows do against machine-guns and
aeroplanes? It is true that *Watu wa Mngu* had adopted
bows and arrows as a symbol of their fight against the
evil spirits, but owing to the attitude of *mzungu* towards
the African customs, this fact was not given its due
consideration.

It was also stated that very offensive and unedifying
attacks were made, in the name of Christ, on the
Christian neighbours of missionaries. But nothing was

done to investigate the religious aspects of this group, to show the connection between it and Christianity on the one hand and Gikuyu religion on the other. A careful study of a sect of this nature would have revealed its real African setting.

As far as I know this religious group is still functioning in various parts of Gikuyu country, but at present it has little influence with the general population, its appeal being to such individuals as have been pronounced "sinners" by the missionaries, and to others who have been cured of diseases. The sect is still in its infancy, and its future growth and activities remain to be investigated by anthropological field-workers.

12

MAGICAL AND MEDICAL PRACTICES

GIKUYU RELIGION, in the wider sense, enters into magical and herbal practices. In many cases magical practices and religious rites go hand in hand, and sometimes it is not easy to separate the two, especially in dealing with beneficial magical practices. Apart from herbs used purely for medical purposes, for curing diseases of both human beings and animals, there are varieties of herbs used for magical purposes. We will first deal categorically with magical practices of various kinds employed by individuals, groups, families, or the tribe.

The magic used by the Gikuyu can be classified in the following order:

1. Charms or protective magic (*gethiito*).
2. Hate or despising magic (*monuunga* or *roruto*).
3. Love magic (*monyenye* or *moreria*).
4. Defensive magic (*kerigiti, keheenga*).
5. Destructive magic, witchcraft (*orogi*, i.e. poison).
6. Healing magic (*kehonia, gethiito gia kohuuha morimo*).

7. Enticing and attracting magic (*rothuko*).
8. Silencing and surprising magic (*ngiria, itwanda*).
9. Fertilising magic (*mothaiga wa onoru*).
10. Wealth and agricultural magic (*mothaiga wa otonga*).
11. Purifying magic (*mokoora, mohoko,* or *ndahekio*).

In order to judge the value or the futility of these forms of magical practices it is necessary to explain in some detail the way and method in which each is brought into action, and the influence it has in the life of the Gikuyu community.

CHARM OR PROTECTIVE MAGIC

The majority of the Gikuyu people carry a charm (*gethiito*) in one way or another, according to the particular danger against which a person wishes to be protected. This we can definitely call individual magic, and its presence is considered as a symbol of security in the daily life of the community. Sometimes charms can be manufactured for a group, especially a family group, but the use of such charms is entirely an individual matter except, of course, when the father of a homestead or an age-group leader is performing his magical duties on behalf of the group. If a man is engaged in hunting or other enterprises he approaches a professional magician who dispenses the desired magic. The people respect and have confidence in a magician who has acquired the profession hereditarily and has gone through long years of training, at the end of which he has been initiated into the cult through payment of some sheep and goats or a cow, according to the amount required by the magician's initiating secret council.

The hunter, on desiring to possess the magical power, goes secretly and asks the magician (*mothinga wa*

ithiito, i.e. manufacturer of charms) to provide him
with a charm which will protect him against fierce wild
animals and enemies of all kinds. The magician, whose
duty it is to defend the community from all dangers
(*morigiti wa mogwati*), proceeds to prescribe magic for
his client. He takes some powders made from various
herbs known to have the magical power, then he mixes
these with some magical particles, and finally puts the
required quantity into a small, narrow horn. While
doing this the magician recites some magical formula,
swinging the horn ritually round his head and then
sealing it. The horn is handed to the hunter with
magical instructions as to the use of the charm. On
receiving the charm the hunter gives a small token to
the magician, to indicate that he obtained the charm
by lawful means and that the magician has given it to
him in good faith. When the ritual of giving and receiving is over, the hunter is instructed to wear the
charm on his person and never to part with it. He is
also asked to take the following oath:

> "I promise you faithfully not to reveal the mag-
> ical secret to anyone outside the magician's secret
> council. From now on I am under the most solemn
> ties and engagements of honour, as well as the
> most religious and magical vows and protestations,
> to conceal the secret formula of the magical power.
> I shall never sacrifice my honour or my religion."
>
> (*"Ngokwera na mwehetwa monene ate ndiko-
> imbora hitho ya othingi wa gethiito geeke, kore
> mondo otare wa ndundu ya athingi a ithiito.
> Kuuma reu ngoikara na mwehetwa worindereri na
> muuma wa okamini, negwo ninderere hitho ya
> othingi na hinya wa githiito. Ndiri hingo ngatengora
> okamini wakwa ona kana mambura makwa."*)

On entering the forest the hunter takes the magic
and, after passing it over his left shoulder and between

his legs up and down seven times, he utters the following ritual words:

"Riu ndemogitere mogwati moothe, gotire nyamo njoru engenguhereria. Reke mogwati moothe magarorwo ne meruke eo ndahuhokia na gethiito geke. Nderigita na gethiio geke ndikoneke ne tho ona emwe."

Which means:

"I am now protected from all dangers. There is no bad animal which will approach me. Let all dangers be turned away by the breath which I blow over this charm. I cover myself with this magical power that no enemy can see me."

When the hunter completes this ritual he moves in the forests and jungles with his confidence doubled; on the one hand he trusts his skill and the power of his spear, bow and arrows; on the other hand, his belief in the protective magic strengthens his courage and enables him to penetrate into the heart of the dense forest, and act firmly without fear of the unexpected.

LOVE MAGIC

There are two kinds of love magic, each of which serves an important function in the field of love. There is magic which exerts its power on behalf of the seeker after the love of many (*moreria* or *monyenye*), and the magic which helps him who seeks the love of one (*mothaiga wa rwendo*).

Before we go further, it is necessary to give a brief account of the steps and ceremonies by which these two elements of love magic are brought into action. *Moreria* is considered as a dangerous magic in certain respects, for its handling involves certain risks in the economic and social life of the individual. The magician, before performing the ritual of imparting the magical power of general attraction and enticement, demands that a man who desires to possess this power shall in the first place make a declaration and vow to the magical spirits of the ancestors to the effect that he will devote his life to love. In this declaration he is asked to denounce property, such as cattle, sheep, and goats. Instead of these he desires to have as many girls to love as he possibly can. When a man has made this declaration, then and then only can the magician proceed to perform the ceremony of imparting into the heart of the love-seeker the power of general attraction and enticement.

After these preliminary questions have been answered satisfactorily, the magician, carrying his magical bag, leads the love-seeker into a lonely place. This must be an empty hole in the ground used by the hyenas as their dwelling-place (*oruma-wa-hiti*). It is believed that a place of this nature is the one where the ancestral spirits connected with this kind of love magic will choose to live. For this reason the place is selected for the ceremony of initiating a man into the magical power of attraction and enticement.

When the two arrive at the *oruma-wa-hiti* the love-seeker sits down facing the hole; the magician stands with his hands raised over the head of his client. In this position he calls aloud for the ancestral spirits: *"Ngoma cia ago! Ngoma cia ago!"* ("Magician spirits! Magician spirits!"). *"Yokiai ngoro ya mondo oyo okwenda akundia moreria!"* "Take (occupy) the heart of this man who wants the *moreria* to be imparted into him"). He repeats this seven times, at the same time swinging the magical bag over the love-seeker's head. Then, abruptly, he orders his client to kneel down and put his head into the hyena's hole. While the love-seeker is in this position, the magician starts to beat him rhythmically on the buttocks with the magical bag; at the same time the magician, in a groaning voice, asks the following ritual questions:

"Love-seeker, by your free will you swear by the spirits of love that you will not desire to seek possession of sheep, goats, or cattle? Your intention is to pursue gluttonously the art of love, and just as the hyena devours human flesh you will do likewise in love-making? You swear by the spirits of love that you will not seek purification or any other magic to counteract the love magic? You agree that you will spend most of your time in love-making?"

While the love-seeker is answering these questions the magician hits him on the buttocks seven times with the magical bag. He is then asked to stand up, looking skywards. At this juncture the magician, pointing with his right forefinger towards the sky, declares that:

"Your heart shall be as wide as the sky, you shall have as many girls to love as there are stars in the heaven."

After this, the magician makes small cuts on all the joints of his client's body. On these cuts the magic of love is rubbed in and thus, as the magicians say, mingles with the blood. This treatment is followed by a mixture of love magic which the love-seeker is given to drink to prepare his internal organs for their future activities in love-making.

A man thus treated becomes so possessed with the enticing magical power that he is almost regarded as dangerous for the community. Magic of this nature is rarely used, for people who are known to have taken it are looked upon with contempt, especially in the men's circle. They are debarred from holding any important position in the tribal organisation. The lives of such people generally end in disaster, because instead of doing something constructive, they spend most of their youth in pursuing pleasure, the futility of which they do not realise until they are well over middle-age. At this time they look with envious eyes upon the well-developed homes of the members of their age-groups who have retired from the active life of warriors. They themselves are unable to afford such homes.

Having described the function and the nature of the extreme love magic, we will now enter the field of the more popular love magic. This is used only when a man is desperately in love with someone in particular and has tried all his personal charm and influence and failed. In this desperate moment the man turns to magic. If it happens that there is someone else who is in his way, the first thing would be to get rid of his opponent, by way of separating him from the girl he is in love with. To achieve this, the help of magic of dislike is sought. When he has succeeded in separating his competitor from his beloved, he proceeds to procure the love magic and at once starts acting, for the ground has been prepared.

There are different methods through which the love magic can be put into action, but all of them require personal contact with the person to whom the love magic is directed; without establishing this link, the love magic cannot be effective.

Before a magician gives away his love magic he has to ask the man who requires it if he has any opportunity of speaking with the girl whose affection he wishes to win, or if he has any access to her homestead or garden. In the case of a man who has the opportunity to speak with the girl he loves the matter is easy. The magician supplies his client with a root taken out of the tree of love, *mote wa ombani*. He is also instructed how to recite correctly the magical formula in the traditional language of the magicians. It is very important to acquire the correct use of magical words and their proper intonations, for the progress in applying magic effectively depends on uttering these words in their ritual order.

When finally the man has passed the test which the magician puts to him, and has now got the weapon which he has so much desired, he pays the magician his due and goes away to put his newly acquired magic into practice. He takes special care to locate the girl with whom he is in love. On seeing her, he immediately places a piece of the root in his mouth and conceals it under his tongue. In this way he acquires magnetic or hypnotising power. While he is so possessed he dare not speak to anyone but to the particular person to whom the love magic has been directed in its magical formula. On meeting the one he loves, he directly talks to her and explains frankly what he really wants. The girl, if the magic is strong (because the practical use of magic is based on trial and success), agrees with him and promises to marry him.

Another way of using the love magic, especially when the application of it verbally is impossible, is to take the magic into the hut where the girl sleeps. In this case the magic is put in the fireplace, so that whenever the fire burns, the smoke will reach the girl's nostrils. This effect will induce her to turn her thoughts and love towards the man who loves her. The magic administered in this way is considered more effective for the reason that it has a direct contact with the person's external and internal organs. Another way of bringing the love magic into close quarters with its desired destination is to sprinkle love magic in the form of powder ground from the roots and bark of the *mote wa ombani*. The powder is sprinkled along the entrance of the girl's hut, thus bringing the girl's bare feet into direct contact with the love magic.

If the above procedure fails, an attempt is made to get hold of something which personally belongs to the girl. It must be her hair, finger-nails or a piece of ornament. On this point it is worth while noting that it is a custom among the Gikuyu to take infinite care in disposing of the articles just mentioned; they are carefully hidden to avoid their being used for selfish motives.

When the love-seeker obtains one of these articles it is tied in a small parcel together with love magic and then divided into two. One part is worn by the man and the other half is taken to the girl's sleeping quarters. To deliver this is taking a risk, because the magic must be concealed in the girl's bed. In performing these acts of love magic the performer has to recite a magical formula, as quoted below:

"Love magic, your magnetic and hypnotising power is great.
You are now in my service and you will act as I shall direct you.
My faithful servant, go and enter in the heart of So-and-so; make her think of nothing else but me, who love her so tenderly.
Magnetic power, cause her to dream of my love, join her thoughts with mine, let her hear my whisper so that she may come nearer to my bosom.
Oh, magnetic power, I got you through lawful means; in agreement with the ancestral magical spirits.
Oh, magnetic power, I recite the spells in magical language; you will not therefore fail to serve me faithfully."

After this recitation he calls the name of the girl loudly and starts to address her as though she were listening:

"My beloved, open your heart and get ready to receive my words of love.

> I want you to know that I love you. To me you are like the rays of the sun, the moon, and the morning star.
>
> When you hear my words of love you will, I am sure, give me a positive answer, for there is no room in my heart for a negative reply.
>
> I have sent you my love magic wrapped in the rays of the sun. This will manifest my real love to you.
>
> Through the warmth of the morning sun, the magnetic power will penetrate into your heart. Do not fail to receive my words of love with an open and tender heart."

This form of love magic is very popular; it is practised by almost every tribe in East Africa. The recitation of the spells may differ here and there, but the essence is fundamentally the same in that particular part of the world. The writer is happy to say that he had the privilege of trying one of the spells, and it undoubtedly proved successful.

From personal experience, like that quoted above, and many more in various branches of magical treatment, it can be safely said that this is one way of transmitting thoughts telepathically from one mind to another. It seems that, through concentration, the magician or the possessor of love magic is able to penetrate into the mental mechanism of the person with whom he desires to establish communication. In this form the magician's suggestions are easily transmitted by means of vibration to the brain, and thence to the mind. If the functions and the methods of magic of this nature are studied carefully and scientifically, it will most probably be proved that there is something in it which can be classified as occultism, and, as such, it cannot be dismissed as merely superstition.

HEALING MAGIC

The Gikuyu have clear ideas as to the nature of
diseases and of the treatment required in various cases.
Some diseases are due to natural causes, controllable
by medicine; and a wide range of herbs is used for
medical purposes. Other diseases are beyond ordinary
control and call for magical treatment.

Illnesses which seem to defy the wisdom of man are
attributed to a supernatural power, or to the agency of
ancestral evil spirits. When dealing with them, healing
magic has to be employed, for a magician is believed to
possess the power of second sight. This faculty, it is
believed, enables him to locate the evil spirit or spirits
which are causing the mischief. By invoking the supreme
council of the ancestral magical spirits, and by having
communion with them, the magician is able, through
invisible power, to chase away the evil spirits from their
victim.

The magician's functions include prophecy, purification, divination, and the curing of sickness, and he is
consulted in all perplexing occasions of life. With the
elders of his age-grade he is the guardian of the ancestral
cult, *ogo,* and he tells the community when to sacrifice
to the ancestral spirits and gives instructions for carrying out the ritual ceremonies.

The magician, when summoned to perform a ritual
for magical cure, appears dressed in all his magical at-
tire suitable for the occasion. The patient, who has been
already informed about the coming of the magician,
and who has also been waiting anxiously to receive
blessing from the supernatural power, is called out. He
is seated before the magician, supported by one of his
relatives. After the necessary arrangements for performing the ritual are completed, the magician takes out the
healing magic, *gethiito kia ogo,* from his magical bag.
He holds it in his right hand. In his left hand he holds a

small bell, *rogambi;* this is very important, for almost every Gikuyu magician has one. It is necessary here to explain the nature of healing magic. It is put in the horn of a particular animal, generally *ndongoro,* or in a small, narrow gourd from six to twelve inches. In one of these articles some magical particles, believed to have healing power, are put and sealed therein. The *rogambi* is made of brass and is considered part and parcel not only of the healing magic but of all other magics. *Rogambi* is entirely different from all other Gikuyu bells; it is easily recognised by its peculiar sound, which is believed to have the power of frightening the evil spirits.

With these few remarks we will now proceed to witness the performance of the healing ritual. Before the magician proceeds with his actual work of healing, the sick man who is about to be treated is asked to spit on the healing magic or to lick it. In this way a direct communication with the ancestral spirits is established through the medium of the magician. At this juncture the magician starts to chant the healing ritual with a strong voice and unusual tone and rhythm, accompanied by the tinkling of the *rogambi.* At the same time he swings the magical horn over the head of his patient. Suddenly, in a mystical state of mind, he stops chanting and, looking the sick man straight in the face, he addresses a few words of a magical formula to him, saying:

"Mondo morwaru, njokeete koingata morimo ooyo
  waku, ohamwe na ngoma iria ioreheete.
Umbora migiro irea ooe, ona eeria ootoe.
Wethagathage, amu ni okometahika yoothe."

That is:

"Sick man, I have come to chase away your illness.
  I will also chase away the evil spirits which have
  brought it.
Confess the evils which you know, and also those

you do not know. Prepare yourself, for you are
about to vomit all these evils."

After this, the magician digs a round hole in the
ground. In this he lays a well-prepared banana leaf for
ritual purposes. He then pours in it water which has
been kept in a ceremonial gourd, called *mbotho ya
ndahekio*. The magician puts into the water a carefully
prepared herbal compound. This is believed to contain
some magical influence which will induce the evil spirits
to come out. The magician at once begins to fight the
illness. The sick man kneels, facing the water, as though
he was in a state of vomiting. The magician squats on
the other side of the water, facing the sick man. He
dips the healing magic in the water and, in a magical
language, he proceeds to recite the following spell:

> *"Ne mokoora, ndagokoora megiro erea e mwere.*
> *Ne mohoka, ndakohokora megiro erea e mwere.*
> *Ne moniginia, ndaniginora ngoma iria ire mwere.*
> *Taheka, no taheke wariga iria iriganeire mwere.*
> *Ne mohoroha, ndahorohia morimo orea we
> mwere."*

This spell can be translated to mean:

> "This is (*pointing to the healing magic*) a root. I
> root up the evils which are in your body.
> This is clearing away. I clear away the evils which
> are in your body.
> This is a weakening. I weaken the evil spirits which
> are in your body.
> Vomit, and vomit the unknown evils which are
> concealed in your body.
> This is a calming. I calm the illness which is in
> your body."

At the end of every sentence the sick man licks the
gethiito and spits in the water. In doing this he pretends

that he is vomiting by saying: "I vomit the illness and the evil spirits that are in my body."

When the recital of this spell is completed, the magician enters into the sick man's hut. He takes with him some magical leaves, called *mokenia* and *moimba-igoro,* in the case of a man. If it is a woman, different leaves have to be used, which are called *marerema* and *makohokoho.* The former mean, as their names signify, happiness and prosperity; the latter stand for fertilising and spreading. With these leaves the magician sweeps all the corners of the hut. While doing this inside the hut by himself, the magician recites the following spells in a drawling, low voice used only by magicians:

"Ngohurora nyomba eno, timahuti ngohurora;
   Ngohurora Megiro, na ngoma iria ciekonyanetie
      toturi-ine tooto
   Ngoma cia ago ne ndeciitangeire, na nekio ngohur-
      ora morimo oria werigiceirie moci oyo.
   Megiro, ngoma ici cia wee, hurorokal ohamwe na
      morimo oyo we moci oyo ngamoiterere ndia
      ngiri."

That is:

"I sweep this hut; it is not the dust that I sweep, I am sweeping the evils and the evil spirits which have concealed themselves in these corners.

I have communed with the ancestral spirits of my cult; it is with their power and agreement that I am sweeping away the illness that has surrounded this homestead.

Defilement, evil spirits, come out together with the illness that is in this homestead.

I am going to sink you in the deep, silent water."

On reaching the entrance of the hut the magician intensifies his voice and begins to tinkle his little bell, *ro gambi.* Then, with a jerking gesture, he takes the dust which he has swept and, holding it tight in his left hand, he thrusts the dust into the water, saying in a loud and angry voice:

> "Look at these mischief makers. They shall not dare to approach any homestead again, for they are now going to be drowned in the 'deep, silent water,' *ndia ngiri,* and will be driven to the unknown corner of the earth, *meri ya mekongoe.*"

He then gives the ritual leaves to the sick man and asks him to dust his whole body to make sure that none of these evil spirits has been left behind. These magical leaves are then put into the water contained in the banana leaf, in which the healing magic has been performed. The magician asks one of his assistants to take the water, with its contents, and throw it into a river at a point where it is deep and silent.

Immediately this is finished the magician orders that the old fire in the sick man's hut be extinguished and the ashes removed. He takes out his fire-sticks, *geka na gethegethi,* and makes a new fire. This he lights in the hut. He then calls the sick man and, pointing to the flaming new fire, he declares that the illness has been cleared away; that the soul of the sick man has now been brightened like the flame of the new fire; and that in a few days the sick man will be in perfect health.

When the magician finishes his declaration he ends the ceremony by receiving a small token for his magical duty. The present given at this time may be the skin of a sheep or a goat or something else, according to the possessions of the sick man. The proper payment for this function is left until the man is in good health. Any magician who claims payment before the sick man is better again is looked upon with suspicion; for it is said that if a magician knows that his magic is a good one, he will never hesitate to wait for the result. It is after a man has been restored to health that he not only pays the price of treatment, but also pays it with gratitude.

Following the description of the healing magic given here, it can be said that this way of curing diseases can be attributed to the psychological influence of the magical beliefs on the patient's organism. The suggestions put to him by the magician penetrate to the conscious and unconscious mind. In this way belief in magical power as an instrument of supernatural healing is intensified. This influence helps the sick man, who is in a state of anxiety to be cured, to create in his mind a picture of perfect health and avoid mentally seeing the manifestation of disease. I will venture to say here that treatment of this kind is associated with what is known in certain European quarters as "spiritual healing."

HATE OR DESPISING MAGIC.
MONUUNGA OR RORUTO

Magic of this nature is used to destroy a friendship between two individuals or between groups of people. Its use is not limited to the field of love-making, but is extended to other institutions in the community. The chief function of *monuunga* is when a man wishes to establish a friendship with a man or a woman and he sees that there is someone who is hampering his progress. He at once seeks the power of *monuunga* to assist him in gaining the desired affection. To achieve this end he has, in the first place, to smash up the existing friendship. When he has succeeded in getting his rival out of the way he starts to cultivate the desired friendship. This is in keeping with a well-known Gikuyu proverb which says that if you want to have a good crop, you must dig out well the couch-grass from the field. *Mogonda okegea irio wambaga korutwo thunguri.*

In describing love magic, we saw how a man desperately in love resorted to magical power to gain the entrance to his lover's heart. For our example we will now take a business man who is faced with competition, which hampers his popularity in business. If a man is engaged in an enterprise, say, pottery or ironwork, and he sees that there is another who is doing the same with better results, his progress is at once attributed to a superior magic. The unprogressive one, whose business is declining, at once consults his magician and demands that the matter be looked into, and that he should be supplied with a powerful magical substance to counter-act that which has been employed against him. Then a magician is faced with a situation like this: He puts all his powers and experience together and starts to work, for he knows full well that his reward and popularity depend on the success of his magic. Before giving his magic, he reviews the whole situation to make sure that the failure is not due to the inefficiency of his client in business, and that there is a superior magic which is being employed against him. At the same time the source of such magic has to be located. This is done by means of divination.

When this enquiry is completed, the business man is given the magical substance required to protect his business. On the one hand he has to employ it to entice customers to his business, and on the other hand to turn them away from his competitor. This action, of course, is the last resort when the man has tried all his personal influence and failed. In this desperate moment the man takes it for granted that there is some power beyond his physical ability which he could not command without the aid of the magician's mysterious power and the influence of the spiritual world.

DEFENSIVE AND HYPNOTISING MAGIC. ITWANDA

The hypnotising magic, *itwanda,* is closely connected with the protective magic, but *itwanda* is used for different functions. Its chief use is in arguments, in court cases, and other disputes. It is interesting to watch people displaying their hypnotic power, especially in a Gikuyu criminal or civil court where the defendant, plaintiff, defending and prosecuting counsel are in possession of *itwanda* magic; each employing the magical power and trying to influence the court for his own good, namely, that the magnetic power may hypnotise the judges and the elders and all those connected with the case, and therefore force them to decide the case in his favour.

Without going into details, it is worth while mentioning that *itwanda* has a wide range, and not only that it is used in the Gikuyu courts, but also that the people use it in defending themselves in police and other European courts.

Hypnotising magic can be transmitted to a person or persons only through the medium of speech or close personal contact. For fear of being hypnotised, it is not unusual to see a man refusing to talk to a man against whom he has a case and leaving their talk to be conducted through a third party.

This form of magic was formerly used extensively in tribal warfares, for it was truly believed that by the spell of this magic the enemy could be put to flight or be paralysed and destroyed without showing any resistance. A magician of war had to ensure his position and the confidence of the general public by leading a successful battle. In this he was required not only to cast spells against the enemy, but also to show his dexterity in handling his spear and shield and other weapons of war. When a magician had thus proved himself to possess the qualities required for a leader, namely, the unification of mental and bodily power in action, the warriors guarded him jealously, for his presence on battle-fields was looked upon as a stimulus to the fighting warriors.

The fundamental rules of this institution are still adhered to in many parts of Africa, and it is generally found that the majority of chiefs and other rulers of the African peoples are magicians in one way or another, especially if they command the respect and the leadership of the tribal organisation. The qualifications for this position require, from the African's point of view, that the chief must be brave, courageous, a philosopher, and a seer; that is to say, to be practically a magician.

DESTRUCTIVE MAGIC (WITCHCRAFT). OROGI. POISON

The most hated and unpopular magic among the Gikuyu is *orogi*. The possessor of such magic is looked upon as a dangerous and destructive individual. *Orogi* is used exclusively for nefarious purposes and, as such, its practice is against the ethical and moral laws of the community.

In former days, before the advent of the white man, anyone guilty of the offence of practising *orogi* was punished by death. The way in which a *morogi* was executed acted as a great warning to other members of the community. Before we begin to describe how *orogi* is made, we will, in the first place, give the whole description of the procedure at an execution. Information about this was handed to me by my grandfather, Kongo wa Magana, who took part as a leading elder in many of these unhappy events.

Before a man was executed it had to be proved by witnesses on oath that he had practised *orogi,* namely, that he had killed by poisoning a man, a woman, or a child. The action was brought before the *kiama* by the family of the victim. After the *kiama's* approval of the grounds for arrest, the *njama ya ita,* namely, council of senior warriors, were given instructions to go and arrest the accused person and bring him before the *kiama* for

a trial. In this respect it was necessary to bring a
morogi to the court with all his magics, bad and good,
to be exhibited in testifying that the man was really a
(proper) *morogi*.

Njama took great care to secure good evidence for
the trial; for without strong evidence against the accused
a clash in the community would have been inevitable.
In the first place the *morogi* and his associates were
spied upon, because it was important to catch him red-
handed—that is, to arrest him while at work in his
secret hiding-places, in a cave or in a dense forest. It is
necessary to mention here that *orogi* was never kept or
practised in or near a homestead. Magic of this nature
is extremely feared, for not only does it cause death
when it is administered to a person, but its nearness to
a homestead is considered as bringing misery and suffering which will dog the footsteps of those who dwell
therein. Because of its anti-social character it was, and
still is, practised in the most secret way, whereas other
magics are performed openly and in ways well known to
the community. A magician after handling *orogi* must
go through a purifying ritual ceremony before he enters
his own homestead, for it is feared that unless he is
ceremonially clean he is liable to bring defilement to
his family.

We will now proceed to witness the trial and the
execution. When a *morogi* was arrested he was brought
before the *kiama,* together with his *orogi*. This consisted
of many small horns, calabashes (the size of a small
medicine bottle), and parcels of banana leaves, and
sometimes animal bones are to be found among the
orogi carriers. These articles contained different kinds
of poisoning and curing powders. The latter were a
disguise to cover the nefarious motives of the former. It
should be realised that a *morogi,* in order to conceal
his malicious activities, had to practise as an ordinary
mondo-mogo—namely, a doctor of Gikuyu medicine.

When the magician was finally brought to trial the *kiama* would ask him to taste powder from each horn, calabash, or parcel, giving him, of course, a few minutes in between, and at the same time watching carefully the result of each taste. If the *morogi* was successful in going through this practical trial without showing any sign of reluctance, this was taken as a proof that his medicine and magical substances were harmless.

The next thing then was to find out if, instead of poisoning people himself, he had employed an agent to act for him. In this respect he was asked to take an oath, *muuma* or *koringa thenge,* the taking of which, if he was guilty, meant disaster to his family and kinsmen. His guilt on this point was proved either by refusing, for the sake of his kinsmen, to go through with the oath, or by refusing to taste some of the powders for fear of taking his own life in a way certain to make his spirit eternally unhappy and pernicious, since it is looked upon by the community as ritually unclean. Should he be guilty his choice is between losing his own life disgracefully by taking one of the poisons or producing the extermination of his family and clan by taking the oath falsely. Or, on the other hand, for the sake of the continuation of his clan, he would plead guilty and face the execution boldly.

If the *kiama* found the *morogi* to be innocent he was released, but the *njama ya ita* kept spying on him for a few moons. If he was found guilty, the *kiama* announced the verdict and imposed the death sentence. At once a day was appointed for the execution. This took place almost immediately. All the *morogi's* relatives were summoned to appear on the day of execution.

Early in the morning on the day of the event ceremonial horns were sounded. On hearing these the *kiama* of the district formed a procession towards the place selected for the execution. At this juncture a war horn was blown, calling the warriors to take the prisoner and follow behind the *kiama's* procession. People in the district were also informed and attended. The place chosen for this purpose was always away from home-steads, and had to be an open place which people could see for miles around.

On reaching the place appointed the *kiama* formed a ring. Immediately the *morogi* was brought in under the escort of the *njama ya ita*. He was made to stand inside the ring while preparations for his execution were being made. First, a small he-goat from the *morogi's* flock was brought and handed to him. He was asked to kill it, to symbolise his own death. At the same time he was asked to declare that he had not, and would not, at the time of his death, utter, silently or loudly, curses on anyone; and that he was willing to die silently for his wickedness. After the *morogi* had completed this, he was given the heart of the goat to eat and thus brighten his own heart before he was put to death. Then a short concluding ceremony was performed. It consisted of mixing the blood of the goat with cow's milk. This mixture was poured on the *morogi's* head, and thence on his whole body. During this act the assembly stood in dead silence. After a few moments a few verses of a ritual song were sung, the officiating elder leading the ceremony.

> *"O-o-o-kiama-e, morogi ne egocinwo, o-o-o-kiama-*
>   *e!*
> *O-o-o-kiama-e, morogi ndaremwene, o-o-o-kiama-*
>   *e.*
> *O-o-o-njama-e, morogi neohwo matharara, o-o-o-*
>   *njama-e!*
> *O-o-o-njama-e, oyai matimo na ngo, morekanerie*
>   *ate.*
> *Morogi neahie; o-o-o-njama-e.*
> *O-o-o-kerende kia mogongo, rekaneria inyuothe*
>   *morogi ndare momoreria, hio hoo-o-o-morogi*
>   *neahie curu.*

Hio-hoo-oo-kiama na njama ya ita, na ando a
   mogongo inyuothe, ugai morogi ndare mwene.
Hio-hoo-o-o, morogi neahie curu curu.
Rekaneriai morogi ndare mocie, hio-hoo-oo-o,
Morogi ne ahie curu curu.
Rekaneria morogi ndare ciana, hio-hoo-oo-o,
Morogi ne ahie curu curu.
Rekaneriai morogi ndare moherega, hio-hoo-oo-o,
Morogi ne ahie curu curu."

The spirit of this ritual song can be translated to mean:

"Harken, elders, the wizard is to be burnt, oh, yes,
   elders.
Harken, elders, wizard has no friends or relatives,
   no one has sympathy with him. Oh, yes, elders.
Harken, warriors, let *morogi* be tied with dry
   banana leaves.
Oh, yes, warriors.
Harken, warriors, lift up your spears and shields
   and say with one voice: Let the wizard be burnt.
Oh, yes, warriors!
Harken, people of the district, say with one voice
   that
Morogi has no one to claim him.
Oh, yes, let the *morogi* be burnt completely.
Harken, the elders, the warriors and the people of
   the district agree unanimously that the *morogi*
   stands alone.
Oh, yes, let the *morogi* be burnt completely.
Let us say with one voice that *morogi* has no
   homestead,
Oh, yes, let the wizard be burnt completely.
Let us say with one voice that the *morogi* has no
   children,
Oh, yes, let the *morogi* be burnt completely.

Let us say with one voice that the *morogi* has no clan,

Oh, yes, let the wizard be burnt completely."

While the elders and the warriors were singing this song they went round and round, circling the wizard. Everyone present put a dry banana leaf, *itharara,* on the condemned man. At the end of the ritual song the leading elder called upon one or two of the *morogi's* close relatives. They were asked to tie the banana leaves on their kinsman. By performing this act they signified that the *morogi* was disowned by them and by their clan; they handed him over completely to the authorities and, for example, could never afterwards bring a claim for blood money or any compensation on account of losing one of their clansmen. After the relatives had taken the initial steps and had shown their willingness to get rid of the *morogi,* they were helped by others, and the banana leaves were tied on the *morogi* from head to foot. On the top of the banana leaves dry grass and other inflammable substances were added.

In the meantime ceremonial elders were busy drilling fire from sacred fire-sticks. Immediately the fire was ready the *morogi* was asked to make his will, and at the same time to confess the names of the men he had killed by poisoning. After his confession, one of his relatives was given a brand from the sacred fire and requested to set fire to the *morogi.* As soon as the fire was lit the assembly rose and stood at a little distance with their backs turned to the scene, leaving the guard who acted as executioner to keep the fire burning.

This was one way of getting rid of a *morogi* and of discouraging others from indulging in the nefarious profession. Another way was to crucify a *morogi* at the junction of main roads, but this method was less used.

When the business was over a ceremonial horn was

blown and the elders formed a procession towards a sacred grove. Here a ceremony of purification was performed to provide a ritual cleansing to the assembled public before they returned home.

Nowadays, even though a *morogi* be really an undesirable or dangerous character, he has no fear of this punishment. For the white man's administration does not usually differentiate between a purely medical and a ceremonial doctor (magician) and the nefarious practitioner, *morogi,* but all go under the name of "witch-doctors." All "doctors" and "seers" of every type, even men who can do nothing but good, are liable to prosecution. Indeed, it is now the innocent who suffer. My grandfather was a "seer,". *morathi,* or "wise man," whose duty it was to give general advice and foretell the future as far as he could, especially in connection with the war expeditions. He bequeathed his profession, together with some calabashes which were his insignia, to my father, who, however, did not practise, since there were no more tribal wars to be conducted.

But missionaries, aided by Government officials, searched the homesteads for the "works of the devil." My father's calabashes were taken as evidence of guilt, and he, with many others in the same position, served a period of imprisonment. Although they preserved these traditional symbols they had not taken part in any nefarious activities; it was simply the policy that everything to do with "magic" was to be stamped out, for the missionaries to get rid of "Satan's" influence, and to clear the ground for their proselytising work.

Up to this point we have followed the description of how a *morogi* was dealt with, namely, his trial and execution. It would be worth our while to know a little of how the *orogi* (poison) was, and still is, manufactured. Before we proceed, let us make it quite clear that *orogi* is pure and simple poison. It cannot be confused with magic or miracles; it is deadly poison in the

European sense of the word. It is manufactured from various poisonous herbs, known by magicians specialising in that branch of nefarious activities. Some of these herbs are known to a good number of men and women in the community; but the key point of it all, and one which is jealously guarded, is how to make *orogi*. The formula connected with the manufacturing and administering of *orogi* is, strictly speaking, the property of the *arogi* (wizards') secret council, *njama ya arogi*. This group conduct their business in great secrecy and terror. Even the members of the group do not know the proper names of their fellow-members. They meet very rarely and even then they go in disguise. They paint their faces with very black powder (*mbiro*) and then paint white dots round their eyes and noses. While conducting their business, no member is allowed to wear any clothes. Each member has his own hiding place, known only to himself; it is there that he discards his garment. Every *morogi* goes by himself, and they see one another only at the appointed place. The isolated behaviour of *morogi* can be well illustrated by the well-known Gikuyu proverb which says: *"Ndoire nyiki ta morogi,"* i.e. "I live alone like a wizard."

When the *arogi* complete their business, everyone departs alone, taking great care that no one sees or follows him. A *morogi* generally goes a zigzag way, sometimes going backwards and then forwards so as to confuse anyone who might try to follow him. All this takes place at the dead hours of the night when ordinary men and women are sleeping. The people in a district where such a group of *arogi* is known to exist are in such terror that no one dares to speak about their activities for fear of the consequences which will follow if the *morogi* should know that there is someone who speaks against him.

The substance of *orogi* consists of burnt ashes, or ground powder from poisonous herbs and roots. This toxin and the ritual ingredients go together, because into the toxin a powder ground from human, animal, and reptile flesh is mixed. In this form the mixture is ready to fulfil its deadly purposes. The chief parts of the human or animal body required for the manufacture of *orogi* are the following: genital organs of both male and female, breasts, tongues, ears, hands and feet, blood, eyes, and noses. These articles are extracted from human bodies, the victims of the magician's work. They keep watch over the persons whom they have poisoned, to find out when they die and where their bodies are laid; then they go stealthily at dead of night and extract the required parts. But from animals and reptiles the list is enlarged by adding the internal organs such as heart, kidneys, part of the stomach and intestines, liver, testicles, and fat. The materials collected in this way are dried and then preserved for immediate or future use.

While we maintain that *orogi,* when administered, acts strictly as a poison, we cannot help thinking that the magical aspects of its preparation and administering have their importance. On the one hand the magic rites dramatise the preparations, which are accompanied by complicated ritual formulæ, and on the other hand the implication of supernatural powers, which the magicians are supposed to transmit into the herbs or flesh of human beings and animals through long recitations of magic spells, help to conceal from the ordinary man the real secret of manufacturing toxin. In this way the trade is regulated, and carefully restricted in the hands of a few nefarious men and women.

13

CONCLUSION

IN CONCLUDING this study we cannot too strongly emphasise that the various sides of Gikuyu life here described are the parts of an integrated culture. No single part is detachable; each has its context and is fully understandable only in relation to the whole. The reader who has begun at the beginning and read through will appreciate this for himself, but it is worth while to point out briefly some of the implications.

The key to this culture is the tribal system, and the bases of the tribal system are the family group and the age-grades, which between them shape the character and determine the outlook of every man, woman, and child in Gikuyu society. According to Gikuyu ways of thinking, nobody is an isolated individual. Or rather, his uniqueness is a secondary fact about him: first and foremost he is several people's relative and several people's contemporary. His life is founded on this fact spiritually and economically, just as much as biologically; the work he does every day is determined by it, and it is the basis of his sense of moral responsibility and social obligation. His personal needs, physical and psychological, are satisfied incidentally while he plays his part as member of a family group, and cannot be fully satisfied in any other way. The fact that in Gikuyu language individualism is associated with black magic, and that a man or woman is honoured by being addressed as somebody's parent, or somebody's uncle or aunt, shows how indispensably kinship is at the root of Gikuyu ideas of good and evil.

This vital reality of the family group is an important thing for Europeans to bear in mind, since it underlies the whole social and economic organisation of the Gikuyu. It means, for instance, that the authority of the tribe is different in kind from that of the European national State. The Gikuyu does not think of his tribe as a group of individuals organised collectively, for he does not think of himself as a social unit. It is rather the widening-out of the family by a natural process of growth and division. He participates in tribal affairs through belonging to his family, and his status in the larger organisation reflects his status in the family circle. The average European observer, not being trained in comparative sociology, takes his own fundamental assumptions for granted without realising that he is doing so. He thinks of the tribe as if it must be analogous to the European Sovereign State, and draws the conclusion that the executive authority for that sovereignty must be vested in the Chief, as if he were a Prime Minister or a President. In doing so he makes a huge mistake, which makes it impossible for him to enter into intelligible relations with the Gikuyu people. They simply do not know where he gets his ideas from, since to them the family rather than the larger unit is the primary reality on which power is based.

The visible symbol of this bond of kinship is the family land, which is the source of livelihood and the field of labour. In an agricultural community the whole social organisation must derive from the land, and without understanding the system on which it is held and worked it will be impossible to see the meaning of other aspects of life. In Gikuyu society the system of land tenure can only be understood by reference to the ties of kinship. It is no more true to say that the land is collectively owned by the tribe than that it is privately owned by the individual. In relation to the tribe, a man is the owner of his land, and there is no official and no committee with authority to deprive him of it or to levy a tax on his produce. But in so far as there are other people of his own flesh and blood who depend on that land for their daily bread, he is not the owner, but a partner, or at the most a trustee for the others. Since the land is held in trust for the unborn as well as for the living, and since it represents his partnership in the common life of generations, he will not lightly take upon himself to dispose of it. But in so far as he is cultivating a field for the maintenance of himself and his wives and children, he is the undisputed owner of that field and all that grows in it. In the same way a woman is the owner of her land and her hut as far as outside people, even her husband's other wives, are concerned, and in her management of her property she expresses her initiative as well as contributes to the family budget. But her ownership is not irresponsible; her chief function in the group is the bringing up of her own children, and it would not occur to her that the land was hers for any other purpose.

At the same time, since the Gikuyu outlook is essentially social, there are certain mutual claims which are generally assumed. Relatives help and consult one another in matters of common concern; anyone who is in need will go to his nearest prosperous kinsman as a matter of course, and hospitality is taken for granted. These things are a matter of good breeding and custom rather than of legal enactment, but to understand their gradations in detail would be to understand the real bonds which hold Gikuyu society together.

Economic life, of course, depends on the land. Cer-

tain things have to be done, some of them collectively
and some of them by individuals, and the stages of life
and division of labour are regulated by these necessities.
Traditional usage has allotted to every person at every
age the tasks best suited to him and the group with
whom to work, and in every collective activity certain
jobs are taken over by men and others by women,
while children undertake the responsibilities for which
their strength and experience are suited. Thus there is
no master-and-man relationship in economic life, and
there need be little or no argument about the division
of labour; people grow up to know what is expected of
them and what are the limits of their obligations.

For such a complex community life a careful training
is required and the Gikuyu educational system supplies
it. On its technical side it is practical from the earliest
years. The Gikuyu child does not need Montessori
exercises or class-room lessons in manual dexterity, for
with plenty of space to tumble about in, and with older
people around him doing interesting manual jobs, he
will naturally learn by real experiments. There is work
for him to do as soon as he has acquired the skill to do
it properly, and he hardly distinguishes work from play.
As he grows older the age-group gives him the democratic companionship of equals, and he learns by competition with other children the keenness of sense and
agility of limb which will equip him for his life, as well
as skill in the various operations of agricultural and
pastoral work. He learns these things by imitation and
free exercise, and to some extent at his own risk, and
in doing so he learns how to behave to his seniors and
how to get along with comrades of his own age. And
since there is plenty of necessary activity, of a kind
suited for every age, the steps of his education are not
just exercises for his own improvement, but real contributions to the needs of the group life.

It is therefore difficult to separate cultural from

technical training, but something must be said about the cultural side. The Gikuyu child does not go to school to acquire his tribal education, because he does not need to do so. In the first place the normal life of the community is a healthy environment for him to grow and learn in, and the family scheme has room for him; it is not necessary, either for his own good or for his parents' convenience, to keep him in a special sheltered reservation. Secondly, detachment from the family is no part of the Gikuyu scheme of training. In a European's life the school is usually the first big influence which takes him away from his parents and brings him as an individual into a separate relationship with the State, but Gikuyu boys and girls do not have to make this break. They naturally learn their tribal traditions and moral values from their parents and grandparents, so that they grow up with a simple family allegiance through which they come to understand their duties to the rest of the world. At the same time a great deal of their life and activity is carried on with their own age-group, through whom they learn the lessons of equality and co-operation. By going through their initiation rites together, Gikuyu boys and girls are given an understanding in common, which in some ways is like that of Englishmen who graduate from a college in the same year, though it is much more sacred and binding, and is a vital element in Gikuyu government.

In trying to understand these initiation ceremonies, one must bear in mind the difference between Gikuyu and European culture. The latter is mainly literary; every English child is compelled by law to go through several years of schooling, after which he is expected to be able to read at least his Bible, his ballot-paper, and his newspaper, and thus pick up his social inheritance. The Gikuyu does not use printed books; instead, his social education is imparted to him by image and ritual, the rhythm of the dance and the words of the ceremonial song. For every stage of life there is an appropriate course of instruction through these means, and it is made as unforgettably dramatic as possible. At adolescence especially, when boys and girls begin to take their place as responsible members of the community, it is necessary to impress upon them exactly what is expected of them in their new station in life, and what new obligations are imposed on them by the development of their sexual powers, as well as of their general mental and physical growth.

Again, sexual practices have to be related to the economic life of a community. Children are a social responsibility, and in agricultural life a man cannot afford a wife and family until he has a hut and land, and the power to cultivate it. Therefore, sexual intercourse must be restricted, but for the individual's health and happiness it must not be altogether frustrated. On reaching the proper age, the young initiates are given the benefit of tribal experience and taught how to strike the right balance. If there are breaches of the code, or adjustments to be made between one and another, there is the age-group to take the matter in hand and impress the young offender with a proper sense of the importance of public opinion.

Before entering on marriage, they must again be instructed in the new duties which belong to this new advance in status. For marriage has two sides; it is a free choice of one another by the boy and girl, and this side of it is their own affair. The choice is not a complete leap in the dark, for the freedom of association and physical intercourse which has been allowed to them before marriage ought to have made each of them competent to select a mate with good judgment. But beyond this, it means the linking of two families in bonds which are social and economic as well as biological, and which are, in fact, the connecting-links of tribal life. The code which regulates the behaviour of relations by marriage is, therefore, a most important matter in its bearing on the whole of social life, and has to be very carefully learnt and punctiliously followed.

Marriage, and especially parenthood, gives a man his full share in the common happiness and qualifies him to think for the common good. It is not till he has a son or daughter entering on adolescence that he is regarded as really mature enough to take part in the tribal government, and here again we see that the guiding principles are his family experience, and the opinion of him which his contemporaries have formed. It is not until he has a family growing up that he has had a chance to show his capacity for wise administration and for dealing intelligently and justly with other people, and what he can do in the family group he is expected to do on a larger scale in the interests of the community as a whole. Among his equals in age a man may be selected as a leader or spokesman by reason of his innate gifts and understanding, for the age-group system gives the Gikuyu a good grasp of the principles of democratic selection. If so, he will be marked out by the elders as one who will play an important part in public affairs later on, but not until he has passed successive age-grades and acquired the experience of life which will qualify him to take full responsibility in tribal matters. By that time he is probably the leader of almost a miniature tribe of his own relatives, as well as his age-grade, and his family life will give evidence of his ability in government.

When we come to religion, we see again that Gikuyu religion is integrated with the whole of Gikuyu life. Religion is a dramatisation of belief, and belief is a matter of social experience of the things that are most significant to human life. In Gikuyu life the earth is so visibly the mother of all things animate, and the generations are so closely linked together by their common participation in the land, that agricultural ritual, and reverence for ancestral spirits, must naturally play the foremost part in religious ceremonial.

The new religious movement is interesting because of its bearing on the question of social change. It is not reasonable to expect the Gikuyu to assimilate Christianity whole as the European missionary expounds it. Its language and its traditions have no relation to his daily life, its ceremony is meaningless to him, and its moral code, with its insistence on monogamy for which Gikuyu economy is not planned, and its objection to the central rituals of his own society, strikes him as subversive of all intelligible social values. But the new religious movement does show that Africans, under the influence of new forces, are not incapable of a spontaneous adaptation. It is an effort from within, to assimilate what seems to them valuable in the Christian code and the culture of which it is a part, while at the same time adapting it to the needs of Gikuyu life.

Lastly, we come to magical practices and see how they, like religion, are inspired by the daily economic and social activities of the people, and how they run through and fertilise these activities and refer them to the mysterious forces which surround human life. Even here it is clear how everything good comes from the collective life of the community, while the wizard practises his works of darkness alone. And when a man has been convicted of the capital crime of anti-social wizardry, his offence is against the whole of society, but it is one of his own kinsmen who has to pass final judgment against him by lighting the fire of his execution.

It is all these different aspects of life together that make up a social culture. And it is the culture which he inherits that gives a man his human dignity as well as his material prosperity. It teaches him his mental and moral values and makes him feel it worth while to work and fight for liberty.

But a culture has no meaning apart from the social organisation of life on which it is built. When the European comes to the Gikuyu country and robs the people of their land, he is taking away not only their livelihood, but the material symbol that holds family and tribe together. In doing this he gives one blow which cuts away the foundations from the whole of Gikuyu life, social, moral, and economic. When he explains, to his own satisfaction and after the most superficial glance at the issues involved, that he is doing this for the sake of the Africans, to "civilise" them, "teach them the disciplinary value of regular work," and "give them the benefit of European progressive ideas," he is adding insult to injury, and need expect to convince no one but himself.

There certainly are some progressive ideas among the Europeans. They include the ideas of material prosperity, of medicine, and hygiene, and literacy which enables people to take part in world culture. But so far the Europeans who visit Africa have not been conspicuously zealous in imparting these parts of their inheritance to the Africans, and seem to think that the only way to do it is by police discipline and armed force. They speak as if it was somehow beneficial to an African to work for them instead of for himself, and to make sure that he will receive this benefit they do their best to take away his land and leave him with no alternative. Along with his land they rob him of his government, condemn his religious ideas, and ignore his fundamental conceptions of justice and morals, all in the name of civilisation and progress.

If Africans were left in peace on their own lands, Europeans would have to offer them the benefits of white civilisation in real earnest before they could obtain the African labour which they want so much. They would have to offer the African a way of life which was really superior to the one his fathers lived before him, and a share in the prosperity given them by their command of science. They would have to let the African choose what parts of European culture could be beneficially transplanted, and how they could be adapted. He would probably not choose the gas bomb or the armed police force, but he might ask for some other things of which he does not get so much to-day. As it is, by driving him off his ancestral lands, the Europeans have robbed him of the material foundations of his culture, and reduced him to a state of serfdom incompatible with human happiness. The African is conditioned, by the cultural and social institutions of centuries, to a freedom of which Europe has little conception, and it is not in his nature to accept serfdom for ever. He realises that he must fight unceasingly for his own complete emancipation; for without this he is doomed to remain the prey of rival imperialisms, which in every successive year will drive their fangs more deeply into his vitality and strength.

GLOSSARY

In this Glossary the following phonetic symbols are introduced to avoid using diacritic marks used in current Gikuyu orthography.

Phonetic.	Current Orthography.
e	$\tilde{i}$
ϵ	e
$\mathcal{o}$	o
o	$\tilde{u}$

NOTE.—Plural nouns beginning with A should be looked for under the singular form, beginning with M.

A

Acheera.   Name of a clan.
Agachiko.   Name of a clan.
Agu, "Agu na Agu."   Name of an age-grade of a very remote past. Time immemorial.
Airimo.   Name of a clan.
Aitherando.   Name of a clan.
Amboi.   Name of a clan.
Aka.   Women.
Amboi.   Name of a clan.
Angare.   Name of a clan.
Anjiro.   Name of a clan.
Angoi.   Name of a clan.

B

Baba. Father (my or our).
Borori. Country.

C

Ciana. Children.
Ciana ciaku. Your children.
Ciana ciito. Our children.
Ciana irɔgea thaai. Peace be with the children.
Coco. Grandmother (my or our).
Cɔɔmba. Europeans, foreigners.
Cɔrɔ (pl. *macɔrɔ*). Horn, trumpet; long curved horn.
Cɔrɔ wa ita. War-horn.
Cɔrɔ wa igɔngɔna. Ceremonial horn.

E

Emwɛ. One.
Ɛmbu. Name of a district and of its people.
Ɛthaga. Name of a clan.

G

Gatɛgɔ. Syphilis. Name of an age-group, recording the first appearance of the disease in the country.
Gaturi. Name of a district in Central Gikuyu.
Gecohe (pl. *icohe*). A ring.
Gechukia. Name of certain moonlight dances and songs for young people.
Geka (pl. *ika*). The bottom part of a stick from which fire is drilled.
Gekama (pl. *ikama*). Iron ore, iron slag.
Gekonyi. A prolific creeper with small black seeds used for making beads.
Gekoyo. Name of both the country and the people.
Getara (pl. *itara*). A platform or nest.
Getaroro. A tray for winnowing or spreading grain in the sun.
Gethaka (pl. *ithaka*). Land in a general sense, bush-land.
Gethamarɔ. A roaring sound uttered by warriors.
Gethambiɔ. Uncooked gruel used generally for ceremonial purposes.
Getharia. Lady-killer, or heart-breaker.
Gethathi. An oath-symbol. A stone used for taking oaths and for pronouncing comminations.
Gethegɛthi. Top part of fire-drilling stick. Drill.
Gethemɛngo (pl. *ith emengo*). The evil eye.
Gethɛrɛ (pl. *ithɛrɛ*). Apron worn at back by warriors for dancing.

Gethii (pl. *ithii*). A cloak or mantle made of skin for men only.

Gethiito (pl. *ithiito*). Amulet, charm.

Gethiito kea ogɔ. Magician's charm, or magic.

Gethori. Chest, breast, selfishness.

Gethuuri. Reverend Elder. Mountain.

Getiirɔ. A dance and song for women only.

Getiti (pl. *ititi*). A kind of wicker tray, used as a plate or dish.

Getɔɔka (pl. *matɔɔka*). Lily, used for marking boundaries.

Getonganɔ. A place where dancers assemble before going to dance.

Getungati (pl. *itungati*). Rear-guard.

Gociarwɔ. To be born.

Gocinwɔ. To be burnt.

Gocinwɔ ne ɛgocinwɔ. He is to be burnt.

Goitanga. To sprinkle ceremonially, libation.

I

Ithanwa (pl. *mathanwa*). An axe.

Ithɛ. Father (his, hers, thine).

Ithombe (pl. *mathombe*). Spear-head.

Itimo (pl. *matimo*). Spears.

Itoora (pl. *matoora*). Village, town, city.

Ituranguru (pl. *maturanguru*). Leaves used for ceremonial purposes.

Itwanda. Hypnotising or surprising magic.

Itweka. A peaceful revolution in which one generation takes over the government from the preceding one.

K

Kaare. Ceremonial song, sung only by warriors who have killed an enemy in battle.

Kagutwe (pl. *togutwe*). Leaves used by girls after circumcision, to prevent the lips of the vagina from sticking together.

Kamatimo. Elders of lesser grade, lower rank of the *kiama*.

Kamoinge. A group of people acting together.

"Kamoinge kɔyaga ndere." Unity is strength.

Kanya. A small gourd.

"Kanya gatunɛ ne mwamokanero." "Give and take," reciprocity.

Kanya ka ɩgɔngɔna. A calabash used in religious ceremonies.

Kareng'a. A pure-blooded Gikuyu, a nationalist.

Kebata. A popular spectacular day-dance for warriors only, a display of physical fitness.

Kebɛrɛthi (pl. *ibɛrɛthi*). A wide spear used by elders.

Kegeena (pl. *igeena*). A special calabash in which seeds are kept.

Keguni. Benefit, beneficial.

Kehaarɔ (pl. *ihaarɔ*). An open-air place for meeting or dancing.

Kehee. A big boy who is not yet circumcised.

Keheenga. An obstacle.

Kehɛmbe (pl. *ihɛmbɛ*). Drum, used either for beating or as a receptacle.

Kehɛti. An old woman past child-bearing.

Kehinganda. Last born, the one that closes the womb.

Kehɔnia. Curative, that which cures.

Kehongoyɔ. A useless or thoughtless person. Babbler.

Kehurokɔ. A resting-place, place of retirement.

Keimba (pl. *ciimba*). Corpse.

Keombani. Lady-killer or heart-breaker.

Kohɔnia. To cure.

Koina. To dance or sing.

Koingata ngɔma. To chase away evil spirits.

Kɔirugɔ. Taking an oath by tasting the soil, swearing by the earth.

Komɛmɛnda. To smash to smithereens.

Komenya ooru na wɛga. To know good and evil.

Korɔra. To be fat or fertile.

Koraria morongo. A ceremony of keeping the gods awake.

Konyitwɔ ne ngɔma. To be possessed by evil spirits.

Korathimithia. To ask for blessing, to lead a prayer.

Koringa thɛngɛ. Swearing by killing a goat, by breaking its bones.

Koruta. To take out, to do, to train.

Koruta igɔngɔna. To offer a sacrifice.

Koruta mogirɔ. To purify, remove pollution.

Kuɔha Nyɛki. To tie the grass; phrase used in asking a girl to select her partner for talking or playing with.

Kuuna mogumɔ. The breaking of branches from the sacred tree for circumcision ceremony.

Kwɛnja. To shave, to dig.

M

Macɔrɔ (sing. *cɔrɔ*). Horns, trumpets.

Mae. Water.

Mae maithanwa. "Axe water"; cold water used for numbing the sexual organ before operating.

Mae mɛ gotherɛra matiɛtagerera mondo. Flowing water waits for no man.

Magɛriɔ. Temptations, trials.

Magɛtha. Harvests.

Magetha ma Njahe. The season of harvesting Njahe.

Magetha ma mwɛrɛ. The season of harvesting millet.

Maguta. Oil, fat.

Maguta ma mbareki. Raw castor oil.

Mahoithia. Herb used for embrocation.

Mahiɔ. Flocks and herds.

Mahori. Lungs.

Mahuti. Rubbish.

Mbare. Family group, clan or sub-clan.

Mbare ya Moombi. Moombi's family group, Moombi's tribe or nation, Gikuyu people.

Mbare ya Abaci. Ethiopians.

Mbɛo. Seeds.

Mbirɔ. Soot, black powder; lamp-black.

Mbɔcɔ. Beans.

Mbootho ya Ndahekiɔ. A small calabash in which purification water is carried.

Mbori ya ihaki. A goat or sheep given by a junior warrior to his seniors as entrance fee to a higher grade.

Mbuku. A book.

Mbura. Rain.

Mbura ya mwɛrɛ. The season of short rain commencing in October.

Mbura ya Njahe. The season of long rain commencing in March.

Mɛnjɔ. Shaving ceremony, performed a few days after circumcision.

Menɔga. Fatigue.

Merɪ ya Mekɔngoɛ. Oblivion.

Meruke. Breadth.

Metugɔ ya Nganjiiti. Noble character, good behaviour.

Moburabureki. "Nosy Parker"; fussy, interfering person.

Mocɛɛ (pl. *mecɛɛ*). Sticks used by initiates after circumcision.

Mociari (pl. *aciari*). Parent.

Mociarithania. Midwife.

Mociarwa (pl. *aciarwa*). One who is ceremonially adopted, blood-brother.

Mocie. Home, homestead, village, town.

Mociiri. A judge, a spokesman with legal training.

Mogai. Divider, benefactor, God, testator.

Mogathe wa Mwɛnji. Barber's present; a string of beads given by the initiate to her or his sponsor.

Mogɛndi. Traveller.

Mogɛrɛ. A shrub used in taking oaths or uttering curses.

Mogiɔ (pl. *megiɔ*). A shrub whose bark is used for making strings.

Mogirɔ (pl. *megirɔ*). Taboo, defilement.

Mogonda (pl. *megonda*).   Garden, plantation, farm.

Mogori (pl. *agori*).   Buyer, purchaser.

Mogotha (pl. *megotha*).   A shrub whose bark is used for making strings.

Mogumɔ.   A sacred tree, parasitic wild fig under which sacrifices are offered to Ngai.

Moigwithania.   Uniter, arbitrator, the one who unites in one cause (a Gikuyu journal).   Unifier.

Mohari wa njoa.   One who scrapes the hair from skins.

Moherega (pl. *meherega*).   Clan, division of a tribe.

Mohiki.   A bride, from day of marriage to childbirth.

Mohɔi (pl. *ahɔi*).   One who is given cultivation rights on another man's land.

Mohɔkɔ.   Herb used for purification and other ceremonies.

Mohɔrɔha.   Herb used for purification and other ceremonies.

Moihwa (pl. *aihwa*).   Cousin.

Moireetu (pl. *aireetu*).   Young unmarried woman, circumcised girl.

Moiru.   A partner, co-wife.

Mokɛngɛria.   A creeper used for ceremonial and curative purposes.

Mokɛnia.   A herb used for purification and magical purposes.

Mokɛo.   A shrub whose bark is used for making strings.

Mokoora.   A herb used for purification ceremonies.

Mokoro.   Elderly person, senior.

Mokorwɛ wa Gathanga.   A traditional sacred place where the Gikuyu people are believed to have originated, the first Gikuyu homestead.

Mokoyo (pl. *mekoyo*).   Fig tree (sacred).

Mondo.   A man, person.

Mondo-maromɛ.   A he-man; a title attained after circumcision.

Mondo-mogɔ.   Medicine man, magician.

Mondo-mogo-wa-ita.   A war magician.

Mondo-moroaru.   A sick man.

Monɛnɛ.   A chief, ruler.

Moniginia.   A herb used in purification ceremonies.

Monyinyi.   Junior, younger. Small.

Monunga.   Deciduous tree; stinkwood, a herb used for magical purposes.

Monyaka.   Good luck.

Moogo (pl. *meogo*).   A creeper used for making platters.

Moombi.   Moulder, potter, creator; name of the first Gikuyu woman. The mother of the Gikuyu nation.

"*Moombi arugaga na ngeɔ*."   A potter cooks with broken pots.

Mɔɔndo.   Pocket.

Mora wa itimo.   The bottom part of a spear.

Morathi (pl. *arathi*).   Seers, prophets.

Morigiti wa Mɔgwati. Preventer of dangers, magical protector.

Morᴏ (pl. *ariᴏ*). Son of.

Morɔ (pl. *merɔ*). A digging-stick.

Morɔgi (pl. *arɔgi*). Wizard, witch. One who practises black magic.

Morɔki wa mocie. One who sets foot in a homestead first thing in the morning.

Morongo. Ancestral god.

Moroori (pl. *ɔrori*). Wanderer.

Moruna. Younger brother or sister.

Moruru. Liquid honey.

Moruithia. Circumciser, operator.

Motaathi, Mongirima. Wood from which the staffs of the *kiama* are made.

Motahekania. Purifier.

Motamayᴏ. Sacred tree used in initiation and other ceremonies.

Mote wa igɔngɔna. Sacred grove, under which rituals are performed.

Mote wa itimo. A stick which joins the two halves of a spear.

Mote wa Ngai. Tree of God, sacred tree.

Mote wa ombani. Attraction magic.

Moteei. Shrub used in purification ceremony.

Motɛgi (pl. *atɛgi*). Trapper.

Mothaiga. Medicine.

Mothaiga wa rwɛnda. Love magic.

Mothamaki (pl. *athamaki*). Judge, ruler, spokesman.

Mothamaki wa riika. Leader or spokesman of an age-group.

Mothamaki wa borori. Ruler of a country, a king.

Mothami (pl. *athami*). One who is given cultivation and building rights on another man's land.

Motheegi. A staff of office carried by elders of the *kiama*.

Mothɛnya (pl. *methɛnya*). Day.

Mothingi wa ithito. A maker of charms or amulets.

Mothɔni (pl. *athɔni*). A relative-in-law.

Mothuri (pl. *athuri*). An elder. A married man with grown-up children.

Mothuri wa igɔngɔna. Elder of the Ceremonial Council.

Mothuri wa kerera. Elder of the Traditional Council, educator.

Motiiri (pl. *atiiri*). A sponsor, a supporter.

Motinɔ. Bad luck.

Motirima (pl. *metirima*). A staff of office carried by elders of the *Kiama*.

Motɔngɔrɔ. A procession.

Motoriro (pl. *metoriro*). Flute.

Motumia (pl. *atumia*).   Lady.
Mumɔ.   Youths.
Mungu (*pl. miungu*).   Tunnel, underground passage.
Muuma.   Oath.
Muuma wa anake.   Warriors' oath.
Mwakɔ.   The work of building.
Mwambaigoro.   Creeper used in purification ceremony.
Mwamokanerɔ.   Reciprocity.
Mwanakɛ (pl. *anakɛ*).   Warrior.
Mwangi.   The name of an age-group.
Mwate (pl. *meate*).   Ewe.
Mwathi (pl. *aathi*).   Hunter, bush-man.
Mwehetwa wa anakɛ.   Warriors' oath.
Mwɛnɛ (pl. *ɛnɛ*).   Owner.
Mwɛnɛ-Nyaga.   God.
Mwengo (pl. *Mɛɛngo*).   A small apron worn by women.
Mwɛnjɛrɛrɛ.   Warriors' long spears.
Mwɛnji.   Barber.
Mwere.   Body, millet.
Mwɛri (pl. *mɛɛri*).   Moon, month.
Mwɔndwɛ.   A shrub used for making strings.
Mzungu.   A European (Swahili).

N

Nda.   Stomach, womb.
Ndamathia.   A sacred monster which is believed to have lived
     in rivers.   National totem.
Ndɛmi.   An age-group of the remote past.
Ndere.   Mortar.
Ndereri.   *"Getire ondo wa ndereri"*—Nothing is impossible.
Ndia ngiri.   Deep, still water; deep pool in a river.
Ndɔgamoki.   Herb used for curing wounds and sores.
"Ndoirɛ nyiki ta morɔgi."   I live like a wizard.
Ndokoyo, thiya na ndokoyo.   Axe used for carving hives, etc.
Ndoma.   Arum lily.
Ndoogo.   Warriors' war-dance.
Ndoogo ya ita.   A war-cry accompanied with jumping dance.
Ndorobo.   Hunter, a race of hunters.
Ndoromɛ.   A fat ram.
Ndua.   A large calabash for fermenting beer.
Nduma.   Darkness.
Ndundu ya athamaki.   Council of judges, spokesmen.
Ndundu ya atumia.   Council of women.
Ndundu ya mocie.   Family council.
Ngai.   God.
"Ngai ndegiagiagwɔ."   God is not pestered.
Ngangae.   Slags, blooms.

Nganyiti. Fineness, high quality.

Ngaragari. Balls, pellets.

Ng'aragu. Hunger, famine.

Ngatha. Noble, generous person.

Ngɛmi. Thrilling sounds uttered by women in applause.

Ng'ɛnda the ndiagaga motɛgi. Nothing treads that cannot be trapped.

Ngeɔ. Pieces of a broken pot.

Ngerɛwani. Advance guard.

Ngiri. A thousand.

Ngiria. A beetle used for magical purposes.

Ngɔima (1). A ceremony for sealing marriage arrangements.

Ngɔima (2). A fat sheep.

Ngɔma. Spirits, good or bad.

Ngɔma cia aciari. Spirits of parents.

Ngɔma cia agɔ. Spirits of magicians.

Ngɔma cia ritka. Spirits of an age-group.

Ng'ɔmbɛ. A cow, cattle.

Ng'ɔmbɛ ya igɔngɔna. A ceremonial cow.

Ng'ondo. Land, cultivated or uncultivated; *Gethaka.*

Ngɔrɔ. A branch of banana tree, banana bark.

Nguɔ. Clothes, garments.

Nguɔ ya maribɛ. A kind of women's dress.

Nguɔ ya ngɔrɔ. A cloak worn by women.

Ngurariɔ. A sheep killed in the preliminary arrangements for matrimony.

Nguro. A dance in the form of drill, for men only.

Ngwati. A tassel, below the head of the male organ.

Ngwatanerɔ. Joint property, partnership.

Ngwekɔ. Fondling, caressing.

Ngwekɔ ya Gecɔmba. European (i.e. vulgar or lustful) sexual intercourse.

Njahe. A kind of Gikuyu bean.

Njama. Council.

Njama ya arɔgi. Council of wizards.

Njama ya ita. Council of war.

Njama ya itwika. Council of the Revolution.

Njama ya kerera. Traditional Council.

Njamba. A brave man, hero.

Njɛgɛni. Stinging-nettle.

Njera. Road, path.

Njingiri. Small rattles.

Njogo. Tree peas.

Njongwa. A specialised dance for young men only.

Njɔhi. Beer, any alcoholic drink.

Njɔhi ya gothugumitheria mbori. Beer given in celebration of the first instalment of *roracio.*

Njɔhi ya ngorariɔ. Beer for celebrating an engagement.
Njɔhi ya njooriɔ. Beer given to a girl's parents in a formal
    proposal.
Njɔhi ya ooke. Honey beer.
Nyakiambi. Head wife, first wife.
Nyamo-Njoru. A fierce animal.
Nyina. Mother (his, hers, theirs).
Nyokwa. Mother (your).
Nyɔndɔ. Breasts.
Nyɔni. A bird.
Nyɔni ya monyaka. Lucky bird, i.e. lucky omen.
Nyɔta. Thirsty.

O

Ocoro. Gruel.
Ogembe. Millet (small).
Ohɔrɔ. News, affairs, matters.
Oiru. Jealousy.
Okamini. Generosity, nobility.
Ombani. Attractiveness to the opposite sex.
Ombani na ngwekɔ. Attractiveness to the opposite sex, friend-
    ship based on sexual intercourse. Platonic love and fon-
    dling.
Onɔru. Fatness, fertility.
Ooke. Honey.
Oomo. A kind of medicine to stimulate bravery and per-
    severance.
Oriro. Mystery, wonder.
Orɔgi. Poison. Witchcraft.
Ororo. Bitterness; poison for arrows.
Orugare wa nyɔndɔ. Warmth of the breast.
Oruma-wa-hiti. Hyena's pit or cave.
Otaari wa mocie. The family's traditional education.
Othamaki. Kingdom.
Otɔnga. Wealth.

R

Riige (pl. *mariige*). Door.
Riika (pl. *mariika*). Age-grade.
Riika remwε. Belonging to one age-grade.
Rogambi. A small bell for ceremonial purposes.
Rohuhɔ. Wind, evil spirit, spirit of wind.
Rokwarɔ. A strip of goat or sheepskin worn ceremonially.
Rong'otho. Clitoris.
Rooa (pl. *Njoa*). Skin.
Rooe (pl. *Njooe*). Rivers.
Roraciɔ. "Dowry," lobola.

Rorere. Tribe, nation, race.
Rothukɔ. Enticement, magic, magnetic power.
Rwenji. Razor.

T

Tata. Aunt.
Taatha. Contents of the stomach.
Tɛnɛ. Long time ago, *tɛnɛ na tɛnɛ,* ever and ever.
Thaai. Peace, tranquillity.
Thaata. Barren.
Thahu (pl. *mathahu*). Taboo, defilement.
Thaithayai. Praise, beseech.
Thaka. Handsome, beautiful, beauty.
Thakamɛ. Blood.
Thangari. Couch-grass.
Thɛ. The world, the earth.
Thɛgo. A small calabash used for carrying gruel in circumcision dances.
Thɛngɛ. He-goat.
Thingira. Man's hut, bachelor-hut.
Thɔ. Enemy.
Thɔgwɔ. Father (yours).
Toturi. Corners.

W

Wainɛ. Initiates' song after circumcision.
Wakeri. Form of greeting used by a girl to her sponsor.
Wakia-maito. Form of greeting used by a child to her aunt.
Wakia-mware. Form of greeting used by an aunt to her niece.
Wakine. Form of greeting used between members of the same age-grade.
Watu wa Mngu. People of God; prophets, seers (Swahili).

Index

JOMO KENYATTA, the grandson of a Kikuyu medicine man, is among the foremost leaders of African nationalism and one of the great men of the modern world. In the 1930's he studied at the London School of Economics and took his degree in anthropology under Bronislav Malinowski, one result of which is this now famous account of his own Kikuyu tribe.

Facing Mount Kenya is a central document of the highest distinction in anthropological literature, an invaluable key to the structure of African society and the nature of the African mind. *Facing Mount Kenya* is not only a formal study of life and death, work and play, sex and the family in one of the greatest tribes of contemporary Africa, but a work of considerable literary merit. The very sight and sound of Kikuyu tribal life presented here are at once comprehensive and intimate, and as precise as they are compassionate.

THE TEXT of this book was set on the Linotype in Times Roman, designed by Stanley Morison for *The Times* (London), and first introduced by that newspaper in 1932. The book was composed, printed, and bound by THE COLONIAL PRESS INC., Clinton, Massachusetts.